Achieving Market Integration

Achieving Market Integration

Best Execution, Fragmentation and the Free Flow of Capital

Scott McCleskey

ELSEVIER
BUTTERWORTH
HEINEMANN

AMSTERDAM BOSTON HEIDELBERG LONDON NEW YORK OXFORD
PARIS SAN DIEGO SAN FRANCISCO SINGAPORE SYDNEY TOKYO

Butterworth-Heinemann
An imprint of Elsevier
Linacre House, Jordan Hill, Oxford OX2 8DP
200 Wheeler Road, Burlington MA 01803

First published 2004

British Library Cataloguing in Publication Data
A catalogue record for this book is available from the British Library

Library of Congress Cataloguing in Publication Data
A catalogue record for this book is available from the Library of Congress

ISBN 0 750 65745 6

> For information on all Butterworth-Heinemann
> publications visit our website at www.bh.com

The views of the author are solely his own and do not necessarily represent the policy
or views of virt-x Exchange Limited or the SWX Group.

Use of material from the various regulatory bodies and trade organisations cited in this
work, specifically the Financial Services Authority (FSA), its predecessor (the Securities
and Investments Board), or the Self-Regulatory Organisations (Securities and Futures
Authority, the Investment Management Regulatory Organisation, and the Financial
Intermediaries Managers and Brokers Regulatory Association) does not indicate any
endorsement by the source of this publication, or the material or views contained
within it.

Typeset by Integra Software Services Pvt. Ltd, Pondicherry, India
www.integra-india.com
Printed and bound in Great Britain

To my parents, Gene and Loraine McCleskey

Contents

Acknowledgements

Writing is often a solitary, but never a solo, endeavour. In writing this book, I have had the pleasure and fortune to discuss ideas with a number of colleagues who have been as supportive as they have been informative. These include practitioners and academics in the United Kingdom, elsewhere in Europe, and in the United States. In some cases, their contribution lies in the normal interactions and debates around which my work revolves, in other cases through focused discussion and guidance.

A few individuals and organisations deserve particular mention. First amongst these are the staff and management of virt-x Exchange Limited, where I was employed throughout this endeavour. Though the thoughts, and any mistakes, in these pages are my own and not those of virt-x, I have benefited greatly from the experience and comments of the professionals there with whom I am privileged to work. Secondly, two academic institutions – London Guildhall University and the University of Cambridge – have nurtured my research for the past four years. They have not only provided a valuable academic foundation for my research, but have also encouraged the exploration of new and creative approaches which I hope will be reflected in the chapters which follow. I am also indebted to Nick Idelson and Nicholas Hallam of TraderServe Limited, who have shared their thorough knowledge of market technology in a way that even I can comprehend.

Lastly, I am deeply grateful to my loved ones for the moral support, encouragement and tolerance without which this book would have died an ignominious death long ago.

Preface

As is apparent from a glance at the table of contents, this book takes on a rather unusual structure. After a brief introduction, it begins with a section of six chapters focusing on the reform of best execution policy to ensure it reflects modern technology and market developments. It then sets best execution aside for the moment to discuss the idea of how to integrate securities markets effectively. It concludes with a section which brings the two parts together, showing the relationship between the two issues and recommending policy actions based upon the conclusions drawn in the preceding chapters.

The book takes this unusual structure deliberately, and by necessity. The two issues are in fact so inextricably intertwined that neither can adequately be addressed without reference to the other. Best execution requires integrated markets to be effective, and market integration requires a best execution policy which mandates the routing of orders across borders to the market representing best execution. Though best execution and market integration are examined in two separate sections, the interdependence of the two is a major theme of this book.

The book has been written at a time when the idea of integrating markets is a high political and commercial priority. This is the case in many areas, but especially so in the European Union (EU). The idea that securities markets in Europe must be integrated has been accepted as gospel for decades. In fact, it finds its roots in the Treaty of Rome which in the late 1950s established the forerunner of the European Union, calling for the free movement of capital within the Union's borders. Yet, despite this mandate, and even despite the move to a more or less single currency, little has been achieved. This began to change in the late 1990s with the production of a Financial Services Action Plan (FSAP), which hopes to be a blueprint to the integration of European financial markets. Yet, as we shall see in these pages, the blueprint is more a checklist which is not likely to overcome the market inefficiencies which hold capital within the national borders.

At the same time, the idea of best execution has received renewed attention. Originally a fairly straightforward proposition that an investor should get the best "price" available on "the market", the march of progress has rendered this concept both more complex and more controversial.

These two issues have been dealt with as largely separate problems. One lies within the lofty heights of grand market structure and international economics, the other within the trenches of customer protection. To this point, little has been done to make the connection between these two (and other) issues. The connection needs to be recognised and explored in order to lay the foundation for an integrated approach, dealing with the issues as parts of a whole. This challenge was the genesis of the present work.

The book is not aimed at a single audience. Policy makers, market participants and even investors have much at stake in the successful resolution of the issues explored in these pages. Each also has a voice in developing solutions to these problems. This book attempts to provide a new and hopefully useful perspective, drawing on both theoretical and practical arguments. Theory is useful only to the extent that it can be applied in practice, but in focusing on "how things are" we risk losing sight of how things could be. This book attempts to strike an appropriate balance.

The chapters that follow cover a number of issues related to the twin subjects of best execution and market integration. These include such important and topical issues as the treatment of internalisation, cross-border clearing and settlement issues, and the treatment of Alternative Trading Systems (ATSs). In most cases, these issues are not covered in the level of detail they would normally deserve. Each is so complex that they deserve separate book-length works to fully explore them. While recognising the need to bring up these topics, the scope of this work requires that their treatment be limited to their fundamental issues and their relationship with the topics which are the focus of this book. To go into each issue in full would only bog down and divert the reader from the task at hand.

This book reflects my view that those who comment on policy – especially those whose experience in the markets provides them some level of expertise – should help to provide alternatives, not merely resist change and point out the difficulties that lie ahead. Progress is made by proposing solutions, which if not implemented can at least serve as the basis for discussion and an eventual workable solution. Such is the goal of this book. While it is hoped that the proposals contained here are seen to be logical, cogent and workable, there will most certainly be many who will disagree with parts or all of it. Whether accepted or rejected, though, it should be counted a success if it at least serves as a catalyst for discussion and for the recognition that the many issues discussed are all part of the same puzzle which must be solved if the goal of an integrated market is ever to be achieved.

London
March 2003

Foreword

It is in very few markets that public authorities all over the world intervene as consistently, as widely and as deeply as in financial markets. Beyond the important role in past, less in present and undoubtedly more in the future of self-regulatory and contractual arrangements, public legislation at various levels remains a crucial instrument to help ensure that capital markets function fairly and efficiently.

When making choices public and private authorities need to take into account the new factors created by competition, much more pervasive than in the past, and by technology the input of which is beyond anyone's wildest imagination. Moreover, mechanisms and modalities invented specially in equity cash and later in derivatives markets find more and more application in other types of markets and products as well.

Whether it is the US Congress and the SEC or the EU Authorities including CESR that try to exercise their influence, the main issues are very similar. Some of them are best execution, competitive venues and approaches, private investor protection, effectiveness of enforcement and so forth. Within the European Union, the additional challenges flowing from a multi-jurisdictional system soon to be expanded to 25 countries and followed by a number of others are just enormous. Although there is a lot to complain about the EU's Financial Services Action Plan, the accomplishments so far should not be underrated.

Market structures resulting from market forces and regulation of all types benefit greatly from contributions by academics and practitioners alike. Dr Benn Steil on Transatlantic Markets, or in this case Scott McCleskey on Market Structure and Integrity stand out by clarity of vision and detachment of vested interests. Scott's efforts to link best execution and market integration deserve particular attention. His comparisons between the US, London and the EU deserve to be studied. The flow of lessons is definitely not one way across the Atlantic. The advances that Europe's electronic markets have taken on some of the more old-fashioned American market places are a case in point. Time/price priority in electronic markets is certainly only one example. Redress for private investors in America means paying up front lawyers and slow courts; in Europe it means often fast and cheap procedures before ombudsmen and Complaints Committees. Added to this as potentially important for European enforcement is FESE's proposal to establish a professional's ombudsman.

Scott McCleskey's book is an ambitious enterprise. He will agree with me that his propositions are not necessarily final words in a long discussion. They are very timely in view especially of the upcoming discussions on the final draft text of the EU's 2nd Investment Services Directive and the renewed discussion on market structure in the US.

I would wish the book many attentive readers.

Paul Arlman
Secretary General,
Federation of European Securities Exchanges

1 Introduction

Markets evolve; so, too, must the regulation of markets. The days are past when each country was an insulated and self-contained market, where investors, traders and companies all operated within the isolated confines of a single national exchange. The day of the insulated national market has, in short, gone the way of the trading pit.

The development of cross-border trading has long been recognised as an essential element in the integration of regional or even global capital markets. Within the European Union, it has been recognised as a necessary step towards the free movement of capital, one of the fundamental goals set forth by the founding Treaty of Rome a half-century ago. Yet, in many cases, market integration has been inhibited by a "regulatory lag", as rules and regulations fail to keep pace with the evolution of the markets. As the United Nations put it, "Financial regulation is constantly struggling to keep up with financial innovation, and in this struggle it is not always successful".[1]

The application of "best execution" policies is a prime example of this phenomenon. Originally formulated in the days of single national markets, regulation on the subject has not kept pace with current technology or business practice. Regulators are, in a sense, fighting the last war.

What makes the problem of best execution more and more difficult is the proliferation of venues in which securities simultaneously trade. This proliferation is itself viewed by some as an obstruction to the successful integration of securities markets into a single consolidated pool of supply and demand.

Though best execution is not often viewed as a component of market integration, this book will seek to demonstrate that the two issues are intimately connected. Best execution cannot be solved without reference to market integration, and at the same time a cross-market best execution policy is an indispensable prerequisite for market integration.

This book will seek to examine the two issues with respect to each other. It will examine existing approaches to each, and will ask whether these approaches and the assumptions on which they are founded remain valid. To do so, the book will begin with an exploration of best execution. Applying this apparently simple concept to the real world is a bit like stepping into quicksand. The first part of this book will examine the thorny issues which must be considered to make best execution work in today's environment.

The book will then change course and look into the problems of market integration. It will examine the relationship between liquidity, market fragmentation and the price formation process, followed by a review of previous efforts to integrate markets. The part will conclude with a series of measures which are necessary to link isolated markets.

The final portion of the book, then, will bring together best execution and market integration. Taking the points made in the first two parts to their logical conclusion, the final part will integrate best execution and market integration into a single framework

---

[1]   UN Conference on Trade and Development (UNCTAD), *Trade and Development Report 2001*, p. 102.

which, it is hoped, can serve as a framework for the long-sought goal of an effective, fair and integrated market.

The book will focus on the equity markets. It is equities – stocks – that have been the focus of market integration and consumer protection initiatives for the past several decades. They are the securities which benefit most from order interaction and market integration. Equities also play a particularly central role in the movement of capital across borders and in the economy's capital formation process. Still, many of the principles developed in these pages can be applied to the markets for other types of securities as well.

This work is meant to be an examination of approaches taken in a number of environments, though much of the material discussed in this book refers to developments in the United States. This was deemed appropriate for two reasons. First, there is an abundance of material from the US market concerning best execution, fragmentation and market structure. These issues have been the subject of intense scrutiny in the United States at least since the early 1970s, when the idea of a National Market System (NMS) was first proposed. This long-standing debate leads to the second reason for including material from the United States. In the course of developing the NMS with its attendant regulation and technology, the US market has encountered and considered issues which have not yet surfaced in the European (or other) markets. Even though some of the US material is of limited application to other markets, the greater sin would lie in ignoring the lessons of the US market when considering solutions for the United Kingdom and Europe.

Many terms are used, sometimes interchangeably, to refer to the facility where trades actually occur – these include market, exchange and trading venue. At the fairly high level of discussion which this paper inhabits, the distinction between these terms is not critical, and the term "market" should be construed to encompass the various exchanges, trading systems and venues in which the operations of a market take place.

With respect to best execution, the book starts from the premise that it is fundamentally an investor-protection measure. This has important consequences to the development of the discussion. It means that the starting point would be a theoretical policy which requires each trade to be done at the absolute best conditions, and that any measure which steps away from this ideal must be justified. Much of the debate on best execution appears to start from the other end of the spectrum – a market-centred approach in which any additional cost to the market must be justified. Some even question whether the concept of best execution is relevant to today's complex markets. The two approaches become somewhat blurred in practice (as will be seen in the chapters which follow); still, the approach to be taken has a significant impact on the final shape of the policy.

Market integration, as a concept, is far less controversial. In the United States, the integration of the securities markets was mandated by Congress in 1975, and current debate concerns modernising the methods of integration to fit the modern market. In Europe, the markets are not appreciably integrated, yet the goal of an integrated market can be traced back to the very roots of the European Union. No one publicly speaks out against the integration of the market, yet the implementation of this goal has eluded Europe for decades.

Since this book hopes to contribute to the current regulatory debate, the reader should view it critically. Accordingly, there are certain questions in particular which should be asked. Are the arguments logical and based on valid assumptions? More to the point, are the arguments forward-looking, based on the present and evolving nature of the markets, or are they designed to meet the needs of the last decade? Lastly, would the measures proposed actually accomplish what they set out to achieve?

The chapters that follow aim to present a theoretical framework founded on sound theory and practical application. The end product, it is hoped, will be a new perspective from which to view the issues which touch on the goal of achieving market integration. In dealing with issues at this level, the book has avoided a highly technical approach packed with statistics and complex theory. Yet, further research would be useful to affirm or refute the ideas put forward in these pages.

Part I
Best Execution

What is best execution – an introduction to the concept

At the outset, it would be fair to ask why best execution policy should be examined, or more precisely why it should be examined now. The short answer is that the speed and magnitude of change in the financial markets – both in terms of technology and market structure – have been so profound as to call into question the adequacy of existing policies and standards.

An assumption implicit in undertaking this examination is that best execution, however it is defined, is a thing worth having. As investors maximise their profits by minimising costs and maximising proceeds, we are likely to be on safe ground when making this assumption. It is not, however, assumed from the outset that regulatory intervention is necessary to achieve this goal, and the effectiveness of a *caveat emptor* approach is discussed before proceeding to regulatory approaches. The succeeding chapters explore some of the fundamental questions which must be addressed in devising a best execution policy. The approaches which have been taken in different jurisdictions, and their historical roots, are also examined in some detail. The final two chapters in this part provide a look at best execution from a legal, and then technological, perspective.

2 Is this Regulation Necessary?

During the gas-rationing days of the Second World War, signs posted in public areas encouraged motorists to ask themselves, "Is this trip necessary?" before embarking on the journey. To formulate an effective best execution policy, with all the attendant regulatory cost and effort, we would do well to ask ourselves a similar question – is this regulation *really* necessary?

The idea that a customer should be entitled to the best price for a security would appear so obvious as to require no further discussion. Like a mosaic, though, the picture is much less clear the closer one looks at it. There is no "typical" market, no "typical" investor and no "typical" order. Also like a mosaic, the picture is constructed from many subordinate elements – concepts, assumptions, questions and problems. It is therefore necessary to explore a number of fundamental yet complex questions when examining best execution. Perhaps the most basic, though, is why best execution needs to be regulated at all. This question will be the focus of this chapter.

2.1   Why should best execution be regulated?

Why not leave it to the market to ensure that customers receive best execution? Surely the invisible hand of the market would guide each trader to select the best price for executions in his or her care. We can only answer this question by asking what the purpose of regulation is. A familiar refrain amongst those who work with markets is that formal regulation should only be used when all other means are inadequate. This chapter will take such an approach, and will explore why regulation is not only necessary for ensuring best execution, but why other means cannot meet this need.

One view holds that there are three main reasons for regulation by the public sector – to protect the customer against monopolistic exploitation, to provide presumably less-informed retail customers with protection and to ensure systemic stability.[1] Putting best execution in this context, it can be argued that regulation is necessary in the second sense – that is, to protect the less-informed retail customer from the adverse effects of the *information asymmetry* which arises from the workings of the marketplace.[2]

This relationship between regulation and information asymmetry is more fully described by Keenan and Riches. As they put it:

> The earliest forms of consumer protection were designed to discourage fraudulent trading practices and to protect the consumer from danger. *The main justification for intervening on behalf of consumers today is that the nature of*

---

[1]   Goodhart, Charles, Philip Hartmann, David Llewellyn and Liliana Rojas-Suarez. *Financial Regulation: Why, How and Where Now?* (London: Routledge), 1999, p. l4.

[2]   See Financial Services Authority (FSA), *Best Execution*, Discussion Paper ("FSA Discussion Paper"), April 2001, p. 12.

modern markets is such that consumers can no longer make prudent shopping decisions [emphasis added].[3]

Put simply, retail investors generally do not have the information needed to protect themselves in the market. It could be said, of course, that retail customers in all industries suffer from a degree of information asymmetry. This may be true, but not to the same extent or with the same consequences as in the stock market. First, the retail shopper for other goods and services is more directly involved in the process of buying or selling. The main exception would be in purchasing or selling of a house. But the prices for houses are more stable than most securities, enabling the purchaser or seller to make a reasonable assessment of whether the agent has acted in his or her best interest. Also, the agent in a real estate transaction does not generally have the final say in whether a price is acceptable.

These factors, and the potential impact on an investor's long-term financial well-being, make the retail investor particularly vulnerable and therefore needy of adequate protection.

It seems clear that best execution rules would fall within the legitimate sphere of customer protection. But does this necessarily mean that regulation is the only, or best, method of protecting the consumer? A widely accepted view holds that regulation should only be used to achieve objectives which are in the public interest but which *cannot* be achieved without regulation.[4] The question of whether best execution is in the public interest has been raised with respect to the particular customer protection requirements of retail investors (this point will be further developed later). This brings us to the second question, whether this need can be met without regulation.

In the absence of regulation, it would be left to customers to determine whether or not they were receiving best, or even satisfactory, execution. As has been noted, this *caveat emptor* approach cannot be relied upon in securities markets in the way that is appropriate in other industries. A customer rarely, if ever, knows the precise time when his or her trade is executed. Even after knowing the time of execution, very few retail customers have routine access to the detailed audit trails necessary to show the best price at the time of the execution. In short, investors lack the specific information necessary to judge whether they received the best price.

The investor's information disadvantage would also make enforcement difficult in the absence of regulation. Theoretically, a wronged investor could bring suit in the appropriate court based on the civil law doctrines of agency law and fiduciary responsibility. But an investor could not very well bring suit if he did not know that he had received poor execution.

On both sides of the Atlantic, it has been argued that a best execution policy is unnecessary since few customers complain that they received less-than-best execution.[5] This argument, however, entirely misses the point since very few investors have even the foggiest idea as to whether they received best execution. Rather, small retail investors are

---

[3]   Keenan, Denis and Sarah Riches. *Business Law*, Fifth Edition (Harlow, Essex: Pearson Education Limited), 1998, p. 354.

[4]   Lee, Ruben. *What is an Exchange?* (Oxford: Oxford University Press), 1998, p. 251.

[5]   APCIMS-EASD Letter to the European Commission, 29 May 2002. In the US, the SEC has estimated that best execution complaints comprised only 5% of the complaints received from retail customers in 2000. See the SEC website, at http://www.sec.gov/news/data.htm.

likely to assume that the firm to which they send their order will obtain best execution on their behalf.

In view of this lack of awareness on the part of most retail investors, it is perhaps more surprising that the authorities receive *any*, let alone several hundred, best execution complaints from investors each year. Some would argue that public disclosure of general "execution quality" statistics give the retail investor the necessary information by which to judge their executions. As it will be discussed in Chapter 3, though, such statistics are in fact of little practical value.

Another shortcoming with reliance on agency law is that it only requires the rather unspecific duty of "reasonable care and diligence".[6] Applying such broad concepts to trade executions would be difficult, since there is no clear and agreed standard of the meaning of "reasonable" care or diligence. The need for a clear and enforceable standard is crucial to the effectiveness of a best execution policy, and this point will be examined in further detail in the chapters which follow.

To summarise, the retail customer's informational disadvantage (the lack of "transparency") leads us to conclude that they are not in a position to protect themselves, and so a *cáveat emptor* approach (no regulation) is inappropriate. Reliance on civil law also falls short of the mark because the wronged investor would normally not be aware he was wronged, or at least not in anything like a timely manner, and because the standard of care required by civil law is too broad to be easily enforced in the securities market. Some sort of specific regulation therefore seems appropriate. The UK's Financial Services Authority (FSA) has repeatedly asserted that best execution is a "consumer protection tool", implying that they too have come to this conclusion.[7]

2.2 State or self-regulation?

If some sort of regulation is necessary, need it be *state* regulation, or would voluntary self-regulation by the executing firms be more appropriate? Blundell and Robinson succinctly put the case for self-regulation as follows:

> Broadly, voluntary alternatives to state regulation allow markets to work, ensuring that there are legal or other remedies for those who may suffer from the actions of others, and permit market-based forms of protection, such as voluntary standard-setting, to flourish. The results are 'imperfect', but so are all conceivable outcomes.[8]

Though Blundell and Robinson make a strong case for industry self-regulation in general, much of the discussion rests on the need of companies in a competitive environment to preserve or enhance their reputations.[9] Yet the emphasis on reputation rests on the ability of consumers to know when they have been treated poorly. In a case such as best

---

6   Keenan and Riches, p. 355.

7   FSA Discussion Paper, p. 3, 11, and FSA, *Best Execution*, Issues Paper ("FSA Issues Paper"), July 2000, p. 1.

8   Blundell, John and Colin Robinson. *Regulation Without the State – Occasional Paper 109* (London, Institute for Economic Affairs), 1999, p. 27.

9   *Ibid.*

execution where investors may not know they have been wronged, reputation alone is not sufficient as an alternative to regulation.

Blundell and Robinson also discuss (industry-wide) compliance procedures as an alternative to state regulation. This may be broadly appropriate for securities markets in general, but it would likely not be appropriate for best execution. Effective self-regulation of best execution requires access to, and analysis of, detailed trade-by-trade information from all relevant markets. As most of this information is proprietary in nature, firms may be reluctant to share it with their competitors. Instead, the information would need to be collected and analysed by a neutral third party. This party would also need the resources to conduct the necessary analysis, and the authority to conduct further enquiries.

A well-funded, neutral third party with sufficient authority to conduct this activity is in reality closer to state regulation than to self-regulation. It could be argued that the National Association of Securities Dealers, Inc. (NASD) is an example of the industry regulating itself through a self-regulatory organisation (SRO). However, the NASD's powers are derived from its authorisation by the Securities and Exchange Committee (SEC). The NASD, like all SROs in the United States, is subject to close oversight by the SEC, and all new SRO rules must be approved by the SEC. Moreover, the SEC could conceivably revoke the NASD's status as an SRO. The NASD also exercises a licensing function in that a firm or person expelled from NASD membership would for all intents and purposes be unable to engage in regulated activities in the United States. In practice, the NASD (like the other US SROs) is a quasi-governmental regulator exercising powers devolved from the state.

Additionally, isolated markets have only a limited ability and no incentive to enforce best execution when the best price may be available in a competing market. This point is critical in understanding one of the links between best execution and market integration, and will be developed in subsequent chapters.

So, neither the absence of regulation nor industry self-regulation seems adequate to the task. This brings us to consider regulation by the state itself. In the United Kingdom, the goals of financial regulation are clearly stated in the FSA's Statutory Objectives, enumerated in the Financial Services and Markets Act 2000 (FSMA). These objectives are:

- maintaining confidence in the financial system

- promoting public understanding of the financial system

- securing the appropriate degree of protection for consumers

- reducing the extent to which it is possible for a business carried on by a regulated person, or in contravention of the general prohibition, to be used for a purpose connected with financial crime.[10]

On the face of it, best execution would clearly be within the customer protection remit imposed upon the FSA by Parliament. However, the same legislation injects an element of *caveat emptor*. Specifically, Section 5(2)(d) of the FSMA requires the FSA to have regard to "the general principle that consumers should take responsibility for their decisions".

---

[10]   FSMA 2000, Sections 3–6.

One of the most cogent recent critiques of state regulation has been put forward by George J. Bentson. In his critique of state regulation,[11] he examines consumer protection as a reason for state regulation of financial services. Amongst the four aspects of consumer protection he identifies, the most relevant to best execution is the "protection of consumers from unfair treatment and insufficient information".[12] Quoting the FSA, he asserts that state regulation should only be used where voluntary measures are inadequate:

> in the first instance ... [the FSA should look] to the market and market partici-
> pants to set and enforce high standards in this area [and] should take action
> where such standards are inadequate or are ineffectively enforced.[13]

Bentson rejects the need for state regulation for consumer protection, asserting that, "on balance it is likely to work against the objectives of consumers".[14] He asserts that asymmetric information and other market failures exist equally in other markets, and also refers to the importance of reputation in a competitive environment.

Yet, as we have already seen, reputations are only enhanced or damaged when the consumer knows whether he was treated fairly. While the consumer may know less about the quality of a refrigerator than the producer does, he will eventually *know* that it is a poor quality refrigerator and the manufacturer's reputation will suffer accordingly. No damage to the manufacturer's reputation would occur if this were not the case. Indeed, a customer who has been harmed but is unaware of this fact may in ignorance be a satisfied customer, holding the firm in a higher regard and enhancing its reputation.

FSA Chairman Howard Davies echoes Bentson's assertion that state regulation should only be used where there is a "market imperfection" and that the cure does not cause worse problems elsewhere.[15] Davies does not specifically address best execution in his remarks; however, the existence of a "market imperfection" with respect to best execution is demonstrated elsewhere in this book, specifically with respect to the tendency of order-flow to remain with the principal market for a security even when better prices are available on alternative venues. Given these arguments, it can be concluded that best execution constitutes a market imperfection, which cannot effectively be addressed either by the investor alone or through voluntary alternatives to regulation.

2.3 The state as provider of standardisation

An additional argument for state regulation of best execution is the need to establish a universal standard. Best execution is meant to protect the investor from poor treatment by those on whom he relies to buy and sell securities on his behalf – the "principal/agent" conflict. It is reasonable to assume that a standard of best execution written by consumer

---

[11]   Bentson, George J. *Regulating Financial Markets: A Critique and Some Proposals – Hobart Paper 135* (London: Institute for Economic Affairs), 1998.
[12]   Bentson, p. 56.
[13]   FSA, Report to the Chancellor (1997), p. 1, quoted in Bentson, p. 57.
[14]   Bentson, p. 58.
[15]   Davies, Howard. "Why Regulate", speech to City University Business School, 4 November 1998.

agencies would be different from one written by brokers, dealers or institutional investors. That is, competing interests have different characterisations of best execution. This is clearly demonstrated in the debate currently swirling around the issue, particularly in the responses provided by various interested parties to consultations conducted by the European Commission and the FSA. A universal, clear standard must be written which protects the investor and at the same time has regard to the interests and concerns of other market participants.

This is not to say that a single standard must be applied to all investors, all the time. As we shall see in the following chapters, best execution is not necessary or appropriate to all investors – professional investors or those who might wish to waive best execution, for example. However, it is important that the standard be clearly understood and uniformly applied in those situations where it is appropriate.

It will be seen in due course that regulation can play any one of a range of roles when it is called upon to correct a market imperfection. The least intrusive is to co-ordinate actions and set standards. This is most appropriate when there is little controversy that something needs to be done, but where it is necessary for an outside party with necessary authority to facilitate required actions amongst a variety of participants.

Blundell and Robinson see standard-setting by the industry as a potential area for market self-regulation. This is true in many cases, but such attempts often fall short. One reason is that the resulting standards are written by parties who may share the same interest – and this interest may not be the same as that of the investor. Another reason for such failures is a lack of will on the part of the industry. An example is the origination of the NMS in the United States, where the SEC stepped in to mandate industry action after a lack of progress by the industry acting on its own (see Chapter 5).

A second role, then, arises. This is to mandate action that the regulator determines necessary if the market participants have failed to meet their responsibilities voluntarily. Thus, state regulation may be necessary where the industry cannot provide its own standard; and the threat of the use of this power provides a powerful incentive for the market to succeed in doing so.

Conclusion

In summary, then, state regulation is appropriate in the area of best execution because:

- Consumers cannot assess the quality of their executions on their own, since they do not have access to all the data they would need to perform an accurate analysis. Due to this asymmetry of information, they do not generally know, even after the fact, whether they received good or poor execution.

- Legal remedies are not sufficient in the absence of a clear standard and where the customer does know that he has been harmed.

- If consumers do not know whether they received good or poor execution, reliance cannot be placed on the power of reputation as an incentive to good practice.

- Since it would be difficult to separate proprietary trading information from the rest of the data, a third party is needed to gather and analyse execution data.

- Even with voluntary regulation, a clear standard must be established which is fair to competing interests and which is backed by the necessary level of authority.
- In most jurisdictions, the industry has thus far failed to provide its own effective standard of best execution.

3 Fundamental Issues

Before proceeding any further, it is appropriate to set the stage for the remaining chapters by identifying the fundamental issues which underlie the best execution debate. In this chapter, the questions which form the basis of the debate on how to construct a best execution policy will be introduced. More detailed discussion, and analysis of how they might be resolved, is left for the following chapters; this chapter will serve merely to introduce the issues.

Some of the issues presented in this chapter have wide-ranging consequences and merit chapters or even books of their own. Internalisation, for instance, has become an issue in its own right and we return to it in Part 2 of the book, where we consider its impact on the question of market integration. It is, nonetheless, necessary at least to introduce these issues at this point and to touch upon the ways in which they impact the best execution debate.

3.1 To whom should the standards apply?

Having established that regulation is appropriate for ensuring best execution, the first fundamental issue is to whom this regulatory protection should apply. Should the obligation to provide best execution apply to all transactions?

The short answer is no. First, not all transactions can be said to have a "customer". Firms trading between each other for their own proprietary accounts, for example, do not need best execution protection, partly because of their presumed expertise and partly because there is no "customer" in the transaction.

Nor do all customers need the same level of protection. Best execution is chiefly aimed at protecting retail customers from the adverse effects of "information asymmetry", discussed later in this chapter and in Chapter 4. Unlike retail investors, institutional investors – pension funds, insurance companies and the like – generally have the expertise and resources necessary to protect their own interests in the market. The argument can be made that they need less – or even no – best execution protection.

On the other hand, while it is common to divide the investing world into "institutional" and "retail", or "professional" and "individual" investors, the reality is more complex. Most institutions, for instance, are pooled investments of individual investors. As such, institutions often act on behalf of individual investors, and it can be argued that this means best execution should be applied to institutional investors as well. This issue is discussed in greater detail in the Section 3.11.5.

The more important distinction in respect of best execution is between professional and non-professional investors. Professional investors would commonly include entities which employ full-time trained and licensed professionals to manage the institution's investments. Non-professional investors, roughly equivalent to "retail" investors, are typically individuals handling their own investments either directly (as in internet investing) or through a broker.

This distinction is important in framing the best execution debate, for two reasons. First, professional investors by their nature tend to have greater expertise and better real-time access to information necessary for making investment and trading decisions. It is their job, and they therefore do not have the same need for protection that a non-professional retail investor would have. As a result, professional institutions need less protection, since they possess the knowledge and data to protect themselves, whereas the "information asymmetry" – the relative disadvantage of the retail investor in terms of expertise and information – is one of the principal reasons why non-professional investors do need regulatory protection.

Secondly, the nature of the trades executed by professional institutions is altogether different from retail investors. Dealing in very large orders, they are sometimes more concerned with factors other than strictly price. For example, they may be more concerned in getting fast execution to hedge a position than they are in getting the absolute best price. They may also be more concerned with the "market impact" of buying or selling a large volume onto the market all at once. Non-professional, retail investors, in contrast, tend not to have such concerns and focus on the bottom line – the net price paid or received from their transaction.

As we can see, these short-hand distinctions – retail, institutional, individual, professional and non-professional – cut across and through the strata of investors participating in markets. Insofar as best execution is concerned, the main point is that it is the least knowledgeable investors, whatever they may be called, who require the most protection. The remainder of this book will largely follow the convention of dividing investors into retail and institutional, focusing on the protection of the retail investor. This is done with the understanding that "retail" customers who have the desire and experience to be free of the investor protection rules could waive their application either on an ongoing or on a trade-by-trade basis. This might be the case, for instance, when an individual investor with large sum of money to trade and considerable experience in the market wishes to waive the application of retail best execution rules to his trades.

In sum, best execution is primarily an instrument of *retail investor protection*. This book will argue that it is the most fundamental of all such protections, and that it is more. It is also a necessary ingredient for market integration.

3.2   Assessing execution

It has been established thus far that best execution regulation is necessary, that it is best done under state authority, and that it should focus on retail investors. In other words, it has been decided that best execution regulation needs to be done and on whose trades it should focus. The next fundamental issue is how we should go about the complicated business of accomplishing this simple task.

3.3   The approach: "conceptual" or "prescriptive"?

When regulators write rules, one of their first tasks is to decide how broad or narrow to make them. Making a regulation too narrow not only limits its scope, but could make its application unwieldy or inappropriate in the face of future market developments. On the other hand, an overly broad regulation may be too open to interpretation and therefore lack both clarity and enforceability. This dilemma has been particularly acute in the development of best execution regulation. Some argue that a fairly "prescriptive" approach is necessary, providing a benchmark standard against which executions can clearly be judged by the trader, the customer and the regulator. Others favour a "conceptual" approach, in which the notion of best execution is judged more broadly, taking into consideration all those elements which might constitute the investor's best interests. This issue is so fundamental that little progress or agreement on proposed regulation can be made until it is resolved.

There are of course arguments in favour of and against each approach. Advocates of the prescriptive approach believe that a benchmark of some sort is necessary in order to make the regulation workable. Without a clear distinction between what is allowed and what is not, they argue, there is little point in having regulation at all. The vast majority of traders want to abide by the regulations, and a clear standard assists them in doing so. Regulators require a benchmark in order to be able to establish that a violation has occurred – without it, the regulation is unenforceable. A conceptual approach, they argue, attempts to broaden the regulatory standard so widely that it ends up protecting no one, and amounts to little more than best-practice advice.

Those who advocate a conceptual approach do so on the grounds that the markets, their users and their orders are too varied to allow for a single prescriptive benchmark that is appropriate across the board. In other words, a one-size-fits all approach would in the end fit none.

There are several options under discussion. First, the standard can tend towards the conceptual, "aspirational" standard mentioned by the FSA in its Discussion Paper.[1] On the other end of the continuum, it could be more explicit and quantifiable, as in standards based specifically on price.

In discussing the merits of the conceptual approach, the FSA's Discussion Paper suggests a standard "clear in conceptual terms but which avoids the difficulty of practical application", "...setting a standard to which firms should strive".[2]

Arguably, a policy which "avoids the difficulty of practical application" is of little regulatory value. Practical application is in fact a criterion for a sound policy, not a problem to be avoided. Additionally, the decision of the District Court in the *Newton* case demonstrates the difficulty in enforcing a best execution law which is too ambiguously defined (see Chapter 6).

The FSA also sees potential disadvantages to benchmarks. These include the potential lack of incentive to improve upon the benchmark price, and the stifling of competition, which may arise by designating a particular venue as the benchmark. Price improvement is discussed in the sections that follow; competition concerns could be obviated by the application of an intermarket benchmark, also discussed in further detail below.

On balance, a sound best execution policy should have a clear benchmark against which executions may be judged. The question then becomes what the standard should be.

---

[1]   FSA Discussion Paper, p. 19.
[2]   *Ibid.*

3.4   The scope: single or multiple markets?

The question of whether brokers should be required to check more than one market reflects the historical context in which the best execution debate is set. The very question assumes the extension of the existing one-exchange standard, where it is assumed that only one exchange can be checked at a time.

Chapter 7 will discuss in detail the technology that has made this assumption obsolete. This technology has already begun bringing the best prices of multiple markets onto a single screen. With such a system, it is just as fast for a trader to check five markets as it is to check one. By doing so, these systems have begun the linking of markets into a single, unfragmented pool of liquidity. With such consolidation already present, the question of how many markets to check for the best price is moot. The question should more appropriately be whether brokers should be required to have access to a consolidated price montage, and whether they can be permitted to ignore the best price on that montage, all other factors being equal. The important point to make here is that it is now generally accepted in the best execution debate that multiple markets can be checked as a matter of routine. Given the current state of technology and market structure, it is difficult to see any argument against a requirement to check more than a single market when more than one market for a security exists. This requirement could be deemed to have been met by accessing a consolidated price montage for the security in question, and obtaining the best execution based upon the prices available through the montage.

What if the broker sees a better price, but is not a member of the market on which the price is actually quoted? It would be intuitive to believe that the broker does not have access to prices on markets to which he is not a member, and therefore he should not be required to execute at that price or on that market. But this may be misleading.

Brokers can in fact access markets of which they are not members, via an intermediary. To be sure, this will involve intermediation costs. If the intermediation costs are factored in, they may well make the "best price" an inferior price. However, allowing firms to ignore prices on markets of which they are not a member would disincentivise them from joining markets which may have the best prices, effectively rewarding the firm for staying on the sidelines. To overcome this problem the best execution standard should arguably require firms to provide the best price available even when they are not themselves members of the market in question, and to absorb the intermediation costs themselves rather than pass them on to the customer. If an alternative market is frequently at the best price, firms will find it more economical to acquire membership in that market than to continue paying intermediation costs. This would permit new alternative markets to compete on the basis of the competitiveness of their prices. This approach, though no doubt controversial in some circles, would reward innovation and facilitate competition. Competing markets that provide superior prices and innovative services would be rewarded, whereas the alternative would result in higher costs and inferior prices to the investor and would reward firms for joining as few markets as possible – an outcome which furthers neither investor protection nor market integration.

3.5   The details: what factors constitute best execution?

At first glance, best execution would seem to be about obtaining the best price for the investor. "Price" is a useful shorthand for a rather murky concept which lies at the heart of the best execution issue. Strictly speaking, "price" is by convention the displayed price of a quotation or order. The advantage of using this as the reference price for best execution is that it is clear and widely visible. The primary disadvantage, though, is that the displayed price is not the same as the "paid" price, that is, the price paid by the investor when buying, or received by the investor when selling. In practice, price involves several component factors. These factors can be usefully divided into those directly associated with the cost of the trade and those which are not. The former include transaction fees charged by exchanges and intermediaries, taxes and duties, and clearing and settlement charges. What these fees have in common is that they are charged "per trade" either on a flat fee or *ad valorem* basis. It is in this sense that they are distinguished from the latter category, which are essentially overhead charges which are not specific to the trade in question. When assessing the true price of a transaction, therefore, it is appropriate to factor in those costs which are directly attributable to the trade in question and to leave aside overhead costs such as exchange memberships or staff costs.

Some of the direct costs vary from one market to another, resulting in a situation in which executing at a superior displayed price may result in an *inferior* paid price for the investor. Should these, indeed *can* these, costs be calculated and incorporated into the judgement of best execution? Chapter 4 will consider the elements of a sound best execution policy, and it is left for that discussion to examine the treatment of costs in greater detail.

3.6   Price and non-price dimensions

The inclusion of costs, to be sure, must not come at the expense of practicality. For this reason, only those costs knowable before execution should be included. When purchasing a foreign-listed security, for instance, the trader may not know the clearing and settlement costs before execution because he does not know whether the securities that will ultimately be delivered will need to transfer across multiple depositories (and incur multiple fees). It can be hoped that these unknown fees will fall away in the future, as efforts to rationalise clearing and settlement bear fruit. In the interim, however, the policy should not judge a trader's actions against costs about which he cannot know.[3]

This presents a potential weakness in the argument, because these unknown costs could, in the end, make what appears to be the best price considerably more expensive than alternative prices with lower known costs. In other words, the unknown factor could lead to an incorrect estimate of best execution. This should not be considered grounds for throwing out the entire net-price-based approach, however, since the unknown cost factor serves potentially to diminish, rather than to negate, the value of considering the known costs. It is also worth noting that the march of progress in markets and market technology is in the direction of reducing the number and impact of unknown costs to a level where they are not material to the analysis.

---

[3]   An interesting alternative approach has been suggested in the TraderServe report on best execution and market technology. The authors of that report suggest assuming the maximum "worst-case" costs with the actual cost of all potential execution venues, even if the actual result is lower. A result of such an approach, they argue, is that it will drive the providers of these services to lower the maximum cost of their services, so that the "worst-case" cost will be lower than that of their competitors.

One might well ask how practical it is to expect the trader to check even a limited number of venues with the various known costs associated with them. Fortunately, the trader is not left to do these calculations manually each time a trade is to be executed. As most of these costs – trading fees, taxes and duties, etc. – are at known rates, they can be included in an algorithmic program which calculates and compares net prices. Such an algorithm has not proven difficult to construct, and many such algorithms are currently used in trading. Further discussion of the use of technology to calculate net price can be found in Chapter 7.

So we see that the price dimensions of a trade are not simple, but they are not beyond the reach of a practical and effective assessment. But this is not where the complexity of judging best execution ends. Different investors have different priorities when it comes to effecting a trade, and some, paradoxically, are on the surface not based on price. Some investors, for instance, favour speed or certainty of execution over price. Two questions arise – first, where and to what extent do these "non-price" factors dominate and second, how should these non-price priorities be addressed in a best execution policy? To a great extent, the focus of the best execution debate has revolved around these questions. The only certainty in this issue is that, whatever be the outcome, it will please a few and greatly displease many others. A few of the more prominent non-price dimensions are set out below.

3.7   Speed of execution

Perhaps the most commonly mentioned amongst these is "speed of execution". Under what circumstances might this be the most important factor – so important that the investor is willing to accept a less favourable price than might otherwise be available? Generally, speed is important when the execution in question is part of a trading strategy which involves multiple investments made more or less simultaneously. Such situations might occur when purchasing a basket of securities (or index), or engaging in a hedging strategy which involves purchasing or selling derivatives and their underlying equities at the same time. These strategies are most commonly executed by institutions rather than small investors.[4]

3.8   Certainty of execution

A related factor is that of "certainty" of execution. While it is true that securities often trade simultaneously on multiple markets, it is frequently asserted that one market may be far more liquid than the others. On this assumption, traders sometimes simply send orders to this dominant market, presuming that the larger number of orders increases the certainty of execution for the order.

Implicit in this assumption is the need for immediate execution. If the order were sent instead to a less liquid market, the trader could cancel the order if execution were not

---

[4]   While individual retail investors may indeed buy baskets of securities, they generally do so directly with their broker (acting in the capacity of a dealer) or through a fund rather than directly through the market; the same is often the case in many other circumstances involving retail investors.

forthcoming and enter a new order into the more liquid dominant market. The problem of course is that the trader naturally does not wish to spend the time and effort to do so, when he can instead always send the order to the most liquid market without even bothering to check prices on other markets.

Whether this assumption is valid depends both on the relative liquidity of the markets and on the size of the order to be executed. If one market dominates liquidity to the point that the security is rarely actually available on the other markets, there is good reason to assume it is the only market with "certain execution". On the other hand, if the security is normally available on another market – particularly if it is a market-maker market where some firms have committed to making constant prices – then the question is not the *certainty* of execution, but whether the prices are better on one or the other market. In this situation, where certainty is no longer the issue, it is difficult to argue that the other markets should be ignored. The size of the order is of course a factor in this assessment, as it always is in questions of execution. If the order in question is for a large size – 50 000 shares, for instance – and the sizes normally available on the other markets are only for a few hundred shares, there may indeed be difficulty in executing the order away from the main market. As is the case with speed of execution, questions of certainty are generally concerns of large institutional investors rather than retail investors.

3.9 Market impact

It is sometimes the case that a pending order is so large in relation to the market that it will so tip the supply-and-demand balance that it would seriously impact the stability of the market for those shares. Dumping a large order onto a market, especially one which is fairly illiquid, often means driving down the price significantly. By the time the order has been filled (a process which may require many individual transactions over several days), the price can have dropped dramatically, substantially reducing the overall price obtained for the order (this would of course occur in the opposite direction with a large order to buy). For large orders, then, "market impact" can be a factor to consider when deciding when, where and how to execute an order.

Though market impact is often cited as a non-price factor for best execution, its relevance to the issue is not immediately clear. Suppose the best bid for a security is for 10 000 shares at €20, and an order to sell is for one million shares. Is the trader to obtain a price of €20 for all one million shares? Clearly not, and no existing best execution policy would say otherwise. However, some might argue that the order should continue down the bids, taking out all orders at successively lower prices until a million shares have been bought. It is in this sense that market impact connects with best execution, and many have argued that the market impact of an order should be a factor which permits discretion on the part of the trader.

The market impact of large orders is, however, an issue which relates to the stability of markets in general and is not limited to best execution. Other, more appropriate measures have been introduced to reduce market impact, such as "block trade" provisions in the United Kingdom which permit delayed reporting of large trades. In short, market impact is better addressed by transparency regulations than by best execution policies.

3.10 Non-standard settlement

On some markets in some circumstances, the period over which settlement takes place can rather perversely take precedence over price. In the United Kingdom, for instance, final settlement of a trade between two parties takes place on the third business day following the trade ("T + 3"). For those (primarily retail) investors who still hold shares in paper form ("certificated shares"), however, settlement may not be possible until later, as long as T + 5. Since it is necessary for both parties of a transaction to agree as to the day on which money will be exchanged for securities, the non-standard order can only match against other orders willing to settle on a later date. If the order representing best net price cannot be done for late settlement, the trader must look down the queue for other orders. In such a case, settlement terms can indeed be more important than the price. Non-standard settlement may also be required on occasion by institutions for various reasons. With respect to retail trades, at least, the need for non-standard settlement is driven mostly by the continued but diminishing presence of certificated shares, and can be expected to become less important as more shares become electronic "book entry" securities.

3.11 Counterparty risk limits

A common risk-management tool is to spread risk amongst a number of counterparties, so that the failure of one counterparty will not have disproportionate effects on the firm's own business. This leads to the practice of establishing exposure limits to each counterparty, and thus to limitations on the amount of business to be transacted with each. Counterparty risk limits have been identified by some as an additional non-price factor to be considered in best execution, since a strict best execution requirement could force firms to exceed these risk limits. Setting aside the question of whether risk management should trump best execution, it is worth noting that more and more markets are moving to anonymous trading where the counterparty is not known until after the trade has been agreed and settlement instructions need to be exchanged. Where the counterparty is not known, there is obviously no way to follow counterparty risk limits anyway. Even more, many markets are moving towards a central counterparty model, where a separate entity stands in the middle, acting as the "buyer" to all sellers and the "seller" to all buyers. Central counterparties assume the risk of either party defaulting on the transaction, virtually eliminating counterparty risk. Like non-standard settlement, then, we can foresee this factor becoming less and less important with respect to best execution.

Drafting language in policies to cover non-price factors has not proven easy. Making reference to all potential (current and future) non-price factors is not possible, so language such as "the overall condition of the market" or "best overall result" taking into account "all relevant factors" is often used. As we see below, this creates a new set of problems.

The preceding pages highlight some of the non-price factors which may be involved in determining the best execution for an order. It is not meant to be an exhaustive list, but rather to discuss some of the more frequently mentioned factors and why they may (or may not) bear on execution decisions. From this discussion, a few common threads are apparent.

First, non-price factors may, at their core, still be about achieving the best price. The danger behind slow or uncertain execution is usually that the best available price will move in an unfavourable direction while the trader is awaiting execution. Hedging and settlement cycles aside, the bottom line motivation behind any investment is after all to maximise profit by buying at the lowest net price and selling at the highest net price. In no other sense does speed, certainty, or "market impact" influence profitability than to the extent it impacts on the final cost, through the price of execution.

Secondly, we see that changes to market structure are making some of these factors less of a concern. The move towards fully electronic shares will reduce the need, particularly amongst retail investors, for non-standard settlement; moves towards anonymous and central counterparties reduce the relevance of counterparty risk limits.

The major non-price factors are fundamentally associated with the large trades and complex strategies of professional, institutional investors and not with the smaller and more straightforward trades of private retail investors. This is a critical point. It makes sense to differentiate between the two, applying the broad range of price and non-price factors to the institutional trades for which they are appropriate, and applying to retail trades *only* those factors appropriate to the protection of retail investors. This implied division in the standard of best execution has important implications, and is often overlooked.

Consider a retail order, of normal size and for normal settlement, which is received by a trader for execution. Whatever the range of factors to be considered, the trader is obliged to obtain the best execution for that order. If the range of factors is broad, using the general language described above ("overall condition of the market", "best possible result"), the trader has a wide degree of discretion in determining where to execute the order. A trader could, for instance, send orders consistently to the same market because it is faster for him not to check other markets, because his compensation is partly based on his market share of the main market, or for any one of a number of reasons which would not exist in the perfect markets of an Economics textbook. In doing so, he may not receive the best price for the customer, or even the second-best price, but could justify the execution based on a murky concept of overall market conditions or overall best interests.

On the other hand, if the best execution for retail orders were limited to those factors which really matter to most retail investors – price and direct costs – the trader would not have the latitude to send the order to any market. His next order may be a large order from an institution, in which case it is entirely appropriate for him to take into account the range of non-price factors.

Here, then, we see one reason for distinguishing between retail and institutional best execution. This is that the factors which are relevant to the institutions are drastically more complex than those relevant to retail investors, and that applying institutional factors to retail trades confers an inappropriate degree of discretion which can be abused to the detriment of the retail customer.

The second rationale for the retail/institutional distinction is associated with this danger of abuse. It is retail investors who are at the heart of investor protection measures such as best execution. If the whole point behind such a measure is to protect investors, it should focus first on those who most *need* protection, making appropriate accommodation for the professionals, rather than the reverse. The most effective way to protect retail investors is to draft a policy around their needs and grant wider discretion for institutions, or even to disapply best execution altogether from institutional trades.

This approach implies that there must be a way of distinguishing a retail trade from an institutional one. Should it be done by the size of the order? If so, what should the threshold between a retail (protected) trade and an institutional one be? Is it not true that retail investors sometimes make large trades and institutions small ones?

Perhaps, then, the distinction should be based on the assets and investment experience of the investor. Again, this is a rather rough-and-ready means of distinction, but one which is already used effectively in other circumstances. Certain securities in the US market are considered inappropriate for retail investors, and those who wish to purchase them must self-certify that they meet certain eligibility criteria (usually related to their primary business or the assets they have under investment). The presumption is that investors are not eligible for these risky investments unless they "opt in" through self-certification.

This approach helps us to understand how to make the distinction between retail and institutional investors for best execution purposes. After all, it may be the case that a retail investor wishes the trader to consider non-price factors either for one trade or for all trades. The policy can start with the presumption that the trade is to receive retail protection – that is, retail best execution is the "default" standard. Investors could waive this protection and opt in to institutional protection either on a one-time-only or a continuing basis.

This brings us to the end of a fairly lengthy logical chain, but one which is central to making best execution work. Best execution needs to encompass all price factors, but non-price factors may be more important for some investors, some or all of the time. These investors should be accommodated with a separate, appropriately broad standard, but those retail investors most in need of protection must be afforded the protection of tighter, net-price-based standards. These retail standards should be presumed to be in effect for all retail investors, but any investor could waive retail protection and opt in to the broader standard either as needed or on an until-revoked basis.

3.12 Other issues

3.12.1 *Internalisation*

The practice of "internalising" orders was the focus of considerable debate in the course of the European Commission's review of the Investment Services Directive begun in 2001 and has been a topic of debate in the United States for some years. Internalisation, simply put, occurs when a firm executes incoming customer orders "internally" either against other customer orders or against its own account. They therefore do not execute on any exchange, though their execution may be reported to an exchange afterwards.

Internalisation can be beneficial to the retail customer in some circumstances. Internalised orders do not require certain operational services, potentially reducing the cost of the trade (assuming that the lower cost is passed on to the customer). The magnitude of this saving varies, however, since the fees associated with trading on some exchanges are considerably lower than on others. Orders could also potentially receive faster execution in-house, though again the impact would vary and is likely to diminish as technologies to route orders to exchanges become more and more advanced.

The implications for best execution are twofold. First, is an internalised order isolated from the wider market, depriving it of potentially better execution outside the internalising firm? In other words, how is the best price defined for internalised orders – the best price amongst those with which it interacts (other internalised orders and the firm's own positions), or the best price in the market as a whole?

The second implication takes the reverse view. What impact does the internalisation of orders have on the rest of the market? If an order held within a firm is in fact better than that displayed on any exchange, should the rest of the market be entitled to see (and interact with) that order?

It seems evident that orders should not be internalised at prices inferior to the best price on the wider market. It would also seem logical that the rest of the market should be entitled to interact with the order. Internalisation, though, is a broader market issue with important consequences for market transparency and consolidation. In this respect, it is discussed in more detail in Chapter 9.

3.12.2 *Order routing vs price matching*

Once the best price is determined, does it matter to the customer *where* the execution is done? On the face of it, the answer is no. If the net price is the same to the customer, it seems to make little difference whether his firm routes the order to the venue with the best price, or the firm matches that price itself (or routes it to a third party which will match the best price). There are two potential reservations about the practice of price matching. The first is the question of whether the trade would receive an equivalent level of regulatory protection if executed internally by the firm or with the third party. This question, though, is a larger one which deals with the general problem of internalisation and the regulation of alternative trading systems (discussed in later chapters), and so the answer to this question depends largely on how the larger issue is addressed. The second reservation concerns incentives. If a firm takes the risk of advancing to the best price in the open market, is it fair that another takes the business? If price makers lose their business to price takers who essentially free ride off their business, will there be any incentive to take the risk of advancing to the superior price? The question of order routing vs price matching is one which will likely receive increased attention as best execution policies are worked out in greater detail.

3.12.3 *Price improvement*

The preceding discussion has examined best execution with the assumption that all available prices are displayed, so that the starting point, at least, for finding best execution is to find the best displayed price. But the best displayed prices are not necessarily the best available prices. As long as the spread between the best bid and the best offer is greater than one tick size (quote increment), there is room for improvement within the spread and there may be a trader who would be willing to trade at a better price if approached. This poses a problem for best execution – should traders be required to shop around for better undisplayed prices, or would this be overly burdensome?

Taking this argument further, it has been asserted that a benchmark provides little or no incentive for price improvement, since traders will simply execute at the best displayed price and not seek improvement. As the FSA pointed out in its Best Execution Discussion Paper, "A minimum price may provide little incentive to improve. A benchmark or safe harbour price can define only what is not best execution (i.e. poor execution – execution at prices less than the benchmark). A benchmark price cannot define 'best execution' ".[5]

---

[5]   FSA Discussion Paper, pp. 16–17.

Some participants take the reverse view – that customers are more interested in avoiding price *disimprovement*, that is, obtaining a price inferior to that which is displayed at the time of their investment decision.[6] In this respect, the term "best execution" may be misleading. Instead of establishing a standard which implies no better price is available, best execution could be viewed as establishing the *minimum acceptable* standard.[7] If this is the case, then it should not be necessary to shop for undisplayed prices, since the investor has made the buy or sell decision based on the prices which are visible to him on the markets.

The *Newton* and *Geman* cases in the United States described in Chapter 6 provide useful illustrations of the price improvement dilemma. These cases attack the notion of whether the intermarket best price benchmark always constitutes best execution. As we shall see, though, the facts in the cases show that the decisions do not substantially erode the idea that the best displayed price can be used as the starting point for best execution. In each of the cases, the regulators alleged that the firm in question *knew* that a better price was available, and in fact obtained the better price for its own proprietary trades. Following on from these cases, it seems logical that a sound policy would generally require a firm to obtain a better price it already *knows to be available*, and certainly to refrain from profiting by dealing with the customer at the best displayed price while dealing for itself at the better undisplayed price. Put differently, these cases reaffirm the value of a benchmark, and focus their decisions more on discriminatory pricing.

The US experience is also instructive in another sense. The intermarket benchmark standard has been applied to best execution in the United States for over two decades. As technology advanced, a niche was created to provide price improvement on a regular basis, and the market filled this void. The SEC decision in the Geman case described the service, noting that one firm in particular offered price improvement over the best displayed price for any market order it received for a security in which the firm made a market and in which the bid/offer spread was greater than one tick size. Firms in the United States have been offering these services at least as far back as 1990.

The existence of firms offering guaranteed price improvement – for over a decade – demonstrates that the use of a benchmark does not necessarily discourage price improvement, because the void can be, and is, filled by the market itself. The question then becomes, as it was in the Geman case, whether these improved prices are "reasonably available".

Legal arguments aside, there is perhaps a simpler way to address price improvement in a best execution policy. In cases where the investor wishes the firm to seek price improvement (i.e. shop for a better undisplayed price), the customer should be able to instruct the firm to do so. This would be done by entering a "discretionary" or "not held" order, as is common practice in the United States. These are market orders which permit the trader to use his discretion to attempt to improve upon the current best price. This is done with the understanding that the price may actually move away while the trader is looking for better prices. Where this happens, the trader is not held responsible for the inferior price. "Not held" orders provide an important element of flexibility and should be established amongst the exchanges in conjunction with the new best execution policy.

---

[6]   Letter from Charles Schwab & Co., Inc. to Securities and Exchange Commission, 5 July 2000.

[7]   It would be a mistake, however, to confuse the issue with semantics. As the convention is to refer to the issue as "best" execution, the term should continue to be used.

3.12.4 *Limit orders*

Discussion of best execution normally is phrased in terms of "market" orders, those for which no specific price is provided by the investor. In placing a market order, the customer implicitly instructs the trader to obtain best execution (however that is defined). Little attention is paid to how best execution should apply to limit orders, or other conditional orders. A simple limit order is one in which the investor specifies the price at which he is willing to buy or sell the securities. For example, a limit order to buy 1000 shares of XYZ at a limit of €20 would instruct the trader to buy the shares only if he can do so at a price of €20 or less. Such an order would be placed when the offered price for XYZ is greater than €20, with the investor betting that the price will fall to (or below) €20. Unless and until this happens, the order remains unexecuted. In fact, if the price of the security *rises*, the investor will not receive an execution at all. In effect, the investor is willing to risk non-execution in order to benefit from the predicted fall in the price of the shares.

In a sense, limit orders are a convenience for investors who do not have the time or facilities to monitor the price of the security and then execute when the price is at the appropriate level (i.e. patiently watch the market and enter a market order when the price reaches €20). That is, the investor is placing a reservation to trade when the market reaches a particular level, rather than waiting until it happens and then fighting the crowds. The existence of limit orders is in this sense a recognition of the fact that investors do not have the time, information and resources to monitor the markets and react quickly to maximise their own trading profits (though limit orders are in fact also used by institutions and traders who cannot watch the prices on all their securities at once).

This brings us to the application of best execution to limit orders. Since limit orders are essentially a reserved market order, it seems appropriate that the investor should be as entitled to best execution for a limit order as for a market order. The difference lies merely in the way the order is placed – immediate (market) or reserved (limit) – and this difference would not justify a lower level of protection.

3.12.5 *Soft commissions, bundling and misaligned incentives*

Institutional investors are often given the opportunity to receive monetary or non-monetary incentives for routing order flow to specific trading firms or venues. In the United States, this may take the form of "payment for order flow", in the form of rebates or in-kind services such as the provision of investment research or information technology. In the United Kingdom, monetary payment for order flow is not permitted, but the provision of non-monetary goods and services ("soft commissions") is allowed to take place. The use of these incentives is relevant to best execution to the extent that it may artificially influence the choice of execution agent, or may be used to justify a less-than-best execution price.

The issue of soft commissions is as broad and deep as the best execution debate itself. In 2000, the UK government ordered a review of institutional investing, resulting in a 200-plus page report (the "Myners Report"), which recommended broad reform of the soft commission practice. Specifically, the Myners Report recommends that institutional investors should pay for the services currently being provided under soft-dollar arrangements in order to make the costs transparent to the individual investor.

The use of soft commissions is a practice common amongst institutions in both the United States and United Kingdom. Schwartz and Steil found that, on average, 26% of the order flow of those surveyed was directed to broker-dealers "as payment for 'research, trading or information services or third-party services' ".[8] In the United States, an inspection by the SEC of seventy-five broker-dealers found that seventy-one had soft commission arrangements in place.[9] A study commissioned by FSA in the United Kingdom found the practice to be widespread as well, finding that up to 40% of commissions paid by fund managers to brokers went to pay for services other than trade execution.[10] This figure represents both soft commission arrangements (such as the provision of data vendor terminals and company or market research) and "bundled" services. Bundling of services is the practice of providing additional services not directly related to trade execution, and charging a single inclusive price for both these services and executions.

Both soft commissioning and bundling bring the potential for conflicts of interest arising from the incentives they provide to route order flow to particular brokers or venues. According to the FSA, both bundled services and soft commissions are normally supplied on the understanding, implied or explicit, that the fund manager will send a specific volume of business to the executing broker.[11] Indeed, where the provision of these services is based on a multiple of the order flow (i.e. £100 of data terminal subscriptions for every £115 in order flow sent to the broker), a perverse reversal of incentives occurs – order flow decisions are based on the need to pay for support services, rather than the reverse. A fund manager who knows that he needs to pay for ten data terminals knows that they will be paid for by the broker, and need not come from his own budget, if he routes a certain amount of order flow to the broker.

Soft commissions interfere with best execution in two ways. First, brokers compete for institutional order flow not by making, or seeking out, the best possible trade prices for their institutional clients, but rather by offering them services unrelated to trade execution, which these clients may purchase using their fundholders' assets. Second, institutional clients select brokers based not on minimising the cost of executing orders, but rather on the basis of brokers' packages of ancillary services which can be purchased with trading commissions. In the absence of such soft and bundled commission arrangements, institutions have an unambiguous commercial incentive to pursue best execution on each and every transaction, thus significantly mitigating the need for regulatory monitoring and intervention.[12]

An objection may be raised that the use of soft commissions and bundling is not harmful to best execution, since the brokers are themselves obliged to obtain best execution once they receive the order from the fund manager. This objection is based on two assumptions, however. First is that the best execution policy is formulated in a way that provides an effective control on the broker. In other words, it must employ an enforceable

---

[8]   Schwartz, Robert A. and Steil Benn. "Controlling Institutional Trading Costs: We Have Met the Enemy, and it is Us", in *The Journal Portfolio Management*, Spring 2002, p. 41.

[9]   Securities and Exchange Commission (SEC), *Inspection Report on the Soft Dollar Practices of Broker-Dealers, Investment Advisors and Mutual Funds*, 22 September 1998, at IV.a.

[10] Oxford Economic Research Associates, *An Assessment of Soft Commission Arrangements and Bundled Brokerage Services in the UK*, March 2003, cited in FSA Consultation Paper 176, *Bundled Brokerage and Soft Commission Arrangements*, April 2003.

[11] FSA, CP 176, pp. 8–9.

[12] E-mail to the author from Dr Benn Steil, 7 April 2003.

benchmark for the execution of an institution's trades in the same way as it does for retail trades. Yet this poses practical problems. Broader standards are likely more appropriate for institutions, yet a standard such as the best interests of the customer would be of no help in ensuring best execution, since the provision of these services could be loosely judged by the fund manager and the broker to be in the customer's best interests. Secondly, the fund managers would presumably be entitled to waive best execution, but would do so based on their own interests and not those of the fund managers' own customers. If the brokers paying soft commissions have access to a limited number of venues, they may not be able to provide the same level of execution quality as other options available to the fund manager, and it may therefore be necessary for the fund manager to waive best execution protection in order to make the soft commission arrangement viable.

In sum, the use of soft commissions and bundling arrangements distorts the execution decision process by providing incentives to base these decisions on factors other than the quality of the execution itself. Like internalisation, the concept of soft commissions is a broad one which cannot be judged solely on its implications for best execution. A full examination of the practice is beyond the scope of this book, and so it is left here, highlighting the fact that it is one of many issues impacting on best execution.

3.12.6 *Statistical disclosure of execution quality*

Another approach to best execution is to eschew trade-by-trade regulation in favour of requiring periodic public disclosure of general execution performance (for execution venues) or order routing practices (for brokerage firms). Such an approach can in fact be taken on its own or in conjunction with trade-by-trade regulation. In the United States, this approach has been formalised as Rules 11Ac1-5 and 11Ac1-6 as discussed below. A similar approach was later proposed by the FSA in the United Kingdom.

The key questions with respect to the disclosure approach are (1) does the benefit to the investor justify the cost to the industry and (2) is disclosure alone sufficient, or need it be complemented by other measures?

The idea of public disclosure of relevant facts and statistics seeks to address the central notion of the best execution problem – the information asymmetry, which puts the investor at a disadvantage *vis-à-vis* the broker. While few would argue against providing information, *more* information is not necessarily the same as *useful* and *timely* information.

In mandating the publication of this information, three assumptions are made. First, it is assumed that investors will look at the information. Do all investors know where it is (if it is all in one place), and will they then bother to look at it on a regular basis? Will it be more relevant to them than the firms' commission rates, which are not given the same level of exposure?

Secondly, it is assumed that investors will comprehend the information and its impact upon them. This means that the investors not only understand the meaning of the information, but also make a comparison with competing firms. Implicit in this assumption is that a uniform methodology can be derived which can be applied to all types of firms and will be meaningful and understandable to all types of investors regardless of the type of investing in which they engage. Yet given the difficulties already discussed in terms of composing a universal definition of best execution, it seems highly improbable that a single, universally applicable measure of execution quality can be devised.

Thirdly, the disclosure of information assumes that investors will actually *do something* with it. If they conclude that their firm does not give them best execution, will individual investors really switch brokers? How often – once a quarter or once a month?

More information can even have a detrimental effect. If disclosure is believed to be more effective than it really is, regulators might forego other policies, which in fact are necessary to supplement disclosure. Put another way, overconfidence in the effectiveness of disclosure could make the financial community complacent that best execution is being looked after. Additionally, disclosure rules could be enormously complex and costly. Regular calculation and publication of statistics and "report cards" involve both expense and manpower. If the information is not serving its goal, this cost likely outweighs the benefits.

Lastly, the accuracy and consistency of the data is itself subject to debate. As the New York Stock Exchange (NYSE) itself pointed out, statistical measurements of best execution vary considerably depending upon the methodology used.[13] This view was also reflected in a letter from the Securities Industry Association (SIA) Trading Committee to NASD Regulation (NASD-R) regarding NASD-R "compliance report cards".[14] In this letter, the SIA noted that it had analysed over one thousand transactions and had found problems with more than 70% of the alerts generated and published by NASD-R in the relevant report cards, primarily due to either "flawed programming logic or inaccurate data".[15] It is difficult to imagine a universally valid and neutral methodology for judging execution quality (particularly if one accepts the argument that so many intangible non-price factors are involved).

So, there is a danger of over-reliance on public disclosure of execution quality data, but can it also be helpful? A useful parallel might be the idea of publishing bank interest rates. These are standardised and relatively simple to understand, but do customers actually switch banks every time they see another bank paying higher interest? The answer is no, but it highlights the actual intent of public disclosure. Publication of interest rates – or execution quality – is a matter of facilitating competition through transparency. Customers might not move to new firms en masse every time a new leader appears, but the firm could use its standings in the tables to enhance its reputation more generally, leading to more new customers in the long run.

Also, some types of information are more easily comprehended and therefore more useful than others. SEC Rule 11Ac1-6 requires firms which accept customer orders to disclose their practices with respect to the market centres to whom they send customer orders for execution. This is much simpler and comprehensible than calculating execution quality on a statistical basis. Information which clearly informs the investor how many (and to which) markets the firm has access would likely be clear of relatively obvious relevance and of minimal cost.

For these reasons, it seems logical that firms which accept customer orders should be required to disclose publicly the information vendors and the markets to which it has access, but detailed statistical information should not be mandated.

---

[13] Bacidore, Jeffrey, Katherine Ross and George Sofiano. "Quantifying Best Execution at the New York Stock Exchange: Market Orders". NYSE Working Paper 99-05, December, 1999, p. 1.
[14] Letter from SIA Trading Committee to NASD Regulation (NASDR), 27 June 2001.
[15] *Ibid.*

Conclusion

Chapter 2 set out the case for a regulatory best execution policy. This chapter has shown how complex a task the formulation of such a policy will be. While the concept of providing the best price may seem a common-sense and straightforward idea, we have seen that there is little here that is straightforward, and that there remains considerable debate as to how such a policy should be framed.

Once best execution is removed from its protective theoretical cocoon and placed in the market, practical considerations begin to raise questions. We see that the concept of price must be qualified by the costs associated with the trade, but even these costs are not always simple to delineate. Further, we find that not all customers have the same priorities or the same idea of what constitutes best execution in their trades. Specifically, we see that retail and institutional customers are vastly different both in the level of protection they need and in the execution factors on which they place highest priority. This division leads to the proposition that two different policies are needed, and the issue of how the market is to distinguish when one should be applied rather than the other.

We have also seen in this chapter that best execution is one of many market-related issues, most of which touch on each other. Internalisation, the use of soft commissions and other topics of current controversy is closely intertwined with best execution (and in fact, we will see in the second half of this book that all of these issues are entwined in the larger issue of market integration).

In pointing out the difficulties, this chapter has also aimed to point out some solutions, or at least compromises. The conclusion from Chapter 2 remains valid – that best execution requires some level of regulatory structure. The complexities raised in this chapter then become issues to address, rather than reasons to shrink from the task. In the next chapter, we will see how a valid best execution policy might be constructed, which optimises investor protection without unduly compromising the operation of the market.

4 Putting it Together: *Elements of a Sound Best Execution Policy*

Up to this point, we have seen that the seemingly simple idea that investors should receive the best available execution for their trades is actually quite complex. It is entangled with several other issues, from the definition of key concepts to the way in which it should be measured. This chapter will aim to put the puzzle back together, examining the ways in which these issues can be tackled. The chapter begins by considering what the finished product should look like – by looking at those elements which must be present in any proposed policy in order for it to be effective. With these elements in mind, a workable best execution policy takes form.

4.1 Elements of an effective best execution policy

A good place to begin is by asking ourselves how we will judge the effectiveness of a best execution policy. Like most other regulatory policies, it must meet three tests if it is to be effective. It must be enforceable, flexible and practical. The sections which follow begin with the problem of composing a policy which is both enforceable and sufficiently flexible, before addressing the question of practicality.

4.2 The enforceability/flexibility dilemma

The first two elements, enforceability and flexibility, are in a sense two directions in a continuum, and regulation is often a matter of finding the point in between which strikes the right balance. Finding this point is a matter of judging how much emphasis to place on each of these two qualities in the matter at hand.

Enforceability concerns tend to dominate when the issue focuses on investor protection, particularly with respect to vulnerable retail investors. These policies require a relatively high level of clarity and certainty so that a violator can be shown to have breached the relevant rules. In the absence of this certainty, two problems arise. First, it would be nearly impossible for regulators or litigators to seek redress. Secondly, without the likelihood of regulatory sanction, the policy's deterrent effect is substantially reduced. To facilitate enforceability, rules should be as clear and straightforward as possible. Fortunately, retail trading (as compared to institutional) itself tends to be fairly straightforward, since individual customers generally tend to invest on the basis of return (i.e. net prices) and are less likely to invest in highly complex instruments or engage in complicated trading strategies.

Many say that it is impossible to judge best execution on a trade-by-trade basis, and that it instead should be judged as a process. While this may be true for institutions, the argument can still be made that a process-based judgement leaves considerable (and unwarranted) room for individual interpretation. Indeed, a process-based approach does not eliminate the trade-by-trade assessment of best execution. Instead, it transfers the trade-by-trade judgement from the customer to the trader – or more precisely, to thousands of traders. Since these traders act based on their own judgement, experience and whims, the resulting application of the policy would lack anything close to consistency. A single enforceable benchmark provides one standard for all, rather than as many standards as there are traders.

Flexibility becomes more important as the issues or instruments subject to the policy become more complex. Consequently, it becomes a priority when working on issues in which there is significant involvement with institutional trading. In order to accommodate the needs of a wide range of actors, business models and situations, these standards need to be high-level, broadly worded principles.

In determining where to place best execution regulation along this continuum, we must first ask ourselves where the focus of the policy lies – with retail or with institutional investors. It has already been established in Chapter 3 that best execution is fundamentally a matter of protecting retail investors, leading to the conclusion that best execution policy, in order to be effective, must lie well along the "enforceability" end of the continuum. This presents two issues: how to construct a policy so that it is sufficiently enforceable, and how to prevent any resulting reduction in flexibility from impairing institutional business.

The Regulatory Policy Continuum

Flexibility	Enforceability
Aspirational/Conceptual	Comprehensive/Prescriptive
General/Non-Price Standards	Benchmark Standards
Less Binding	More Binding
Institutional Investors	Retail Investors

4.3 Enforcement: visibility and clarity

An enforceable policy requires a clear and widely visible standard – a benchmark. In order to be useful as a customer protection measure, it must be clear and demonstrable when the standard has not been met. This serves two functions. First, it facilitates disciplinary action by leaving little room for argument and interpretation over vague concepts such as general market conditions or overall best interests of the customer. The resulting sanctions, publicly enforced, serve both to deter future abuse and to inspire confidence in the market. Sanctions cannot be imposed fairly without some measure which serves as a litmus test as to when a violation has occurred.

The second function served by a benchmark is to provide clear guidance to firms executing customer orders. Market participants do not generally seek additional regulation, but they do seek regulatory clarity. By reducing the level of imprecision and uncertainty, a benchmark permits firms to develop policies and systems to ensure that customer orders in fact receive proper execution. For instance, they can then set automated parameters for trading and for internal monitoring of compliance with the standard – something not possible with indistinct standards. This simplifies procedures and potentially reduces compliance costs. By reducing imprecision, benchmarks also reduce the risk of litigation. The more open the standard is to interpretation, the more vulnerable firms are to costly lawsuits – with or without merit – alleging failure to achieve best execution. When compliance is measured against a clear benchmark, the executions are more easily defended and frivolous lawsuits are discouraged.

Benchmark regulation, then, provides a means of deterring and sanctioning the dishonest broker, and at the same time serves the honest firm by providing clear guidance for compliance purposes.

Consider the alternative. Suppose that a best execution policy were more "aspirational", setting a conceptual standard which a firm should *attempt* to meet, using broad terms such as "the best interests of the customer". Many firms would still strive to achieve the best price for their customers. But regulation must focus on the dishonest broker, who intends to cheat his customer or at least to place his own interests above those of the customer. Studies have demonstrated that, when a trader's compensation is geared towards execution on particular markets, or when a trader executes on dominant markets out of sheer force of habit, the prices on other markets may be ignored.[1] In such circumstances, a trader could easily justify any price given to the customer, based on the broker's broad interpretation of the best interests of the customer. An imprecise and overly broad "aspirational" standard would also fail to deliver the advantages for firms deriving from regulatory clarity.

4.4   Determining the benchmark

How, then, are we to construct a clear standard? The logical starting point is the best displayed price. This price is visible – widely seen by those who make execution decisions (i.e. traders) as well as the public (through the internet and other media). It is also distinct – an execution price is either as good as the displayed price or it is not.

The displayed price has the additional advantage of immediacy – it can be checked before the order is executed. In order for a best execution policy to work, it must not merely be a standard by which regulators can *retrospectively* check to determine whether a trade was done properly. It must be visible to the trader *ex ante* so that he can give best execution, knowing it to be best execution. The purpose of the policy, after all, is to prevent poor executions from happening in the first place, not merely to punish those who have failed to meet the criteria through deliberate or inadvertent negligence. This requires a standard visible before the trade is done.

While the displayed price provides a useful starting point, it is not the price actually paid or received by the investor. Taxes and duties, "wire charges", and other costs associated with the trade affect the final, or net, cost. These charges often vary depending on where the execution is done, and as a result the best displayed price may not result in the best net price to the customer. Since it is the net price which constitutes the customer's bottom line, it is important to take into consideration those costs directly relevant to the trade, and base best execution on the best net price and not merely on the best displayed price.

---

[1]   See for instance European Central Bank (ECB) *The Euro Equity Markets*, August 2001, pp. 37–42 and Charteris Plc, *European Financial Markets 2001: Revolution or Evolution?*, 2001, p. 8.

4.5   Calculating the benchmark

Which costs are directly relevant, and should be included in the net price calculation? Again, the retail focus dictates beginning with the perspective of the investor, who after all is the presumed beneficiary of a best execution policy. The purpose of buying and selling securities, from the investor's point of view, is to make a profit. To do so – to maximise economic benefit – the investor seeks to purchase at the lowest net cost and sell for the highest net proceeds. It is appropriate then to focus on those costs which are added to or subtracted from the gross amount of the trade, and which result in an adjustment to the cost or proceeds to the customer. These include those costs which:

1.   affect the final price paid or received by the investor (*not* the executing firm)

2.   are knowable before the execution of the trade

3.   are readily quantifiable.

The first condition attempts to distinguish direct costs from overhead. Overhead costs are not specific to the trade – membership fees paid by firms to securities markets, for instance – and should not be included in the net price calculation.

Typical direct costs include exchange transaction fees, clearing and settlement charges, taxes and duties (such as Stamp Duty and the Panel on Takeovers and Mergers Levy in the UK). It could also include any fees paid to an intermediary, for instance when a firm wishes to execute a trade on an exchange of which it is not a member.[2]

The second condition almost goes without saying, but it is worth recognising that some costs may not be known before the trade is executed. An example might be the clearing and settlement costs when purchasing a foreign security. Particularly if that security is less liquid, delivery of the shares may involve two or more settlement depositories, resulting in multiple transfer fees. It must be said that this is not a common situation, and that the ongoing rationalisation of clearing and settlement arrangements within Europe will do much to eliminate this problem (at least within Europe).

The third condition is also fairly self-evident. As the calculation of net price is essentially a matter of arithmetic, the values used in the calculation must be clearly identified. It is no problem to subtract two from fifty, but how does one quantify "speed" or "market impact" in such a way that it can be included in the net price calculation? As common sensical as the third condition is, it leads to the heart of one of the most contentious issues in the best execution debate – how, or indeed whether, to account for inexplicit costs and non-price-related factors. The answers to these important questions depend largely on whether the customer is a retail or an institutional investor, and this further illustrates the importance of making a distinction between the two types of investor.

To the retail investor focused on buying low and selling high, elements such as speed and certainty are not irrelevant, but they are incidental. That is, they are relevant only to the extent that they enable the execution to be done at the most favourable price.

---

[2]   The argument could be made, however, that firms should absorb intermediation fees in such circumstances in order to encourage them to join those exchanges which most frequently have superior prices. This is discussed in further detail in Chapter 3.

The point behind a speedy execution is to obtain the best price before it moves in an unfavourable direction. In no other sense do speed, certainty, or "market impact" influence profitability than to the extent they impact on the final cost, through the price of execution. So, these factors are not in and of themselves relevant to best execution for retail investors. The extent to which they might impact cost is not easily quantifiable (if at all) and at any rate cannot be known with any certainty prior to the execution. For these reasons, inexplicit costs and non-price factors cannot be included in the calculation of the net price calculation which forms the benchmark for retail best execution.

It is also worth mentioning that the extent to which non-price factors are demanded by investors has been called into question by regulators.[3] There will be a few retail investors who focus on these factors, but these rare individuals can easily be accommodated by providing for the possibility for such a customer to waive all or some of the best execution protections.

Critics might object that this leaves out the legitimate concerns of institutions, who often place heavy importance on these non-price factors and indefinite costs due to the size and complexity of their transactions. This criticism misses the mark, however, since the net-price-based standard is focused on retail trades, and institutions would likely be made subject to a separate, broader standard.

The foregoing paragraphs have argued the rather obvious point that non-price factors are not suitable for a net-price benchmark. The consideration of non-price and indefinite costs is indeed necessary when addressing institutional trading, and this brings us to the matter of flexibility.

4.5.1 Flexibility – a matter of choice

The great trap set for those attempting to formulate a best execution policy lies in trying to construct a policy which is appropriate to all investors all of the time. Such a one-size-must-fit-all approach is doomed to failure by the complexity of the markets and the diversity of investors. Though the net-price approach in this chapter aims to ensure adequate protection for retail investors, it may well be inappropriate for institutional investors. Retail regulation does not always fit instituional trading, and vice versa.

The first step in addressing this problem is to identify those situations or investors to whom such a policy cannot or should not be applied. Once this has been done, the critical second step is to decide how to accommodate these situations and investors. Two methods come to mind. The first is to loosen the standards until they are broad enough to accommodate all situations and investors. This is a fairly common suggestion in the best execution debate, and takes the form of advocating broad "best interests" standards and "conceptual" approaches rather than benchmarks. Yet the resulting lack of clarity results in enforceability and other issues. The problems associated with these approaches have been described above. Moreover, it seems clear that writing standards broad enough to fit all investors all the time is itself nothing other than a "one-size-fits-all" policy, just making the size larger.

---

[3] Levitt, Arthur. "Best Execution, Price Transparency and Linkages: Protecting the Investor Interest", in *Washington University Law Quarterly*, Vol. 78, pp. 514–515 and SEC, *On Line Brokerage: Keeping Apace of Cyberspace*, Special Study, November 1999 ("Unger Report"), p. 4.

The other method keeps the standards narrow and distinct enough to protect retail investors, but carves specific situations out of the policy and provides the freedom for certain investors to waive the retail standards. This leaves the core standard intact and functioning for those investors most in need of protection, but allows for the disapplication of the standard when (and only when) it is appropriate to do so. As in the case with other regulatory issues, care should be taken to keep the number of carve-outs limited but up to date with market practice. The use of waivers, though, would always permit an institution to waive the more restrictive standard even where there is no carve-out (i.e. no "automatic" waiver). Typical examples of carve-outs and safe harbours for best execution would be large trades, basket trades or trades for non-standard settlement.

In order to guard against abuse, waivers must be "affirmative", meaning that the party waiving retail protection must expressly do so. This can be done on a trade-by-trade basis, or on an until-revoked basis (with proper records recording the waiver). The use of waivers has several attractions. First, it provides flexibility for those rare retail investors who place a priority on a factor other than best price (for instance, selling a certificated share which requires longer-than-standard settlement). Secondly, it permits institutions to exercise flexibility even where there is no existing carve-out.

The different investment needs of retail and institutional customers makes it clear that different approaches to best execution are necessary. What is not as clear is where the distinction between the two types of customer lies. Regulators can (and already do) make the distinction based on credible criteria such as net assets, level of trading activity and order size. Yet there would always remain a grey area of customers who could be considered either retail or professional. Here lies a further attraction of waivers. Small institutions which might find themselves encumbered by retail treatment could simply waive retail protection, effectively using the waiver to self-certify as institutions. Certain asset or experience requirements might be wise to ensure this self-certification is not done inappropriately, but the point remains that waivers help to address the question of who is an institution and who is a retail customer.

All in all, the use of carve-outs and waivers seems much more practical and effective than diluting the standard with potentially overbroad criteria. Their use accomplishes the goal of providing appropriate flexibility while retaining the necessary degree of protection.

Implicit in this is the assumption that retail protection is the "default" standard, from which institutions opt out. The question may fairly be asked, why does it need to be this way, and not the other way around? Why not start with a broad (or no) best execution requirement as the default, with more protection for those who opt *in* to the retail regime? The answer, once again, lies in the investor-protection orientation of best execution policies. By making retail protection the default, brokers must assume that the trade priority is best net price unless specifically directed otherwise by the customer. If the default were reversed, the broker would have wide discretion as to execution, and the retail investor would lose control over the execution factors, venue and price. The choice of execution factor would reside with the trader, and not with the customer; in effect, all trades would be done on a "discretionary" basis.

It is more appropriate to give protection unless that protection is waived, than to provide no protection unless it is asked for. Waivers give the *customer* the choice as to which factor is most important; a general standard leaves this choice to others.

This method is illustrative of a more general concept which can be applied to other areas of regulation which wrestle with the problem of accommodating a wide range of actors. Using a core/periphery approach, the first step is to identify which actors or activities are meant to be the focus of the regulation. Next, a core standard is constructed around this focus, and this core standard is presumed to be in operation except where specifically disapplied. The final but critical task is judging where to draw the perimeter – that is, determine where the core standard is not appropriate. These areas are then excluded using carve-outs and safe habours. Though there may be some "grey areas" where it is not clear whether the standard should apply, the use of waivers would allow the investor to opt-in to or out of the protection as necessary.

We can see, then, that a range of factors may be important to the investor. To some, the level of complexity this introduces to the idea of best execution makes it impossible, or at least inappropriate, to attempt any kind of price-based benchmark. This overlooks the key point that factors regarded as important tend to depend upon the type of investor involved. Factors such as speed or certainty of execution tend to be important because of the size or complexity of the trade, or because the trade is a component of a more complex trading strategy. These trades tend to be the domain of institutional investors not of retail investors. A distinction is thus possible between retail and institutional investors not only in terms of their level of expertise and access to information, but in the types of trades they tend to deal in (and therefore the factors which affect their conception of best execution). This leads us to the same conclusion reached earlier in the chapter – that best execution should be focused on the retail investor, who not only needs the protection most but for whom it is far more practical to establish a benchmark by which execution can be judged.

An objection may be raised to this approach, based on the fact that institutional investors should receive the same level of protection as the retail investor. After all, institutions are essentially intermediaries representing the pooled interests of many individual investors. Indeed, most individual investors do not have the resources to invest in efficient sizes by themselves, and so they turn to institutions (such as investment trusts in the United Kingdom or mutual funds in the United States) for their investments. Should the interests of these investors not also be protected?

On the surface, the answer is yes, though it is important to ask one question: from what are the customers of these institutions to be protected? Given that their investments are handled by professionals employed by the institution, their trades do not suffer from market information asymmetry, at least in the narrow sense of the term. The institution's employees can be expected to have training, experience and access to information on par with the traders in the market. They would therefore be able to monitor the market, and the execution of the orders, in a way which the non-professional customers who invest through the institution cannot.

Still, whenever there is a customer relationship, there is a potential conflict (the principal/agency problem in regulatory parlance). In this case, it manifests itself largely in the form of soft commissions, which could influence the institution's professionals to allow practices contrary to the interests of the customers. If the institution were to receive activity-based incentives such as free research or information technology from a broker-dealer or ATS, it has an incentive to send orders to them regardless of the quality of price received.

So arguments can be made both in favour of and against extending retail protection to the customers of institutional investors. In the end, though, the application of retail protection standards to institutions would be difficult due to the size, complexity and other trading characteristics typical of the way in which institutions trade. Whatever the merits of applying retail protection to institutions, it would be impractical to implement. A more reasonable approach, and one which some regulators have already taken, is to address the potential conflict of interest within the institution by limiting or forbidding the practice of providing soft commissions rather than by applying strict retail standards to the trading of institutions.

Because one size does not fit all, then, flexibility must be written into the best execution policy. But care must be taken not to confuse flexibility with ambiguity. Stretching the standards to the point that they fit everyone and protect no one merely provides ambiguity, and ambiguity is the enemy of market confidence. A properly constructed benchmark standard provides the appropriate level of protection where it is needed, without making its application impractical. In the next section, the issue of practicality is explored further.

4.5.2 *Practicality*

Any proposed regulation must be practical and cost-effective to implement. This requirement has been particularly relevant in the evolution of best execution. In the United Kingdom, for example, the emergence of Tradepoint in 1996 meant for the first time that there was a choice of markets on which UK-listed shares could be bought and sold. This had obvious implications for best execution, given that the existing standard was the best price on the London Stock Exchange (LSE). Yet it was argued that it would not be practical to require traders to compare prices between the two markets, since this would require them to go back and forth between two terminals each time they wanted to do a trade. There was no dispute that a better price might be available on Tradepoint, merely that it would be impractical and inefficient to implement a policy requiring traders to execute trades at the best price on either market.

Time and technology have marched on. Traders can now view and compare prices on multiple markets, in real time, from a single terminal (or even a single window). Still, any proposed policy must stand the test of whether it can be implemented without impeding the market from going about its business.

The question of practicality does not rest merely on the number of screens which must be checked. The calculation of net prices can be complex, certainly too complex for rapid manual calculation of multiple alternatives before each execution. If net price is to be central to the best execution standard, technology must be available to facilitate these rapid calculations. Similarly, technology is necessary to make the routing of orders practical.

Chapter 7 discusses the technological issues in some depth, and comes to the conclusion that the necessary technology already exists and can be expected even to improve in the future. When considering the practicality of the best execution policy, then, those who draft the policy must look forward, not backwards. Like generals fighting the last war, regulators too often draft policies which regulate the markets of ten years ago. Regulation must evolve with the markets or it will be rendered irrelevant at best, and counterproductive at worst.

Many involved in the best execution debate express concern not only about the practicality, but the *costs* which might result from a new policy. A particular concern has been the perceived cost of this new and more advanced technology. As will be discussed in Chapter 7, it should not be assumed that firms will need to incur a burdensome cost in developing radically new technologies. Since the relevant technologies have been in use by large and small firms since the early 1980s, it is more a question of adaptation than invention. Moreover, the increased complexity of the market will continue to drive firms to use sophisticated technology just to keep up with the competition. Technology upgrades are a fact of life in firms of all size, and the inclusion of order management technology in the process hardly represents a radical or prohibitively costly measure.

Costs are, at any rate, sometimes unavoidable in pursuit of protecting investors. The important task is to *minimise* costs, not to eliminate them, and to ensure that they are justified by the benefits gained in the form of maintaining an adequate level of protection as markets become more complex.

Conclusion

This chapter has aimed to construct the outlines of a best execution policy which meets three basic requirements for good regulation – that it is sufficiently enforceable to be effective, that it be flexible enough to accommodate the differences between key actors in the markets, and that it be practical so that it can be implemented without disrupting the markets. Using these criteria as a blueprint, it was established that the investor protection nature of best execution policy requires a clear and visible benchmark against which to measure execution. A policy which fails to set a clear and open standard is unenforceable and of little value to the retail investor or to the market. A benchmark standard serves retail investors by providing an enforceable measure of investor protection, and it serves professional market participants by providing regulatory clarity.

Focusing on retail investors, this leads more specifically to the best (intermarket) net price as the core standard. Flexibility is required to accommodate those professional market participants for whom this standard is too restrictive. Investor protection concerns imply establishing the core retail standards as the "default", providing the necessary flexibility through the judicious use of carve-outs, safe harbours and waivers. The practicality of the proposed best execution policy is established partly by this flexibility, and partly through the use of technologies already available and in many cases being used.

A key point in addressing best execution is striking the right balance between investor protection (prescriptive, benchmark standards) and flexibility for institutions (conceptual, general standards or even no standards). It seems then that the prescriptive approach may be effective but less than practical, while the conceptual approach would be more practical but ineffective in meeting its stated purpose, investor protection. The optimal approach falls somewhere between, combining elements of both. In this chapter a "core standard" approach was developed and proposed. This approach can also be employed usefully with regard to other regulatory issues.

In a complex market, different participants will have competing ideas of what should or should not be included in a best execution policy. Some of these ideas will be diametrically opposed, and there will be trade-offs between them. In the end, then, we are seeking the *optimal* policy, rather than the single perfect policy. In the case of best execution, the optimal policy involves the core standard approach, distinguishing between the needs of the core (retail) and that the periphery (institutions).

The use of an intermarket net-price benchmark also has certain other benefits. First, by extending the standard beyond a single exchange, it encourages competition amongst market venues. The "relevant market" is simply that which has the best price. By encouraging the use of technology and membership in more markets, it encourages innovation and competition as well.

In these first four chapters, a theoretical base has been laid for the examination of best execution. Key concepts were defined, and the central issues examined. Using the criteria of good regulation, a working outline of how an effective best execution policy might look has been proposed. It is appropriate now to leave this theoretical landscape and examine how different markets have historically attempted to deal with best execution. In the next chapter, we will see widely different approaches taken in three different market environments – the United States, the United Kingdom and continental Europe. The chapter will aim to discuss not only what approaches were taken, but why they were taken and what factors have influenced the evolution of best execution policy in each jurisdiction.

5 Comparing Approaches

5.1 Overview

Although there are certain elements which are common amongst markets, there is no global standard for best execution. In two of the most active markets, the United States and the United Kingdom, the policy has a comparatively well-developed history and is now under review. This chapter will examine the current state of best execution in these countries and how these policies have developed to their present form. At the supranational level, important steps have been taken to standardise best execution across the European Union, and this development will also be reviewed.

A survey of current approaches is appropriate here for two reasons. First, best execution is partly determined by the market environment in which it is placed, and a review of practices in a variety of markets demonstrates how the policy can be (or should not be) adapted to reflect different market factors. Best execution has also become a cross-market issue and cannot be viewed in the isolation of a single market. As is pointed out in the second half of this book, cross-market best execution policies are an important element of integrating previously isolated markets. Yet, extending best execution to, say, the Pan-European level becomes difficult if the existing polices of the constituent markets are materially different. It would be helpful to observe the lack of cohesion amongst European policies and the efforts being made to form a unified policy. Secondly, particularly with respect to the United States, issues occurring in one jurisdiction may later arise in others, and it would be useful to know how the issues arose and were addressed. This is certainly not to say the approaches should be copied wholesale, but they often provide useful ideas.

The chapter does not seek to provide an up-to-the-minute account of best execution policy in these markets. Any such attempt would be futile, given the pace with which changes are contemplated and made. Instead, it aims to show the evolution of the policies and the factors which have influenced their development.

5.2 Best execution in the US markets

5.2.1 *The regulatory environment*

There are three things worth knowing about the US regulatory and market environment before embarking on a discussion of its best execution regulation. These are that the US market is actually a network of linked but competing markets, that the markets are subject to a unified and hierarchical structure of regulation and that the US approach to best execution has historically been based upon a price benchmark. Each of these three points will be discussed in turn.

The US "market" is actually a number of markets, which operated independently for decades but which now are effectively consolidated under an NMS. For this reason, the idea

41

of best execution has long been a cross-market concept, distinguishing it from the approach taken in the hitherto fragmented European market. And as is discussed below, the notions of best execution and integration of markets have long been considered to be parts of the same overall goal.

Efforts to integrate US markets can be traced back at least as far as the early 1970s, with a number of studies conducted by the SEC into the future of market structure.[1] Congress, too, saw the importance of integrating the market, and in 1975 passed the Securities Acts Amendments,[2] culminating in the addition of Section 11A to the Securities Exchange Act of 1934. The 1975 Amendments form the statutory basis for the current market structure in the United States, and are noteworthy for two reasons. First, they directed the SEC to facilitate the creation of an "NMS". Secondly, they set specific objectives for this system. Amongst these goals was the consolidation of all buying and selling interest so that each investor would be able to obtain the best possible execution for his order, even if the order originated in a different market.[3]

From the beginning, problems of fragmentation, transparency and best execution were seen as different aspects of a single issue. This was confirmed by a later SEC Release:

> The Commission believes that vigorous competition amongst buyers and sellers in an individual security, particularly through an opportunity for their orders to interact directly, is the only reliable means to achieve the best prices for investors.[4]

In December 1999, the SEC issued a Concept Release concerning the regulation of market information, which functioned essentially as a review of the NMS. In the summer of the following year, the SEC established an independent committee (the "Seligman Committee") to review the structure and operation of the NMS and to assess proposed broad changes to the way market information is processed and disseminated. This Committee was composed of twenty-five members representing a broad range of interests, including exchanges, alternative markets, broker-dealer firms and the public.[5] Though the report dealt more broadly with issues of market structure and information, it expressly recognised the interconnection of structure and order execution. Amongst its recommendations is that the SEC conduct a comprehensive study of securities market structure issues to take full account, amongst other things, of the changes to technology which have arisen since the NMS was originally constructed. The report adds that such a study "could more broadly address such topics as securities market linkage and order execution and such challenges as fragmentation of markets. There is an inevitable interconnectedness to securities market structure issues".[6] The report also confirmed the importance of

---

[1]   For instance, the SEC's *Institutional Investor Study Report to Congress* in 1971, the SEC's *Statement on the Future Structure of the Securities Markets* in 1972, and the SEC's *Policy Statement on the Structure of a Central Market System* in 1973. See also the *Report of the Advisory Committee on Market Information* (the "Seligman Report"), submitted to the SEC in 2001, for a history of the development of the NMS.

[2]   Public Law 94-29, 89 Stat. 97 (1975).

[3]   See Section 11A(a)(1), Exchange Act.

[4]   SEC Release No. 34-43590.

[5]   Seligman Report, Introduction.

[6]   *Ibid.*

price transparency and consolidated markets as core elements of the securities market in the United States, and of the price display rule mandating the centralisation of market information. The report made additional recommendations regarding the structure of price information regulation and the NMS, and these points are covered in more detail in Chapter 11.

The history of the NMS is also useful in demonstrating the importance of regulation in bringing about cross-market initiatives, and the methods by which it does so. Initially, the role of the SEC was facilitation/co-ordination. No coercive action is foreseen in the 1975 Amendments themselves, merely that the SEC, in "facilitating" the creation of the NMS, would co-ordinate and set standards that would apply to all participants. In 1978, the SEC instituted the first consolidated quotation plan, in which all quotes for a security were disseminated in a single quotation stream.[7] But by 1980, it became apparent that more was needed. The market data was being provided, but the markets were not indicating in a clear manner where the best price actually resided (e.g. with a competitor market). As a result, the SEC saw the need to move into the prescriptive mode, enacting a "display rule" *mandating* that all vendors and brokers-dealers display the National Best Bid and Offer (NBBO) for each security.[8] This is a clear demonstration of a regulator starting with a minimal level of coercion and moving "up the scale" as needed. The SEC began with the least intrusive level of its powers – co-ordination – and only mandated a specific action when it became clear that the market had failed to take the necessary action of its own accord.

The SEC has said that the scope of the duty of best execution has evolved over time with changes in technology and transformation of the structure of the financial markets.[9] As time went on, other practices became apparent which called for additional regulation. Amongst them the most significant was the practice of "trading through" customer limit orders. A limit order, it will be recalled, is one which a customer places for execution if and when the market price of the security moves to a specified price or better. In practice, a client could place a limit order at a price superior to the broker-dealer's own displayed quote, and yet never be filled. For example, the inside market for a security might be 10 bid, $10\frac{1}{4}$ offer and a customer places a limit order to buy at $10\frac{1}{8}$. The broker-dealer then receives another order, a market order to sell. He might execute this order at his posted bid – buying for himself at 10 – even though he has a customer willing to buy at $10\frac{1}{8}$.

After a considerable debate and comment period, the SEC in 1996 required the markets to implement a limit order handling rule (Rule 11Ac1-4), requiring firms to display to the market (i.e. on the Consolidated Quotation System (CQS)) any customer limit order which would improve either the price or size of the firm's own best bid or offer (in the previous example, the firm would need to display the customer's $10\frac{1}{8}$ bid). Again, regulation had stepped in where the market had not been driven by the invisible hand to do what was needed. The SEC sees this as an example of carrying out its Congressionally mandated duty when necessary:

---

[7]   Annette Nazareth (Director, SEC Department of Market Regulation), *Minutes of 10 October 2000 meeting of Advisory Committee on Market Information*, available at http://www.sec.gov/divisions/marketreg/marketinfo.shtml.

[8]   *Ibid.*, See Rule 11Ac1-2, effective April 1980.

[9]   SEC, *Inspection Report on the Soft Dollar Practices of Broker-Dealers, Investment Advisers and Mutual Funds*, September 1998, at footnote 55.

...Congress expected that in those situations where competition might not be sufficient to do this, such as the creation of a composite quotation or transaction reporting system, that the Commission would use its powers granted to it under Section 11A to ensure their implementation as rapidly as possible.[10]

Little progress towards a unified market could have been made without the overarching authority of Congress and the SEC to persuade, co-ordinate or compel changes affecting a number of competing markets. Herein lies the importance of a single regulatory authority, as exists in the United States but which is presently absent in the European Union. This brings us to the second important characteristic of US markets. Not surprisingly, the United States benefits from a unified, hierarchical regulatory structure for financial markets. That is, Congress is responsible for the legislation covering all of the markets, and (at least as far as securities are concerned) all of the necessary regulatory powers are delegated to the SEC.[11] Under the provisions of the Securities and Exchange Act of 1934 (the "Exchange Act"), Congress has delegated to the SEC the responsibility for establishing and maintaining standards for fair, orderly and efficient markets. Congress exercises its oversight function by requiring regular and ad hoc reports, as well as testimony before the relevant committees of the Senate and the House. Congress rarely becomes directly involved in the regulation of securities markets, the 1975 Amendments and the more recent Graham-Leach-Bliley Act being the most notable exceptions.

While Congress has delegated overall responsibility for the markets to the SEC, the SEC has itself delegated large portions of the day-to-day regulation of the markets to Self-Regulatory Organisations (SROs) such as the exchanges and the NASD. The SROs are given special rule-making authority by Congress via the Exchange Act, but they are directly supervised by the SEC. Their specific responsibilities involve the establishment, enforcement and review of standards of conduct for their members, as well as the fair and orderly operation of any trading facilities they might operate.[12] It is in this capacity that the SROs have come to address the issue of best execution. Indeed, the fundamental expression of best execution policy in the United States is NASD Rule 2320 and the subsequent interpretive releases issued by the NASD.

In practical terms, Congress establishes the legislative foundation for securities markets regulation, delegating overall responsibility to the SEC and day-to-day responsibility to the markets themselves. This hierarchical structure means that a single regulator (the SEC), operating on behalf of a single legislator, is able to direct, co-ordinate or cajole the markets to implement measures deemed important for the overall good of the integrated marketplace and which require co-ordinated action by more than one market. The importance of this authority is apparent in the discussion below of the situation in the European Union, which lacks such an authority.

The third important point about the US approach is that it is, at its core, based on a price benchmark. Since virtually all markets were linked in the 1980s, and particularly since the

---

[10]   Nazareth, minutes of 10 October 2000 meeting of Advisory Committee on Market Information.

[11]   The regulation of securities markets in the United States is distinguished from other financial markets. For example, the regulation of commodities markets has been delegated to the Commodities and Futures Trading Commission.

[12]   SEC, *Report to the Congress: The Impact of Recent Technological Advances on the Securities Markets* ("SEC Technology Study"), September 1997, at IV.B.

SEC imposed the Display Rule, it has been possible to refer to an NBBO which was visible to all participants and which represented the best available (displayed) price. The NBBO was even given something akin to legal character through judicial and regulatory decisions, described in some detail in the following chapter. The existence of an identifiable best price is also reflected in NASD Rule 2320. Under its provisions, member firms are required to "use reasonable diligence" to execute trades with or for customers "so that the resultant *price to the customer* is as favourable as possible under the prevailing market conditions" (emphasis added).[13]

There is much to be considered in this expression of best execution policy. The first is the explicit reference to price. Though there are qualifications and exceptions, the standard begins with the notion that the price is the central factor to be considered. In many respects, it meets the criteria discussed in Chapter 4, in that it begins with a price benchmark and then makes accommodation as necessary.

Secondly, the phrase "resultant price to the customer" implies that the standard is in fact the net price, as the price to the customer would presumably be net of costs. This leads to the next question, that of scope. Rule 2320 is expressly limited to dealings with (as principal) or for (as agent) a customer, but no distinction between retail and institutional customers is provided in the rule itself. This has recently led to consideration as to whether firms which accept retail orders from other firms have the duty of best execution to the other firm's retail customers, from whom they are once removed. As it stands, the application of Rule 2320 to customer dealings exempts firms trading on their own behalf with other firms. By excluding these interdealer trades, the rule reflects its purpose as a customer protection measure.

Another important clause of Rule 2320 is that which refers to "prevailing market conditions". As was pointed out in the previous chapter, such a clause could be seen to provide necessary flexibility to the application of the price standard, or it could provide a dangerous loophole through which any trader could escape by claiming his execution was acceptable under his assessment of the prevailing market conditions. A similar dilemma arises in the interpretation of "due diligence" in ascertaining this best price. And here it is very important to understand the distinction in how market conditions are used in applying the NASD policy.

In interpreting best execution responsibilities, US judicial and regulatory decisions have held generally that the duty of best execution requires "that a broker/dealer seek to obtain for its customers' orders the most favourable terms reasonable under the circumstances".[14] This "facts and circumstances" determination[15] is roughly equivalent to the NASD provision concerning due diligence in ascertaining the best price. In both cases, the determination can take account of a number of factors such as the trading characteristics of the security and access to competing markets.[16]

On its face, the facts and circumstances test applies not to the standard itself, but rather to the reasonable efforts to *find* the best price. The benchmark remains a price-based standard (best resulting price). In other words, the regulation on its face provides for flexibility in the way in which the best net price is sought, not in the standard itself. This

---

13   National Association of Securities Dealers, Inc. (NASD) Rule 2320(a).
14   NASD, Notice to Members (NTM) 01-22, pp. 201–202, citing Newton *vs* Merrill Lynch (citation below).
15   NASD, NTM 01-22, p. 202.
16   Unger Report, pp. 35–36.

is an important difference from some of the currently proposed policies, which seek to use the facts and circumstances flexibility to the standard itself. However, the use of the facts and circumstances analysis has in practice been extended in the United States to the standard,[17] resulting in a far broader interpretation.

5.2.2 Order handling (Rules 11Ac1-4 and 11Ac1-1)

In 1996, the SEC enacted a set of Order Execution Rules[18] with the aim of increasing transparency and to "improve opportunities for the best execution of customer orders" in the light of the development of "sophisticated technological systems for displaying and routing customer orders".[19] These included the aforementioned Limit Order Display Rule [20] requiring market makers and specialists to include in their bids and offers any customer order which would improve their own displayed prices (subject to certain exceptions). Additionally, the SEC amended the existing Quote Display Rule[21] to require market makers to make public any quotes they make privately (i.e. through an ATS) which are superior to its publicly disseminated quotes. This does not necessarily mean that the firm itself would have to include the price in its own public quotes, because the requirement is deemed to be met if the ATS feeds its prices to the major markets.

The Unger Report

In 1999, SEC Commissioner Laura Unger commissioned a special study of the impact of on-line trading and other new technologies on the regulation of the securities industry.[22] The final report of the study (The Unger Report) identified the impact of new technologies on the concept of best execution as one of the areas requiring consideration.

In its discussion of best execution, the Unger Report provided a brief background of the current requirements for best execution. It connects the requirement for firms to conduct "regular and rigorous review" of order execution quality to the issues of internalisation and payment for order flow.[23] Like soft commissions, these practices had been widely held to present an inherent conflict of interest, potentially inducing firms to route their customers' orders (or execute them internally) based on factors other than the customers' best interests.

The report found that technologies have provided firms with "the opportunity to adopt a new approach to order routing and to meeting their best execution obligations".[24] Significantly, amongst these technologies the Report identified the development of best execution algorithms, which consider a number of factors to determine the best market to which to route an order.[25] An important feature of these algorithms is that they do so on an order-by-order basis,[26] raising

---

[17]   For instance, see NASD, NTM 97-57, providing interpretive guidance to best execution responsibilities in the light of the institution of Limit Order Protection Rules.

[18]   See SEC, *Order Execution Obligations*, Exchange Act Release No. 37619A, September 1996.

[19]   SEC Technology Study, at IV.D.2.a.

[20]   SEC Rule 11Ac1-4.

[21]   SEC Rule 11Ac1-1.

[22]   "On Line Brokerage: Keeping Apace of Cyberspace", Special Study, US Securities and Exchange Commission, 11 November 1999, *op. cit.*

[23]   *Ibid.*, p. 39.

[24]   *Ibid.*, p. 2.

[25]   *Ibid.*, p. 39.

[26]   *Ibid.*, p. 39.

the possibility of applying an order-by-order best execution standard rather than relying on the more general "regular and rigorous review" of execution quality. This possibility is further discussed in Chapter 7.

The study also found that many firms, primarily on-line brokerage firms, contend that factors such as speed and certainty of execution should receive greater emphasis in their regular and rigorous evaluation of execution quality.[27] It is significant to note that the report stops short of endorsing this view, calling instead for the SEC to "encourage the industry to demonstrate the relative importance of factors such as speed and certainty of execution in today's market environment".[28] Also noteworthy is that the increased importance of speed and certainty are attributed partly to the fact that "on-line customers supposedly expect immediate execution at the NBBO".[29] If this expectation is true – the expectation of execution *at the NBBO* – it demonstrates that speed and certainty derive their importance from their relationship to the *price* of the execution. It also demonstrates the focus (at least for one segment of the market) on avoiding price disimprovement rather than achieving price improvement.[30]

Many participants in the Unger study's Roundtable Discussion indicated that it was difficult to obtain sufficient information from various market sites upon which to make their regular and rigorous review, and that the information which was obtainable was not uniform.[31] Consequently, the Unger Report recommended that the SEC "consider requiring market centers to make certain uniform information available on various best execution factors", as well as information concerning order-handling practices and inducements for order flow.[32] These recommendations were followed by the adoption and implementation of the current disclosure rules, Rules 11Ac1-5 and 11Ac1-6.

The report also recommended that the SEC evaluate the impact of technologies such as order-by-order routing algorithms on best execution,[33] and their potential for making order-by-order routing a "practical alternative to the aggregate routing of retail order flow".[34] It left the latter question, however, to the then-forthcoming SEC study into the effects of market fragmentation. The Concept Release resulting from the SEC study noted weaknesses in the way the NMS addresses best execution, such as the fact that orders need not be routed to the firm displaying the best price. It proposed for consideration what would in effect be a national limit-order book, but this proposal met with near universal rejection. The Concept Release dealt more broadly with issues of fragmentation and market linkages, and is discussed in greater length in Chapter 11.

---

[27] *Ibid.*, p. 41.
[28] *Ibid.*, p. 2.
[29] *Ibid.*, p. 41.
[30] Letter from Charles Schwab & Co., Inc. to Securities and Exchange Commission, 5 July 2000.
[31] *Ibid.*
[32] *Ibid.*
[33] *Ibid.*
[34] *Ibid.*

5.2.3 Disclosure (Rules 11Ac1-5 and 11Ac1-6)

In November 2000, the SEC adopted Rules 11Ac1-5 and 11Ac1-6, regarding public disclosure of order execution and routing practices.[35] These rules arose from the SEC's review of market fragmentation[36] and required market centres to provide certain standardised execution quality standards (Rule 11Ac1-5), and broker-dealers to disclose their practices with respect to the market centres to whom they would send customer orders for execution (Rule 11Ac1-6).

The effectiveness of information disclosure has been the subject of some debate in the United States. As part of the requirement for firms to conduct a "regular, rigorous review" of the execution quality of market centres, the NASD regularly publishes "Compliance Report Cards" which measure the quality of executions.[37] Representatives of the industry, however, have indicated that the statistics in these Report Cards are filled with unreliable and misleading data. The SIA conducted its own review of trading data used to compile the report cards, and found that "Of the more than 1000 transactions analyzed, the member firm group found problems with more than 70% of the alerts captured by the Report Cards."[38]

5.2.4 The treatment of soft commissions and payment for order flow

In Chapter 3, the problem posed by "soft commissions" was raised as one which presents potential conflict-of-interest issues with respect to the routing of customer orders. Put bluntly, the danger is that a trader would route orders to that venue or intermediary from which he obtains a "soft commission" (such as free research or IT services) even if he can obtain a better price for the customer elsewhere. The problem is even more stark in the United States, where outright payment for order flow has also been permitted. The effect of these practices has come under increasing scrutiny by the SEC, largely as part of its more comprehensive review of market structure and regulation, and the SEC has indicated that the issue is amongst the areas of particular interest in the course of their examinations of firms.[39]

The potential influence of soft commissions and payment for order flow on routing decisions was also included in a 2002 NASD review of best execution duties for firms which execute trades on behalf of other firms.[40] As previously noted, the NASD has questioned whether the scope of the duty of best execution should be extended to customer orders received by a member firm from another member firm. In seeking comment, the NASD has proposed several alternatives with respect to how far to extend the scope. The options under consideration include both narrow and broad extensions of the scope, but it is worth noting that one proposal would limit the extension to only those situations in which the receiving firm pays the sending firm for the order flow it receives.

---

[35]   SEC, Securities Exchange Act Release No. 34-43590, 17 November 2000.
[36]   Defined in SEC, Securities Exchange Act Release No. 34-43590 as "The trading of orders in multiple locations without interaction among those orders".
[37]   NTM 01-22, p. 205.
[38]   Letter from SIA Trading Committee to NASD Regulation, 27 June 2001.
[39]   Bresiger, Gregory, "Regulator Looks Again at Best Execution: Buysiders Grapple with a Difficult Standard", in *Traders Magazine*, June 2002.
[40]   NASD Notice to Members 02-40.

5.2.5 *Price improvement*

Although best execution in the United States is judged against the NBBO benchmark, it must be added that improvement on this price is expected whenever it is readily accessible. This became an issue in particular with the emergence in the late 1990s of Electronic Communications Networks (ECNs), which function as alternative markets but whose prices are not always included in the NBBO. This expectation took away any status the NBBO might have had as a safe harbour, in which executions at the NBBO could always be presumed to represent best execution. Rather, it now represents a floor beneath which executions cannot generally be done (thus retaining its benchmark value for enforcement purposes). The question which arises from the price improvement expectation is whether and when a particular execution venue becomes readily accessible. The approach taken by US regulators, as seen below, was to require firms to make this assessment themselves on a "regular and rigorous" basis.

5.2.6 *Enforcement and guidance*

Best execution is actively enforced in the United States, and it is through the enforcement of the rule that its interpretation can best be seen. Both the SEC and the NASD actively review firms' handling of customer orders. Indeed, NASD Regulation has noted that best execution is "an important focus" of its "examination, customer compliant and automated surveillance" programmes.[41] Even a casual review of the NASD's disciplinary activities confirms that firms' failures to provide best execution routinely lead to censures, fines and restitution orders.

The NASD has noted four areas in which firms might typically run afoul of their best execution obligations:

1. Executing customer orders at prices inferior to the NBBO without justification;

2. Executing customer orders in an untimely manner;

3. Executing customer orders in a manner designed to allow the member firm to profit at the expense of its customer; and

4. Failing to establish procedures to regularly and rigorously examine execution quality.[42]

Each of these violations is revealing in terms of how the best execution obligation is actually interpreted. The first clearly establishes that price – and specifically the NBBO – is the benchmark standard against which execution is judged. It can easily be argued (as it was in Chapters 3 and 4) that this benchmark is what makes the best execution standard enforceable in the first place. "Without justification", of course, leaves considerable room for flexibility, but the NASD's wording clearly implies that price is assumed to be the "default" standard and it is up to the executing firm to justify any deviation from this standard.

The second violation deals more specifically with "prompt execution" rather than "best execution", and the two concepts are sometimes dealt with separately in discussions of customer protection. Still, the NASD's evident concern over prompt execution is worth

---

[41]   NASD Notice to Members 01-22.
[42]   *Ibid.*

noting, if only because it implies a presumption that customer orders are expected to be executed immediately unless directed otherwise.

The notion of profiting at the expense of the customer has a rather specific application in the United States, but it can be extended theoretically to larger issues raised in this book. The specific application in the United States arises from situations in which a firm obtains a superior price for itself (i.e. a price off the market which is superior to the displayed NBBO) and then fails to pass this price improvement on to its customer (see the discussion of *in re Geman* in the next chapter). Viewed more broadly, the prohibition from profiting at the customer's expense could be applied with equal effect to areas in which the trader is under a potential conflict of interest, whether this conflict arises from payment for order flow, soft commissions, or the trader's own compensation structure within the firm.

The last of the four violations noted by the NASD is of a slightly different character, as it focuses on process rather than on the executions themselves. It also reflects the conviction held by the NASD and the SEC that best execution is an evolving standard, which must necessarily reflect changes to market technology, structure and rules.[43] This has led to the policy that "as these changes in the market occur, broker/dealers must analyse and modify their order execution procedures to consider price opportunities that become 'reasonably available'".[44] In practice, the NASD has advised that this regular and rigorous review be conducted on at least a quarterly basis.

The evolving nature of best execution is also reflected in the ongoing provision of guidance and interpretation by the NASD and the SEC. In the period between 1997 and 2002, the NASD issued six Notices to Members containing guidance on best execution, ranging from general interpretation in the light of other changes to market regulations to the specific responsibilities related to execution of over-the-counter securities. During the same period, the SEC instituted rules mandating the publication of execution quality and order routing data, as well as the aforementioned market structure studies. The frequent provision of interpretive guidance and rules by the NASD and SEC demonstrates their assumption that the regulation of customer order execution must evolve with the markets themselves to ensure that full account of new opportunities is taken to ensure provision of the best overall price to the customer.

In general, the approach to best execution in the United States which has been established over the years is a complex and evolving one. It is characterised by a core benchmark standard (the NBBO), deviations from which must be justified by the executing firm. A degree of flexibility is integral to the approach, as interpretive guidance and rulings have established the need to consider the "facts and circumstances" approach. Nonetheless, the standards are enforced, largely as a result of the presence of a presumed benchmark coupled with close scrutiny of whether firms conduct reviews of their execution procedures which are both regular and rigorous. Lastly, the US policy is strengthened by explicit recognition of its dynamic character, the policy itself requiring regular and rigorous review in order to remain current with developments in technology and market structure.

---

[43]   NASD Notice to Members 01-22; Securities Exchange Act Release No. 37619A.
[44]   NASD Notice to Members 01-22, citing Securities Exchange Act Release No. 37619A.

Best execution in the United States

...in any transaction for or with a customer, a member and persons associated with a member shall use reasonable due diligence to ascertain the best inter-dealer market for a security and buy or sell in such market so that the resultant price to the customer is as favourable as possible under the prevailing market conditions. The factors articulated in NASD Rule 2320(a) to be used when applying... "reasonable diligence" in this area are:

1. The character of the market for the security, e.g. price, volatility, relative liquidity and pressure on available communications;

2. The size and type of transaction;

3. The number of primary markets checked; and

4. The location and accessibility to the customer's broker-dealer of primary markets and quotation sources.

Source: NASD Rule 2320.

5.3   Best execution in the United Kingdom

Best execution in the United Kingdom has developed from different roots and in a different environment. Whereas the US best execution policy has been strongly influenced by the emergence of competing exchanges linked into a single intermarket system, the UK policy has its origins in a single market environment – an environment which existed well in the 1990s.

The historical trail of best execution policies in the United Kingdom is illustrative of many of the issues involved in devising such a policy. It is also a story of the regulatory process – of the review and revision of a regulatory policy in order to reflect technology and market practices which have come to characterise the practice of trading.

The trail begins at a time when best execution was a much simpler concept. For equities at least, there was a single market in the United Kingdom – the LSE – and the level of cross-border activity was low enough that it could effectively be ignored. The trail proceeds through decades of change, both domestic and international, and brings us to a point where both the UK policy itself and the EU regulatory environment in which it will exist are undergoing significant reform.

5.4   Introduction of a multiple exchange environment

To understand the current policy, then, it must be placed in the context of its historical development. Until the introduction of the Tradepoint Investment Exchange (Tradepoint) in September 1995, the LSE was the sole stock exchange in the United Kingdom (with the occasional exception of very small regional exchanges). As such, the question of best execution did not need to consider prices available on competing markets. In October 1986, the LSE instituted a best execution rule which reflected this single-exchange environment. It stated that, for orders within the displayed size and during the mandatory quotation period, a broker would be deemed to have achieved best execution if he obtained the best price displayed on the Stock Exchange Automated Quotation (SEAQ) System.[45] Through the end of the 1990s, the development of the best execution standard resulted from a series of adjustments to this single-exchange orientation.

5.5   The "relevant market" condition

At the same time, the Securities Association (forerunner to the Securities and Futures Authority, SFA) adopted its own rule regarding best execution.[46] This rule stated (in part) that best execution is achieved if the firm: "... takes reasonable care to ascertain the price which is the best available for the customer in the relevant market at the time".[47] The "relevant market" condition was expanded upon in Guidance stating that, in determining which was the "relevant market", the SFA would have regard to "market conventions". Since there was only one stock exchange in the United Kingdom at the time, the market convention for the LSE – its SEAQ standard – prevailed.[48] Similar language, including the "relevant market" condition, was later incorporated into the rules of the SFA's successor, the Securities and Investments Board (SIB)[49] and those of other SROs.[50]

When Tradepoint applied for Recognised Investment Exchange status in 1995, it became clear that the standard of best execution would need to be reviewed in the light of the availability of prices on a competing market. In its 1995 Annual Report, SIB indicated that "... in an environment in which there are competing systems trading the same security, regulators need to be in a position to provide clear and consistent guidance to their members on how best execution rules should operate in practice".[51] As a consequence, SIB initiated a review of existing policy, conducted jointly with the LSE, Tradepoint and other interested recognised bodies.[52] The Treasury included the results of this examination in its review of LSE rules.[53]

The result of the review was the adoption in September 1995 of further SFA guidance.[54] The Notice containing this guidance formally incorporated a two-step approach – first, the "relevant market" is chosen, and only then are prices *on that market* compared in order to determine the best price. No explicit requirement was imposed upon firms to have access to more than one market or to compare prices on two markets even if the firm does have access to both. In practice, then, the standard remained a single-market benchmark, with firms free to ignore prices on competing markets. The Notice did, however, indicate that the guidance would be kept under review.[55]

---

[45]   LSE, *Price Improvement and Best Execution*, in *Stock Exchange Quarterly with Quality of Markets Review*, Spring 1992, p. 25.

[46]   Securities and Futures Authority (SFA) Rule 5-39.

[47]   SFA Rule 5-39(4)(a).

[48]   LSE, p. 25.

[49]   Securities and Investments Board (SIB), Core Conduct of Business Rule 22.

[50]   Such as IMRO Rule 3.8 and FIMBRA Rule 29.16. The SFA was replaced by the FSA on 1 December 2001.

[51]   SIB, "Regulation of the United Kingdom Equity Markets", June 1995, para. 3.29.

[52]   SIB, Report of the Review of Best Execution, 23 August 1995, para. 3.

[53]   Letter from Jeremy Heywood (HMT) to Andrew Whittaker (SIB), 4 August 1995.

[54]   SFA Board Notice 280.

[55]   *Ibid.*

In August 1997, the SFA published further guidance in response to the establishment by the LSE of the Stock Exchange Trading System (SETS), an electronic order book.[56] This guidance affirmed the use of the SETS price as the standard for best execution (for stocks trading on SETS) in a manner similar to that which used the SEAQ standard.[57] In doing so, it affirmed the use of prices on a single market as the benchmark, regardless of activity outside that market.

It should also be noted that, under existing rules, non-private customers (i.e. institutions) were able to waive best execution protection, on the basis that they may then be able to negotiate preferential terms for their business.[58]

In September of the following year, however, the SFA published Board Notice 488A, which gave a more detailed interpretation of the requirement to exercise reasonable care in determining the relevant market. Importantly, it clarified that the SETS standard was subject to the firm's fiduciary obligations to the customer, i.e. to obtain a better price than SETS if one is available to the firm.[59]

5.6   Board Notice 542

The next clarification of the policy came in April 2000, with SFA Board Notice 542. By that time, the presence of alternative trading venues was more widespread (including the establishment of a third equity exchange, Jiway). Board Notice 542 re-stated the SFA's position that firms were not required to obtain access to any particular trading venue or to a minimum number of venues. However, where a firm did have such access, and where it could make a "direct and immediate" comparison of prices, a firm "should ensure that the customer receives the best price available to the firm".[60]

Until the implementation of the present regulatory regime (under the FSMA 2000) in December 2001, then, best execution policy was manifested in SFA Rule 5.39 and the four SFA Board Notices[61] which embodied the gradual modification of the best execution standard from a single- to a multiple-market environment.

5.7   FSMA and the Conduct of Business Sourcebook

The FSMA embodied a broad reform of the regulation of the financial services industry in the United Kingdom. Amongst other things, the Act formally established the FSA as the single regulator for virtually all of the financial services industry. Pursuant to the Act and its implementing legislation, the FSA implemented a new comprehensive rule book containing separate sections (or sourcebooks) for various aspects and activities within the realm of financial services. Amongst these were the Conduct of Business Rules (COB Rules), in which the FSA's views on best execution are contained.

---

[56]   SFA Board Notice 437.
[57]   *Ibid.*
[58]   FSA Discussion Paper, p. 21.
[59]   SFA Board Notice 488A.
[60]   SFA Board Notice 542.
[61]   SFA Board Notices 542, 488A, 437 and 280.

It is important to note that the Act also mandated that the FSA have regard to certain statutory objectives in performing its responsibilities. These included, importantly to this discussion, the protection of customers receiving financial services.[62] The degree to which the rules are compatible with this and other requirements will be discussed later in this chapter.

The best execution rules promulgated under FSMA are found in Section 7.5 of the Conduct of Business Sourcebook. Most specifically, Section 7.5.5 stipulates that in order to provide best execution, a firm must:

■ Take reasonable care to ascertain the price which is the best available for the customer order in the relevant market at the time for transactions of the kind and size concerned; and

■ Execute the customer order at a price which is no less advantageous to the customer, unless the firm has taken reasonable steps to ensure that it would be in the customer's best interests not to do so.

It can readily be seen that this standard has a number of elements which are open to interpretation, such as "reasonable care", "best available" and "relevant market". The Sourcebook attempts to provide a certain degree of guidance by enumerating evidentiary provisions which may be used by a firm in establishing that it has complied with the rule. For example, Rule 7.5.6(1) provides guidance as to how firms can go about establishing that they have taken "reasonable care". The most important of these for our purposes states that firms

> ... need not have access to competing exchanges, or to all, or a minimum number of, available price sources; but if a firm can access prices displayed by different exchanges and trading platforms and make a direct and immediate comparison, it should execute the customer order at the best price available to the firm on such exchanges or trading platforms, if this is in the best interests of the customer ...

This guidance itself is open to a degree of interpretation. On the face of it, the guidance would appear to require all firms with access to any major data vendor to compare prices across markets, since these vendors provide the means by which to compare the prices directly and immediately. It then follows that the firms would be expected to execute at the best price available, but the last phrase – "if this is in the best interests of the customer" – provides an escape for any firm or individual trader who wishes to avoid the obligation. When the decision of what is in the customer's best interests is left in the hands of the trader rather than the customer, control over the implementation of the policy passes to the person whose actions the measure is meant to regulate. It becomes, in short, a *voluntary* practice rather than a regulation.

Adding more uncertainty to the guidance is paragraph (2) of the same rule, which stipulates that for customer orders for shares traded on SETS (the LSE's electronic order book), a firm's best execution will be satisfied if, subject to the multiple market guidance

---

[62]   The other three statutory objectives are the promotion of confidence in the market, promotion of public awareness and the deterrence of financial crime (in particular money laundering). The FSA, in its Consultation Paper, recognised the impact of best execution on the first two of these, but correctly identified consumer protection as the main area in which best execution is concerned.

described above, it executes the orders through SETS. In sum, a firm holding a customer order on a SETS-traded security must, if it has access to multiple price feeds (as through any major vendor such as Reuters or Bloomberg), check those prices and execute at the best price available, unless the trader decides it is in the customer's best interests not to receive the best price, and in any case the trader will know that he has met his obligation if he does the trade on SETS. Rule 7.5 permits traders to execute trades in SETS securities other than on SETS under certain conditions, but the onus is then placed on the trader to demonstrate that the customer was not disadvantaged in so doing.

In practice, it is clear why traders would continue to execute trades in SETS securities on the LSE. As the most widely traded UK securities are SETS securities, the implication for the UK markets is clear, in that the rules effectively reinforce the concentration of trading on a single market.

This regulatory incentive can probably be said to reinforce an existing tendency rather than create a new one. As the Charteris report[63] showed, internal reward and incentive structures encourage trading on the dominant market regardless of the nature of prices elsewhere. Added to this is the more nebulous but just as real inertia which leads traders and firms to stick to practices which they know to have worked well for them in the past rather than to undertake new practices. Whereas regulation could be the remedy to these internal incentives, the COB rules effectively reinforce these patterns.

At about the same time that the COB Rules came into force, the FSA initiated a review of its best execution policy. The process actually began as far back as mid-2000, when the FSA circulated an "issues paper" amongst interested parties to set out the framework for further discussion on best execution. This was followed by a public Discussion Paper in April 2001, in which the FSA set forth its preliminary thinking on the issue for public comment. After reviewing these comments, the FSA issued a Consultation Paper, containing specific proposals, in October 2002. The proposals contained in the Consultation Paper (CP 154) reflected the first real attempt in the United Kingdom, and arguably in Europe, to construct a workable best execution policy which reflects the multiple market environment.

Consultation Paper 154 included four main policy proposals: a restructuring of the best execution obligation itself, provision of information on firms' execution arrangements, ongoing review by the firms of their execution arrangements and regular monitoring by the firms of "execution quality".

5.7.1 *Restructuring the best execution obligation*

Under the CP 154 proposals, the FSA moved away from a standard focused on the price displayed in the market. The proposals embraced the concept of the customer's *net* price, essentially as discussed in Chapter 4. As the Consultation Paper itself pointed out, " … 'best execution' is not to do solely with maximising or minimising price, but also with minimising relevant costs. As such, it is the overall net result to the customer that counts".[64]

Importantly, CP 154 also proposed to include non-price factors in the best execution obligation. These included factors such as order type, size, settlement arrangements and timing. The proposed standard made no distinction in this regard between retail and

---

[63]   Charteris Plc, *European Financial Markets 2001: Revolution or Evolution?*, 2001.
[64]   FSA, *Best Execution*, Consultation Paper 154 (CP 154), October 2002, p. 4.

institutional orders, with their typically different considerations and objectives. As noted in earlier chapters, the application of these institution-focused considerations to retail orders may prove problematic. Nonetheless, the inclusion of these factors departed from the previous best execution standards and demonstrated the degree to which the FSA was willing to start afresh with the new best execution standard.

A third important development in the new proposal was the removal of the SETS safe harbour. We have already seen that the removal of such single-market benchmarks is an important measure. The CP 154 proposals, though, went one step further and asserted that "... (any) fixed benchmark provides no real incentive for a firm to seek out the best deals for its customers". The proposals therefore called for best execution to be judged without reference to any price benchmark.

5.7.2 *Provision of information on firms' execution arrangements*

As is the case with existing best execution regulation in the United States, CP 154 called for firms to be required to provide information to their customers concerning their execution arrangements. The Paper proposed that firms disclose to their customers arrangements such as the venues to which they have direct access, their order routing procedures and any conflicts of interest that might arise (presumably including analyst conflicts, but the case could also be made that incentive conflicts would be covered as well). The FSA asserted in the Paper that such disclosure "should help consumers to compare the execution services on offer from different firms, and to make more informed decisions about the type of service appropriate to their needs".[65] It added that this level of provision would also facilitate competition amongst firms (such an assumption would rest on the information being fully public, rather than provided only to the firm's customers).

5.7.3 *Review of execution arrangements*

Implicit in much of the text of the Consultation Paper was the recognition of the fact that ongoing changes in market structure, technology and practice have a direct effect on the optimal approach to best execution. This theme was perhaps most explicitly expressed in the proposed requirement for firms to review relevant practices and arrangements on a regular basis. The proposal left out many of the details, calling on respondents to the Paper to provide input as to what should be included in the review, how it should be performed and how frequently it should be done.

5.7.4 *Monitoring execution quality*

Lastly, the Paper proposed that firms be required to monitor the "quality" of their executions in order to determine whether their practices resulted in the most favourable executions for their clients. The Paper noted that many firms already performed such reviews, though the frequency of the reviews varied widely (and some firms performed no such reviews). As a concept such as "execution quality" is somewhat vague, the Paper called on respondents to advise on what such a review should involve and whether a uniform approach for all firms would be desirable.

---

[65]   FSA, CP 154, p. 5.

5.8   The FSA's statutory requirements

It was mentioned earlier that the FSA is required by statute to provide for an adequate degree of protection in carrying out its regulatory responsibilities. Most important with regard to best execution is that of customer protection, and this focus on the customer can be seen throughout the process of the FSA's review of best execution. In its earlier Discussion Paper on Best Execution, the FSA made this clear:

> Best execution is a consumer protection tool. It is aimed at requiring firms to exercise reasonable care in the execution of orders for customers, with an emphasis on price.[66]

This sentiment was amplified elsewhere in the Discussion Paper:

> The aim of the best execution rules is to impose an obligation on firms to obtain for their customers the best price available to the firm for the customer (given the characteristics of the customer's order).[67]

In addressing the customer protection aspects of best execution, the FSA indicated in its subsequent Consultation Paper that four considerations were important to consider:

1. the differing degrees of risk involved in different kinds of investment or other transaction;

2. the differing degrees of experience and expertise that different consumers may have in relation to different kinds of regulated activity;

3. the needs that consumers have for advice and accurate information;

4. the general principle that consumers should take responsibility for their decisions.[68]

The FSA proceeded in the Consultation Paper to assess the degree to which its best execution proposal meets the consumer protection requirement of its statutory obligations, emphasising the degree to which the policy would reduce the "information asymmetry" between investors and firms. In considering the differing degrees of experience and expertise amongst customers, for example, it stated:

> Our proposals have considered the differing degrees of experience and expertise of consumers. Firms have a fiduciary responsibility to their customers, and so customers rely on the firm to do its best for them.

> Our proposals, and the emphasis on disclosure of execution arrangements, are aimed at minimising the information asymmetry that exists between firms and private customers. Firms have much better access to information on trading than private customers. The more transparent the process is, the more possible it will be for consumers to evaluate the effectiveness of the firm undertaking the execution and so be in a better position to ensure high quality, value-for-money service.[69]

---

[66]   FSA Discussion Paper, p. 11.
[67]   *Ibid.*, p. 8.
[68]   FSA, CP,154, Annex A, pp. 1–20
[69]   *Ibid.*, p. 2.

In taking this approach, it affirmed and relied upon the role of disclosure in protection of the consumer. Implicit in such an assumption is that the customer will understand the information and its relevance to his or her investment needs. The "public awareness" portion of Annex A, however, only repeats the benefits to be reaped through the provision of advice and does not address how the investors will be made to understand the information and its import. It is also worth noting that the paragraphs dealing with the differing degrees of expertise amongst customers (quoted above) actually only address the information asymmetry between clients as a whole and firms, rather than between, say, individual retail customers and institutional customers.

The Consumer Protection portion of Annex A is key to understanding the FSA's approach to best execution as a means of customer protection. The proposal focuses on information disclosure by the firm, and on the firm's responsibility to review regularly its execution process and "quality". In practice, then, customer protection occurs at the "process" level, rather than in the executions themselves.

Taken as a whole the FSA Consultation Paper made significant changes in the approach to best execution in the United Kingdom. What had once been a displayed-price benchmark standard with a broad safe harbour for trades on the dominant market, had become a disclosure-based standard incorporating both costs (net price) and non-cost factors. The extent to which the new policy could be expected to protect consumers or to facilitate cross-market movement of capital is further described elsewhere in this book.

In general, the most important aspect of best execution policy in the United Kingdom through the 1980s and 1990s was its origin in a single market environment, with gradual adjustments over time to accommodate changes to the market structure. The specific reference to a benchmark standard – the SETS price – is also a defining characteristic of UK policy up to that point. In contrast to the US policy, this benchmark functioned as a safe harbour – executions done at the SETS price were presumed to have met the best execution standard (it will be recalled that the NBBO in the United States became more of a "floor", or minimum standard, than a safe harbour). The existence of a clear benchmark made easy work for traders and compliance officers, and also met the regulator's standard of providing clear and consistent guidance. The adoption of the two-step process and the "relevant market" standard was a reflection (cynics would say a fudge) of the presence of competing, though small, markets. In the second half of this book, the relationship of best execution to market integration will be raised, at which point it will be argued that single-market benchmark standards can be especially pernicious to market integration since they encourage orders to remain in one dominant market.

So, like the United States, the United Kingdom initially adopted a benchmark standard, but this benchmark was based on prices on a single dominant market and functioned as an actual safe harbour. Like the United States, the policy in the United Kingdom came to include an expectation that traders would look outside this established domain for better prices where reasonably practical, with the proviso that the policy should be reviewed periodically to reflect changes to the market.

The review of best execution after the passage of FSMA in 2000 was indeed a break with the past. Not only was emphasis shifted away from a single market standard, but the concept of using a benchmark price of any kind was challenged. After the passage of FSMA, best execution policy in the United Kingdom essentially started from a blank sheet of paper.

As the FSA pointed out in CP 154, the UK best execution policy must fit within the regulatory framework of the European Union. As such, the proposals in the Consultation Paper were made somewhat conditional, contingent upon the outcome of the proposals being considered by the European Union at the same time. For this reason, and because of its broader impact on European market integration in general, we now turn to regulation of best execution at the European level.

Best execution in the United Kingdom

To provide best execution, a firm must:

1. Take reasonable care to ascertain the price which is the best available for the customer order in the relevant market at the time for transactions of the kind and size concerned; and

2. Execute the customer order at a price which is no less advantageous to the customer, unless the firm has taken reasonable steps to ensure that it would be in the customer's best interests not to do so.

Source: FSA Handbook of Rules and Guidance: Conduct of Business, Section 7.5.

5.9   European Union regulation

Historically, there has been no standard definition of best execution in the European Union. Unlike national jurisdictions, and in particular contrast to the US experience, there is no single regulator to co-ordinate or direct changes to regulation. To the extent that such an authority can be argued to exist, this function lies with the Commission, and now the Committee of European Securities Regulators (CESR). The actions and products of these organs, however, are prone to political compromise along national lines, and progress in developing cross-market policies such as best execution has been slow. Each country in Europe has operated under its own concept of best execution, making use of terms with differing emphasis and levels of specificity. Of the fourteen countries represented below, seven make specific reference to "price" (Austria, Denmark, Germany, Greece, Italy, Norway and the UK), while the remaining six make less specific references, using terms such as "best conditions" (Belgium) or "best advantage" (Ireland). In all cases, the standard is qualified in terms of relevant markets or availability.

Best execution in other European countries

Austria	"…at best price on the relevant market within a reasonable period of time…"
Belgium	"Orders must be executed as rapidly as possible and at the best conditions."
Denmark	"…a securities dealer must always have a universal obligation to ensure the customer the best possible price"
Finland	"…shall execute…in the customer's best interest without undue delay."

Box continued

France	"ensure that its orders are executed in the best manner possible"
Germany	"...to obtain the best price on the relevant market..."
Greece	"...within reasonable time period...firms will seek the best price available..."
Ireland	"...deal to the best advantage..."
Italy	"...best possible conditions considering price paid, received and other costs..."
Netherlands	"...as fast as possible in the best possible manner..."
Norway	"...the client shall be given the best price that the firm considers..."
Portugal	"Perform the transactions in the best conditions of market feasibility."
Spain	"in the best terms..."
United Kingdom	"price which is the best available for the customer order in the relevant market at the time for transactions of the kind and size concerned"

Source: *Best Execution*, FSA Discussion Paper, April 2001; FSA Handbook of Rules and Guidance: Conduct of Business, Section 7.5.

The first comprehensive legislation for EU financial services was the 1993 Investment Services Directive (ISD). The ISD was wide-ranging in its scope, but did not specifically discuss best execution, much less provide a common definition or policy. To the extent that it is addressed, best execution would likely fall within the scope of Article 11, which requires Member States to draw up Rules of Conduct for firms under their supervision, in accordance with certain broad principles set out in the Article. Amongst these principles is that which requires investment firms to act "with due skill, care and diligence, in the best interests of its clients and the integrity of the market".[70] A best execution policy could be inferred from this principle and investors' inherent vulnerability in the execution process.[71] Article 11 also provides a basis for differentiation between professional and retail investors, in its requirement that any rules developed by Member States pursuant to the Article 11 principles be "applied in such a way as to take account of the professional nature of the person for whom the service is provided".[72]

Though a best execution rule may be implied from Article 11, the range of best execution policies shown above demonstrates the broad interpretation given to the concept. The increasing complexity of the markets made this situation more and more untenable, particularly in the light of efforts to achieve a single market in securities.

The move towards a single definition of best execution for the European Union gained momentum with the EU's comprehensive review of financial services regulation begun in

---

[70]   Article 11, Council Directive 93/22/EEC of 10 May 1993 on Investment Services in the Securities Field (ISD).

[71]   Moloney, Niamh. *EC Securities Regulation* (Oxford: Oxford University Press), 2002, p. 532.

[72]   Article 11, ISD. See also Moloney, pp. 523–524.

the late 1990s. A consultative body of EU securities regulators, the Forum of European Securities Commissions (FESCO) proposed its own definition in February 2001.[73] The FESCO standard revolved around taking reasonable care to obtain the "best result" available in the "relevant market". Like the UK standard, this seemed to imply that the market should be chosen *first*, based on a number of conceptual factors, *after* which the best price available on that market would be found. The FESCO was subsequently reconstituted as CESR, with a mandate from the Commission under the Lamfalussy Process (see Chapter 12) to provide advice to the Commission on proposed measures to implement the broad principles established by the Commission's Directives on financial services. In April 2001, CESR issued a consultative paper[74] which largely reiterated the position developed in the FESCO paper.

In July 2001, the European Commission began public consultations on the revision of the existing (1993) ISD. Though the 1993 ISD did not directly address the issue of best execution, it was anticipated that the revised ISD should do so. In the Commission's draft of the new ISD in November 2002, best execution was specifically addressed in Article 19.[75] Although much of the original FESCO proposal found its way into Article 19, the reference to the "relevant market" was significantly absent.

Under the procedures for formulating and implementing financial regulation in the European Union, the provisions in the ISD are meant to be broad principles. Detailed implementing measures are left to the remit of CESR. This arrangement is meant to provide a measure of flexibility to the regulations, in that the implementing measures can be amended without the need to rewrite the entire Directive. Upon adoption of a Directive and its implementing legislation, Member States are required to enact national legislation to achieve the aims of the Directive. Once the EU regulation is adopted, then, the United Kingdom and other Member States could find themselves rewriting their own recently developed best execution polices in order to conform to the new EU policy. In all likelihood, though, this will not be required for the United Kingdom since (as we shall see) the development of the EU policy in this area has closely followed that of the United Kingdom.

The upshot of this process is that the approach actually taken towards EU best execution depends largely on the implementing measures ultimately adopted by CESR. Nonetheless, it is worth examining Article 19 as it represents the broad principles which are intended to remain constant even while the detailed measures evolve.

In drafting Article 19, the Commission chose not to adopt a specific price benchmark standard. Instead, the Article refers to executions "on terms most favourable to the client", and to the "best possible result". This best possible result is to be judged with reference to price, but also costs, speed and likelihood of execution. The approach is explicitly a process-based approach, requiring regulators in each of the Member States to verify that firms implement "effective and efficient procedures" which result in a "systematic, repeatable and demonstrable method" for executing client orders on these most favourable terms.

---

[73] Federation of European Securities Commissions (FESCO), *Standards and Rules for Harmonising Core Conduct of Business Rules for Investor Protection*, Consultation Paper, February 2001, Section 5.2.

[74] Committee of European Securities Regulators (CESR), *A European Regime of Investor Protection – The Harmonisation of Conduct of Business Rules*, CESR/01-014d, April 2001.

[75] European Commission, *Proposal For A Directive of the European Parliament and of the Council on Investment Services and Regulated Markets*, COM (2002) 625(01), November 2002, at II.2.3.

Article 19 also established the requirement for firms to review on a regular basis their best execution procedures and the venues to which they (reasonably) have access. The Article specifically expresses the expectation that firms would look for venues which, on a consistent basis, offer the most favourable terms of execution.

The EU approach embodied in Article 19, then, is less specifically oriented towards a clear price benchmark than is the case in certain other jurisdictions, though the move away from a "relevant market" standard marks a step away from single-market standards and towards a truly intermarket approach. Like the United States and the United Kingdom, the EU approach places greatest weight on examining compliance on a procedural, rather than specifically trade-by-trade basis.

Like the United Kingdom, the European Union explicitly identifies best execution as a customer protection measure. It goes further, however, in recognising the importance of best execution in the integration of the European markets. In the commentary to the November 2002 draft of the revised Investment Services Directive, the Commission notes that the best execution obligation "is the mechanism which will ensure that trading information made available under transparency obligations results in changes to the order-routing decisions of investment firms".[76] The mechanics of how this mechanism is to work is discussed further in Part 2 of this book, but it is sufficient to note here that multiple market standards are central to its operation.

Best execution for the European Union

Article 19
Obligation to execute orders on terms most favourable to the client

1. Member States shall require that investment firms providing services which entail the execution, whether by the firm itself or another investment firm, of client orders in financial instruments ensure that those orders are executed in such a way that the client obtains the best possible result in terms of price, costs, speed and likelihood of execution, taking into account the time, size and nature of customer orders, and any specific instructions from the client.

2. The competent authority shall verify that investment firms implement effective and efficient procedures which form a systematic, repeatable and demonstrable method for facilitating execution of client orders on terms that are most favourable to the client. In assessing these procedures, regard shall be had to the extent to which the procedures enable the firm to obtain the best possible result having regard to the conditions prevailing in the marketplace to which the investment firm can reasonably be expected to have access.

3. Member States shall require investment firms to review, on a regular basis, the procedures which they employ to obtain the best possible result for their clients and, where necessary, to adapt those procedures so as to obtain access to the execution venues which, on a consistent basis, offer the most favourable terms of execution available in the marketplace.

---

[76]   *Ibid.*

4. In order to ensure the protection necessary for investors, the fair and orderly functioning of markets, and to ensure the uniform application of paragraphs 1, 2 and 3, the Commission shall, in accordance with the procedure referred to in Article 59(2), adopt implementing measures concerning:

    (a) the factors that may be taken into account for determining best execution or the calculation of best net price prevailing in the marketplace for the size and type of order and type of client;

    (b) the procedures which, taking into account the scale of operations of different investment firms, may be considered as constituting reasonable and effective methods of obtaining access to the execution venues which offer the most favourable terms of execution in the marketplace.

Source: ISD Proposal COM (2002) 625(01), November 2002.

Summary

This review of the development of best execution policy in three jurisdictions has aimed to provide an insight into the similarities and differences in approach, as well as the different regulatory environments which may affect the ultimate shape of the policies. It has avoided detailed enumeration of the nuances and interpretations which determine their application on a day-to-day basis. It enables us, though, to identify certain recurrent issues and to ask where the policies differ, and perhaps why.

Table 5.1 identifies eight issues which help to form the contours of a best execution policy. It is by necessity unscientific due to the ambiguities present in various areas of some policies. It is, nonetheless, useful because it helps us to see the relative stress laid upon certain areas, and the directions in which we can see these policies going.

The first two columns describe the environment in which best execution policy is set. Of the three jurisdictions, only the United States has a consolidated market structure, in which most of the competing markets and their pools of liquidity are linked. Both the United States and the United Kingdom benefit from a unified regulatory/legislative authority with the ability to mandate, co-ordinate and standardise. While the European Union arguably

	Consolidated Market Structure	Unified Regulatory Structure	Price Benchmark	Net of Costs	Multi-Market	Firms Required to Review	Basis of Assessment	Customer Disclosure
US[a]	Yes	Yes	Yes	Yes	Yes	Yes	Process	Detailed
UK[b]	No	Yes	No	Yes	Yes	Yes	Process	General
EU[c]	No	Not in Practice	No	Yes	Yes	Yes	Process	None

Table 5.1: Comparison of regulatory environments and approaches
[a] NASD Rule 2320 and interpretive guidance.
[b] As proposed in CP 154.
[c] As proposed in Article 19 of the November 2002 Draft ISD.

has such a structure in the form of the European Commission and CESR, the degree to which these organs are able to carry out the three functions, free from national interference, remains to be seen.

The remaining columns address the characteristics of the policies in the three jurisdictions (assuming current proposals survive largely intact). The table shows general consensus on certain issues, such as the need for multi-market, rather than single-market, standards and the need to consider customer costs. Each of the jurisdictions has also adopted a largely process-based assessment of firm compliance rather than a trade-by-trade approach. The primary difference in approaches is the degree to which price is used as a benchmark for best execution. Though each jurisdiction makes reference in some manner to price and makes room for some degree of flexibility, the United States remains apart in its approach, which makes specific reference to a benchmark and requires firms to justify deviation from it.

Overall, though, the approaches are probably more similar than they are different. What is not readily apparent from Table 5.1 is where the approaches are becoming more, or less, similar to each other. The abandonment of the two-step, relevant market approach by the United Kingdom and the European Union marked a clear and important trend towards multiple market standards, at the same time that the inclusion of costs in the calculation brought all three jurisdictions into alignment with the end result for the customer. Abandonment of the SETS safe harbour, on the other hand, marked a step by the United Kingdom away from price-based benchmarks and towards a more conceptual approach, an approach shared by the European Union.

Conclusion

This survey of best execution in different jurisdictions highlights the various approaches taken to the problem of best execution. In the United Kingdom, development of the policy has been driven by changes in the national market structure from a single exchange to multiple exchanges. The policy has adjusted periodically to take account of changes to this structure and to new technology, but without taking specific measures to consolidate price or trading information from amongst the various venues. The UK policy, then, has been developed in the context of a shift from a single-exchange environment to a fragmented environment.

In the United States, consolidation of markets through linkages was legislatively mandated, with a view that transparency, fragmentation and best execution are inextricably linked and can only be addressed together. This multiple-exchange environment led to a different set of issues such as "reasonable availability". These issues will become increasingly relevant in markets such as the United Kingdom and the European Union as the movement towards consolidation and linkage makes these markets appear more like a network and less like a patchwork of isolated exchanges.

In Chapter 4, a framework was established for analysing the effectiveness of a best execution policy, and we can use that standard to evaluate the approaches in these jurisdictions. Of the three, the US policy probably best meets the standards, due to its closer focus on price and the existence of the NBBO as a visible benchmark. For the policies proposed for the United Kingdom and the European Union, potential enforceability problems are apparent. Given the customer protection orientation of best execution, the absence of a clear benchmark may sacrifice too much enforceability for the sake of flexibility.

This Chapter has also aimed to show how policies take form in the real world. Here, policies are the result of compromise and negotiation, and policy makers do not have the luxury of political seclusion that theoreticians enjoy. Herein lies a lesson not to be forgotten: the political and regulatory processes and the market environment often determine the final shape of regulatory policy.

6 A Legal Approach

Best execution is not a legal concept in and of itself. Rather, it is generally regarded as an extension of the long-standing legal principles of fiduciary duty and the law of agency.[1] This view has been articulated explicitly by regulators such as the SEC and the FSA. It has also been carried through into relevant court decisions.

The basis for the application of agency and fiduciary responsibility is the nature of the relationship between the investor (principal) and the broker (agent).[2] By accepting an order from a customer, in the absence of any representation to the contrary, the brokers implicitly represent that they will execute the order in accordance with the client's economic interest.[3] A stockbroker acts as agent for his customer, and therefore assumes the duties of agent – amongst these, the duty to exercise due care and skill in carrying out business for the client.[4] Failure to satisfy the requirements of best execution can in fact constitute fraud, in that it could be a breach of the implied representation to exercise due skill and care to execute the order in a way which maximises the client's economic benefit.[5]

6.1   Fiduciary responsibility and the "shingle theory"

Best execution is provided a legal basis in the United States through a concept known as "the shingle theory". This theory states that, by hanging out his "shingle" (holding himself out as a professional broker), a broker makes an implied representation to his customers that he will deal with them fairly and act in their best interest.[6] In effect, the application of the shingle theory to best execution gives the SEC and the courts the grounds to charge violations of best execution obligations under the anti-fraud provisions of the Exchange Act and SRO rules. The shingle theory was directly applied to best execution in *Newton vs Merrill Lynch*, in which the Third Circuit Court of Appeal stated:

> When a market maker accepts a market order it impliedly represents that the order will be executed in a manner consistent with the duty of best execution.[7]

---

[1]   NTM 01-22, p. 201.

[2]   FSA Discussion Paper, p. 12.

[3]   See FSA Discussion Paper at p. 12, and Foley and Lardner LLC analysis of Newton vs Merrill Lynch (citation below), http://www.foleylardner.com/brokerdealer/139838.html.

[4]   Keenan and Riches, pp. 245–246.

[5]   *In the Matter of Marc N. Geman*, SEC Securities Exchange Act Release 34-43963.

[6]   Unger Report, p. 26, citing *In the Matter of Duker vs Duker 6 SEC 386 (1939)* and *Charles Hughes and Co. vs SEC, 139 F.2d 434(2d Circuit 1943), cert. denied, 321 US 786 (1944).*

[7]   See also the analysis of the case by Foley and Lardner, at http://www.foleylardner.com/brokerdealer/139838.html.

6.2   Cases and decisions

The application of these principles can be illustrated by considering a few of the cases in which best execution was at issue. The decisions taken by courts and regulatory bodies not only establish precedent, they also offer a view of how best execution requirements are interpreted in practice. Three cases are discussed below; two from the United States (*Newton vs Merrill Lynch* (*Newton* or the *Newton* case) and *In the Matter of Marc N. Geman* (*Geman* or the *Geman* case))[8] and one from the United Kingdom (ICE Securities Limited).

Both the *Newton* and *Geman* cases addressed the issue of whether the execution of trades at the best displayed price constitutes best execution if better (undisplayed) prices may be "reasonably available". The ICE case focuses specifically on the fiduciary duties owed by a firm to its customers.

6.2.1   *Newton vs Merrill Lynch*

In *Newton*, the plaintiffs (investors) alleged that technological advances made it possible during the class period (4 November 1992 to 4 November 1994) for the defendants (market makers) to execute prices via alternative trading systems at prices better than the NBBO, and that they knowingly failed to do so for their clients while doing so for their own accounts. Both parties agreed that the market makers had implicitly represented that they would seek best execution for the clients by virtue of the fact that they had accepted unpriced (market) orders from the clients (as per the "shingle theory"). The parties disagreed as to whether this duty included the implicit representation that the market makers would execute at a price better than the NBBO if such a price were available from other sources, such as alternative trading systems.

The District Court had granted the defendants' request for a summary dismissal of the case. Amongst the reasons for this decision was that the court considered the definition of best execution to be ill-defined, and that reliance on the NBBO for best execution, even in the face of superior prices elsewhere, could not be found to be inconsistent with the duty of best execution. The Court of Appeals reversed the decision of the District Court, however, on the grounds that accepting a customer order implies execution at the best price reasonably available; the fact that the market makers executed, for their own account, orders for the same securities at essentially the same time at the superior (non-NBBO) prices demonstrated that these prices were reasonably available.[9]

6.2.2   *In re Geman*

The *Geman* case was an administrative law matter heard by the SEC. Marc Geman was Chief Executive Officer of a registered broker-dealer firm and in this capacity he was alleged to have aided and abetted the firm in a number of violations. Amongst the allegations was that he "aided and abetted and caused the firm's breach of its obligation of best execution by executing retail customer orders at the NBBO price and then, in contemporaneous offsetting transactions, obtaining superior prices for itself".[10]

---

8   SEC Administrative Proceeding File No. 3-9032, in SEC Securities Exchange Act Release 34-43963.
9   *Newton vs Merrill Lynch*, 135 F.3d at 271 n.3., see also Foley and Lardner, *op. cit.*
10   *In the Matter of Marc N. Geman*, SEC Securities Exchange Act Release 34-43963.

The SEC agreed with the Third Circuit Court's view on the *Newton* decision that "routine execution of customer orders at the NBBO when better prices are reasonably available can be a violation of the duty of best execution".[11] The decision for the Commission to make was whether prices better than the NBBO were in fact "reasonably available". The Commission found that the record did not substantiate this, and cleared Geman of the best execution charge. It should be noted that the finding was based mostly on the absence of sufficient proof (partly due to the firm's failure to keep required books and records), and that the Commission stated that "... we nevertheless are deeply troubled by the Firm's trading practices".[12]

In the Newton and Geman decisions, the Court and Commission pointed out that the standard applied to best execution should be reassessed from time to time to reflect the current state of technology in the market. That is, what was formerly *not* reasonably available may be commonly available now or in the near future.[13]

Newton (decided in 1998) and Geman (decided in 2001) have certain common findings, which are relevant to this discussion of best execution. First, the NBBO (i.e. the best displayed price) cannot always be assumed to be the standard of best execution. Where better prices are *reasonably available*, the executing firm may not be able to rely on the best displayed price. (As discussed in the previous chapter, this does not remove the NBBO's value as a benchmark, since it still functions as a minimum standard rather than a safe harbour.)

Secondly, the question of whether better prices are in fact "reasonably available" involves a facts-and-circumstances analysis. This is related to the state and availability of technology in the market, a standard which itself changes with time. It is important then to note the context of these decisions (particularly Newton). Phoning around to other brokers is no longer the only alternative to the best displayed price (e.g. NBBO or SETS); rather, the question in these cases was whether better prices were reasonably available via electronic networks such as Selectnet or Instinet.

Thirdly, the fact that the executing firm profited by executing at the superior, non-NBBO, prices whilst filling customer orders at the inferior NBBO price was indicative of the "reasonable availability" of better prices.

It is also worth noting that the superior prices in both cases were available on widely used systems, which were not part of the NMS. It could therefore be argued that the problem was actually a deficiency in the NBBO, in that it did not in fact display the prices available from all widely accessed sources. This point is made more apparent by the inclusion of ECNs into the SuperMontage® consolidated quotation system later developed by NASDAQ®.

What do these decisions tell us with respect to best execution? On the surface, the main import of the decisions might appear to be a rejection of the best-displayed bid and offer as a useful standard for best execution. On deeper analysis, though, it can be seen that the decisions only assert that this is the case when better prices are "reasonably available", and the facts and circumstances – the technological capabilities available at the time – are the

---

[11]   SEC Securities Exchange Act Release 34-43963 at IIIA(iv).
[12]   *Ibid.*
[13]   *Newton vs Merrill Lynch*, 135 F.3d at 271 n.3.

determining factors. This point has been explicitly made in both decisions, as well as in the SEC's Order Execution Obligations, where it states:

> The scope of [the] duty of best execution must evolve as changes occur in the market that give rise to improved executions for customer orders, including opportunities to trade at more advantageous prices. As these changes occur, broker-dealers' procedures for seeking to obtain best execution for customer orders also must be modified to consider price [improvement] opportunities that become "reasonably available".[14]

This reasoning provides a legal foundation to an intuitive conclusion – that the standard of best execution is dependent upon the state of technology, and that the standard must therefore be updated periodically to reflect what is currently "reasonably available". This leads to the line of discussion in the next chapter, the state of technology available and in use by the market.

6.3   ICE securities

In June 1999, the UK Securities and Futures Authority (SFA, since replaced by the FSA) initiated disciplinary proceedings against ICE Securities Ltd and its Chairman for failing to meet its best execution obligations to three customers. The customers were Directors of a small, thinly traded company with operations in Russia in whose shares ICE Securities was making "a quasi-market".[15] The three Directors had wished to sell their shares in the market quickly due to political developments in Russia, and one of the Directors enquired to ICE whether the firm would purchase 500 shares from the Directors at US $3900 per share, the price at which shares of the company had been placed in the public market approximately two weeks earlier.

ICE agreed to buy the shares at US $3900 per share, but did so only after deciding internally that ICE could then sell them in the market at US $18 000 per share. The price increase was due to the fact that the placing two weeks earlier had been "enormously" oversubscribed. ICE was aware that the share price had risen substantially since then, and had even sold shares on its own behalf at prices between US $16 000 and US $19 000. As this was an unquoted stock, the customers would not themselves have seen these prices, and they were therefore unaware that the market price of the shares had risen so dramatically.

The SFA held that ICE owed a duty of best execution to its customers, i.e. the selling Directors. As such, it was obliged to obtain the best price for its customers. In its discussion, the Disciplinary Tribunal used reasoning similar to the shingle theory, stating that "the continuing relationship between ICE and the Directors was based upon the understanding…that ICE would act in the best interests" of the customers.[16] It was further found that, by agreeing to purchase the shares from its customers at a price it knew to be substantially below that available in the market, ICE failed to give best execution to its customers.

---

[14]   SEC, *Order Execution Obligations*, 62 SEC Docket at 2242-43.
[15]   SFA Board Notice 600, 10 October 2001.
[16]   *Ibid.*

The applicability of the ICE case is somewhat limited by the circumstances surrounding the trading. The fact that the shares were not publicly quoted, for example, obviates any reference to the SETS price or any multiple market benchmark. Nonetheless, it does provide insight into the application of fiduciary duty (and to a degree the shingle theory) to best execution in the United Kingdom. There have been few recent cases in the United Kingdom in which best execution is the central issue, and so future cases under the revised regulations will be of particular importance in gaining insight into how the rules will be interpreted and applied in practice.

6.4 Limitations

The foregoing review of recent decisions is useful in providing insight into the reasoning which underlies the interpretation of best execution. By understanding the logic behind the interpretation, we gain a better understanding of the practical application of the regulations. This examination does not, however, imply that best execution is fundamentally a legal issue which can be solved through redress in the civil courts. As was noted in Chapter 2, civil remedies are only useful, indeed are only available, when the customer knows (and can show) that he has not received best execution. This is likely to be rare, given the customer's inherent dependence on his broker and trader, and the three cases described above are as noteworthy in this respect as they are for their legal value.

6.5 Competition issues

The facilitation of competition in the marketplace is of such importance in financial regulation that it is often enshrined in legislation. In discharging its duties, the FSA is required by statute to have regard to, amongst other things, the "desirability of facilitating innovation in connection with regulated activities"[17] and the "desirability of facilitating competition between those who are subject to any form of regulation by the Authority".[18] In the United States, a similar imperative appears in the Exchange Act. Section 23(a) of the Act requires the SEC to consider the impact on competition of the rules it promulgates.[19]

In an environment characterised by competing exchanges, the application of best execution policy inherently impacts upon competition and innovation within the marketplace. The performance of an exchange is often considered in terms of its liquidity, the flow of orders which interact with one another. It is in this respect that best execution touches on market fragmentation and market structure.

Put simply, fragmentation potentially occurs when a security trades simultaneously in more than one venue (exchange, alternative trading system, or other organised venue). Fragmentation is not necessarily a bad thing as long as the benefits of a consolidated market are preserved, as a report by the London School of Economics has indicated.[20]

---

[17] FSMA 2000, Section 2(3)(d).
[18] FSMA 2000, Section 2(3)(f).
[19] Securities and Exchange Act of 1934, Section 23(a)(2).
[20] Board, John, Charles Sutcliffe and Stephen Wells. *Market Regulation in a Dynamic Environment*, London School of Economics, September 2002, p. 9.

Moreover, fragmentation really exists only where the various trading venues are not linked with respect to order or trade information (this notion is developed in detail in Chapter 9).

The existence of competing exchanges presents a major challenge to the formulation of a best execution policy. Some argue that the logical benchmark for best execution (if there is to be one) would be the best price on the market with the most liquidity.[21] This is the crux of the "relevant market" approach as it appeared in the United Kingdom and FESCO policies and which is still put forward occasionally in current debates. But there are two major flaws in such a policy. First, the best price simply may not be on the dominant or "relevant" market at any given time. When this occurs, ignoring all but the dominant market could hardly be in the best interests of the customer. The FSA has identified the possible weakness of the "relevant market" condition in multiple exchange environments. In its best execution Discussion Paper, it noted that "(s)pecifying a price linked to a single exchange fails to recognise the possibility that a better price may be available at a different execution venue".[22]

The second problem with the "relevant" market approach is that it is self-reinforcing. Requiring best execution to be judged against the price on the most active market will logically drive trading to that market, making it more liquid and other markets less so. It would be difficult to reconcile such a policy with the imperatives to encourage competition and innovation. From a competition point of view, reference to relevant markets or markets with dominant liquidity constitutes a true barrier to entry for exchanges.

One alternative is to establish separate benchmarks for each trading venue. This was considered at one point by the FSA:

> If it is considered that the benchmark approach should be retained and if it is inappropriate to use only a single benchmark...then one option might be to define a benchmark in relation to each execution venue...in this way a range of benchmarks could possibly be created for all execution venues.[23]

This approach, however, may also have unintended effects. By treating best execution as a divisible concept, it would reinforce fragmentation and could lead to a "two-tier" market based on the liquidity in each pool. More to the point, a standard involving more than one benchmark is no longer a standard.

A third alternative is to establish the best price, on whichever market it may be, as the benchmark. This is simply another way of describing an intermarket benchmark. This would avoid the undesirable effects of undermining competition or reinforcing fragmentation. The primary drawback to such a policy is that its effectiveness depends greatly on the degree of linkage amongst the markets. It does little good to have a better price, which is not visible to all or most participants. A consolidated quotation montage would help to resolve this problem, and in fact such technology is already in use, as is discussed in the following chapter.

Regulators have shown ambivalence towards their role with respect to market structure and competition. Howard Davies, Chairman of the UK's FSA, has said that "(i)t is not the regulator's job to resolve the competitive issues or to determine the shape of the market.

---

[21]   FSA Discussion Paper, p. 17.
[22]   *Ibid.*
[23]   *Ibid.*, p. 19.

And, as a matter of principle, we welcome competition and innovation, which are likely to be the best guarantees of a fair deal for investors and capital raisers alike".[24] He added, though, that " ... in a period of restructuring and uncertainty we need to be vigilant, and to ensure that market integrity is not compromised as competing trading systems seek competitive advantage".[25]

The SEC sees its role as creating an environment conducive to innovation and solutions driven by the market participants themselves. Speaking of the NMS in the United States, former SEC Chairman Arthur Levitt said:

> The SEC's objective or function is not to dictate a particular market model, but rather, to allow the natural interplay of market forces to shape markets according to the demands of investors. Put another way, the Commission has been charged by Congress to *facilitate the development* of a National Market System.[26]

Levitt expanded upon this sentiment in testimony to Congress in 1999:

> Our role is to maintain and monitor a framework in which fair competition can flourish, and to assure market integrity. It is not now and has never been to dictate the ultimate structure of the markets. As we have for the past 65 years, we expect the markets themselves to develop workable solutions. Our markets have not achieved their great successes as a result of government fiat, but rather through efforts of competing interests working to meet the demands of investors and to fulfil the promises posed by advancing technology. We approach regulation of the markets in this way for a very simple reason – it best serves the interests of investors.[27]

Having said this, the SEC reserves the right to intervene when it does not feel that market-initiated solutions are achieving the desired results:

> ... history and experience presents [*sic*] a stubborn fact about market infrastructure: individual competitive interests cannot always be relied upon to produce a basic framework for competition that serves the *public.*[28]

The SEC points to the creation of the consolidated quote system (and associated consolidated tape) as an important example of it fulfilling Congress's expectation that it would use its Section 11A powers to enact measures where market forces and competition had failed to do so.[29]

---

[24]   FSA, "FSA Chairman Calls For Broader Debate on New Market Structures", Press Release FSA/PN/ 046/2000, 4 April 2000.

[25]   *Ibid.*

[26]   Levitt, Arthur. "The National Market System: A Vision That Endures", speech at Stanford University, 8 January 2001.

[27]   US Senate Banking Committee, Subcommittee on Securities, Hearing on the Changing Face of Capital Markets and the Impact of ECNs, Testimony of Arthur Levitt, 27 October 1999.

[28]   Levitt, 8 January 2001.

[29]   Nazareth, minutes of 10 October 2000 meeting of Advisory Committee on Market Information.

Conclusion

This chapter has aimed to provide a different perspective on best execution, stepping away from the minutiae of regulatory policy and looking at it from a legal point of view. The legal foundation lies universally in the concept of the duty of a firm to act in the best interests of its customers. The question then becomes, as was the situation in the three cases discussed in this chapter, what specific actions are required under the circumstances to meet this obligation.

Some have argued that the existence of this fiduciary duty under civil law renders unnecessary the use of regulatory standards of any kind. This chapter does not make that case, since there are practical difficulties in relying on litigation to protect investors.

Legal matters are not restricted to the rights of the individual investor. This chapter has also viewed best execution from the perspective of fair competition. It has suggested that care should be taken that a best execution policy does not inhibit competition or innovation in the marketplace, and that a policy which uses a "relevant market" or single-market benchmark would likely fail this test. Such policies would permit firms to ignore the multiple-market environment, and would constitute a clear barrier to entry for securities markets.

In the previous chapter, we saw the importance placed on the idea of which price venues are "reasonably available" in the development of regulatory policies. In this chapter, it has been seen that the same concept has become embedded in the legal notion of best execution, in determining the limits of what is expected of a firm doing business with or for a customer. The availability of alternative venues is largely a matter of technological constraints. This being the case, it is appropriate to consider in the next chapter the current (or near future) state of market technology.

7 Technological Considerations

To this point, discussion has centred on the principles and standards which could form the basis of an effective best execution policy. This is all well and good, but principles are useful only if they can be put into practice. It has been argued that the technological and systemic hurdles to achieving a comprehensive best execution policy are so great that they would prevent the implementation of such a policy – that the technological environment is an unalterable constraint which restricts the ability of market forces or regulation to change the way best execution is viewed.

It is undeniable that the technological landscape of the financial services industry is complex. To date, however, there have been few studies which have systematically reviewed the technological aspects of cross-market best execution, let alone ascertained whether current and near-future technology can overcome the hurdles which have been proposed.[1]

This is not to say that the role of technology has gone unrecognised. As was noted in Chapter 5, policy makers have generally accepted the idea that best execution policy must be reviewed and modified from time to time to reflect advances in technology and changes in market structure. The SEC, for instance, made this explicit in its 1996 Order Execution Rules and its 1997 Report to Congress.[2] In this Report, the SEC noted the central role of technology in the securities markets, and the necessity of keeping abreast of these developments by working closely with technical specialists and market participants as the Commission moved forward in the development of regulation.[3]

The processes and technologies discussed in this chapter may strike the reader as enormously, even prohibitively, complex. It is worth taking a moment, then, to consider the degree to which highly sophisticated technologies are already embedded in the trading process today. The speed with which information gathering, consolidation and processing can be automated is often seen by firms as providing that critical competitive edge on which their business depends. This has spurred innovation and made complex technology as commonplace as a desktop computer. Consider just a few of the simultaneous processes routinely integrated into trading desks today:

- order and quote management
- position monitoring
- profit/loss calculation and risk limit monitoring

---

[1] The notable exception is "Breaking the Barriers: A Technological Study of the Obstacles to Pan-European Best Execution in Equities" by Nicholas Hallam and Nick Idelson of TraderServe Ltd (Hallam and Idelson 2002). The report was an important source for the material in this chapter, and readers wishing to find a succinct and understandable review of the technological issues are recommended to read their report.

[2] SEC Technology Study, at IV.E.

[3] *Ibid.*

- trade/transaction reporting
- routing for clearing and settlement
- recording to client account
- export of trade information to back office for processing
- order routing
- automated quote adjustment (quote engines).

And, importantly, many firms already automate the comparison of net prices on various markets for their own (proprietary) trading. In most cases, all of these processes are done simultaneously and in real time. From this perspective, it can be seen that the technological effort to support a best execution policy based on multiple market net price calculations would not start from a blank sheet.

This chapter will begin with the order execution process, breaking best execution down into the steps which must be performed and then discussing the state of technology in each respect. It will then examine broader, but equally important, issues, such as interoperability and affordability. To put things in perspective, a brief description will be given of historical and existing systems constructed to achieve all or some of the steps identified in the process. The chapter will conclude with an assessment of the technological feasibility of a comprehensive cross-market policy and the role of regulation in its implementation.

7.1   The best execution process

When viewed as a process, cross-market best execution consists primarily of three tasks:

- the consolidation of prices from appropriate execution venues;
- calculation of net prices and prioritisation of these net prices; and
- routing of the customer's order for execution at the best net price,

followed by normal post-trade tasks such as regulatory reporting and public dissemination of the trade.

The basic tasks of the best execution process are depicted in Figure 7.1. Additional procedures are involved, but these are "ancillary" to the main tasks, and differ little or not at all from basic domestic execution. These ancillary procedures include trade confirmation and interface with customer account data. Clearing and settlement poses separate issues, and will be addressed in a later chapter. For the moment, discussion will focus on the primary tasks central to cross-market net price execution.

7.1.1 Price consolidation

At any given time, shares of a security may be trading in several locations in isolation from each other. This state of affairs has largely been the case in Europe, where "national" exchanges remain the norm. These exchanges have traditionally – for centuries, in fact – been the exclusive market for companies from the country in which the exchange operates. Both the customers and the firms acting as their intermediaries have also tended to come from the nation in question. While the trend over the past few decades has been towards increased internationalisation, this has manifested itself principally in the

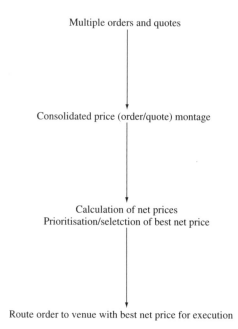

Figure 7.1: The best execution process.

listing of foreign shares and the admission of foreign intermediaries to exchange member-ship. What has been lacking is real interaction between buyers and sellers across these markets. While shares of, for instance, Nokia may trade simultaneously on several markets, a buyer on one market would likely not purchase his shares from a seller on another market. Indeed, the buyer and seller on different markets may not even see each other's bid or offer. As a result, there are multiple markets for the security operating in isolation from, and in ignorance of, one another.

The first step to integrating markets is to bring these isolated markets together. Not by coincidence, it is also the first step to cross-market best execution. We make the presumption here that the securities in each of the markets are "fungible", meaning that they can easily be exchanged for one another. In this way, an investor in Norway could purchase shares in Germany, hold them in his Norwegian account, and eventually sell them to another investor in Ireland. Additional complications are presented if the security is traded in different currencies, though even this does not pose a serious technological obstacle to the process.

The consolidation of prices – orders and quotes, depending on the market structures involved – is neither difficult nor new. Consolidated price montages have been common for a number of years. As is discussed later in this chapter, a consolidated quote montage has been a fixture of the US market for over two decades. In Europe, vendors provide similar montages for securities traded simultaneously on multiple markets. Yet a price montage needs to do more than collecting the prices available on various markets. It should bring the prices together into a single display, arranging the prices from superior (best) to inferior. Volumes available at the various price levels could be displayed either in aggregate (adding together the total volume available at each price from all venues) or on venue-by-venue basis. The venue associated with the prices/volumes is generally displayed along with the price, although it could be argued that this information is superfluous if the associated costs have already been considered and the net price calculations have been performed.

Though the construction of consolidated price montages is becoming relatively routine, there are still technical considerations which must be addressed. First, the data feeds coming from the various exchanges must be compatible. Standardised vocabulary and formats are therefore important. Although these formats do exist, the problem is that they are of limited use unless all or most participants use a single (or at least compatible) format. In the absence of such a common format, the cost of adding data feeds from additional price venues becomes prohibitive.

Synchronisation

Orders and quotes are typically displayed in a price/time or price/size/time priority. For this reason, it is important that the system recognises the sequence in which the prices have been sent to the consolidator. This is potentially dependent on the communications infrastructure employed by the vendor and the market venues – some communications links may be faster than others.

One way to address the problem may be the use of sub-second timestamps to sequence incoming orders and quotes. This would require the acceptance of a common trading clock, but such a measure would merely be an extension of a practice already in use within many markets. The use of sub-second timestamps would not only address the potential disparity in the speed of communication links, it would also prevent a perverse competition amongst execution venues based on the speed of communication links.

Bandwidth and processing speed

Bandwidth constraints are a key consideration not only for determining the number of levels to display, but also for implementation of the system in general. Bandwidth is the rate of data transfer for electronic communications, but can be likened to the size of the pipe through which data flows. If too much data is trying to make it through too little bandwidth, backups and delays will result. These delays can be a major problem if the data is needed in real time, as would be the case with a consolidated price montage. For this reason, consideration must be given to the number of sources (execution venues) sending data and the amount of data each is sending. Additionally, the data processor responsible for the montage must have sufficiently fast processing hardware to prevent bottlenecks occurring once the data is received.[4]

At present, bandwidth amongst exchanges varies considerably. Like other aspects of information technology, though, typical bandwidth size can be anticipated to grow in the ensuing years. Consequently, bandwidth is more a constraint to be considered in constructing a montage than a prohibition against it.

---

[4]   Hallam, Nicholas and Idelson, Nick, *Breaking the Barriers: A Technological Study of the Obstacles to Pan-European Best Execution in Equities*, TraderServe Limited, March 2003, p. 4.

Depth of the display

The total number of shares available at the best price may be rather small, and in fact smaller than the size of an incoming order. Particularly in such situations, it is desirable to see the "depth" of the market, i.e. the next best prices and the volume available at each. Showing the depth also gives market participants an idea of how liquid the market is in general, and how volatile trading may be. Ideally, then, a consolidated price montage would show *all* orders on both sides of the market, regardless of how many levels of prices this might represent.

There are two principal constraints on the number of levels to display. The first is simply the ability to show all levels on one screen, especially in the case of a heavily traded security. Secondly, and more important, are the bandwidth constraints mentioned above. The more levels of depth to be displayed, the more bits of data must fit the pipeline simultaneously. Electronic traffic jams would result in the queuing of orders, not an ideal situation when information is needed in "real time" and when quotes and orders must be properly sequenced. The result of this trade-off is a limitation on the number of displayed levels of interest, with most montages displaying the best three or five levels of prices on each side (buy and sell) of the market.

For the time being, the ability of any montage to fully depict all market interest will remain limited. Even where montages display many levels of interest, these levels are based on the "top of the book" of each submitting firm or venue. That is, montages typically reflect and prioritise only the best bid and offer from each of the submitting parties, while other interest remains out of the picture. Further, the existence of price improvement (trades executed better than the best bid or offer) demonstrates the presence of "hidden interest" available if an order is shopped around.

These factors limit the scope of quote montages, but do not render them ineffectual. The limitations have been present all along, even when restricted to displaying a simple domestic market, yet quote and order screens have always been viewed as essential to the operation of a market. These are not, then, a new problem unique to the creation of consolidated market screens. In fact, it should be remembered that even the single-market quote montages of the domestic exchanges were themselves consolidated montages – they just consolidated data from (largely) domestic sources. Expanding price montages to include multiple markets does not really mean different problems as much as different geography.

As for the undisplayed interest which leads to the potential for price improvement, a comprehensive best execution policy can and should accommodate those investors who wish to have their order "shopped around" to seek a better price. This can be accomplished simply by allowing the customer to waive immediate execution in favour of the trader's discretion – by using discretionary, or "not-held", orders as is the practice in the United States.

Selection and participation of execution venues

This leads to the next question – how does one determine which, and how many, venues to include in the montage? It has been mentioned already that the number of venues feeding data to the montage will impact on the bandwidth and processing hardware requirements. On the face of it, one would logically assume that the montage would ideally include all venues on which a given security trades. For the entire range of covered securities, then, virtually all execution venues would need to be "plugged in" to the montage. This would include not only all exchanges, but also alternative trading systems/electronic communication systems, and potentially also the quotes and orders of internalising firms. From a technical point of view, this raises the level of complexity exponentially, in every aspect from bandwidth to the standardisation of data format.

For the time being at least, the only practical approach to this issue is exactly that expressed or implied by regulators already – regular and rigorous review of the state of technology and available venues. This should be done on two levels – the firms and the regulators. Firms are already required in some jurisdictions to regularly review the venues which they access for price information (not less then quarterly in the US). Regulators would do well to commit themselves to review on a regular basis the state of technology, in order to assess whether processes once written off as impractical are now within reach.

In the meantime, some participation is better than none, and more is better than less. The construction of a consolidated montage should not wait until all venues everywhere can be accommodated, since an incremental development would still facilitate improved best execution and market integration.

Raw vs net prices

Most quote montages consolidate, prioritise and display the "raw" best prices, also referred to as the "displayed" price. The value of raw price data is limited with respect to best execution by the fact that it does not reflect the net price paid to or by the customer. Net prices reflect not only fixed costs attributable to all trades done on certain venues, but also variable costs which may or may not apply to the individual customer based on their status. For this reason, we must ask whether the montage should display raw prices or net prices, and indeed whether a displayed montage is useful at all. To address this question, we should first look at two different trading scenarios – one in which the trader is acting on behalf of an institutional client (or for the firm's own proprietary account), and a second scenario in which the trader acts on behalf of a retail customer.

When dealing for a proprietary account (i.e. the firm is dealing on its own behalf) costs would tend to be less variable. For example, the montage could display net prices of certain static cost information such as exchange fees and taxes due when dealing on each particular venue. These calculations – and therefore the resulting net price – would be relatively constant from trade to trade, and it would be sensible to display and prioritise all (net) prices based on these static costs. The firm could for all intents and purposes "set and forget" the cost data for these types of trades.

For retail customers, the operation may be more complex. Large firms in particular serve widely diverse customer bases to whom different taxes, duties and commission rates, amongst other costs, may apply. For situations such as this, it may be less practical to refer to the quote montage and instead enter the cost information particular to the customer, as well as the specifics of the trade, into a template from which the system will provide information as to the best price and location. This can still be done rapidly if the customer's internal reference/account number is linked to a database of relevant cost information, allowing the trader to simply enter the account number, security, number of shares and special instructions in order to receive a response from the system.

In some scenarios, it may be that the cost data for institutions is as particular as is the case for retail customers. If this is the case, the template procedure may be more appropriate than reference to the montage. This is not fatal to the approach, and merely would indicate a different procedure is to be taken.

If retail, and even some institutional, business is done through a template rather than a montage, it is fair to ask whether it is useful to have a montage at all. This would depend on the nature of the firm's business, but a net price montage would likely be useful for firms which do proprietary trading (in order to make their own trading most efficient), do business for institutional or retail customers for the majority of whom the cost structures are the same, or which "batch" large numbers of customer orders together. It must also be said that a consolidated montage, whether raw or net, provides traders with a feel for the nature and direction of the market, and so it would be useful to have a raw version of the montage available for general (and public) use.

Anonymity of venue

The desirability of bringing together the prices from multiple venues should be evident. But is it necessary, or even desirable, that the system should indicate on which venue the price is available? Traders may have preferences to particular venues on which to trade, and in cases where best execution does *not* apply, this may not be harmful. Where the best execution obligation applies, however, the identity of the venue need not necessarily be displayed, so long as the system is aware of the price's origin and has performed the necessary calculations specific to that market.

This anonymity of execution venue also has the merit of addressing the conflict of interest perceived to exist for traders, in which liquidity remains concentrated on the dominant market because traders' incentives encourage them to trade there (see Chapters 4 and 11).

Consolidated price montages have been operational for some decades now. The CQS, to cite an example, has operated in the United States since the 1980s. While this was the result of a government mandate, the market has also responded (albeit more slowly) with its own solutions, as commercial data vendors have developed their own products. It is important to note in this regard that regulatory goals such as best execution and market consolidation are not the only, or even the primary, rationale for the market to produce such solutions. The ability to view multiple venues for a security permits the firm to shop for the best price for its proprietary account as well. Putting technology to work towards these regulatory goals would be a matter of harnessing the profit-maximising endeavours of market participants for the benefit of the market as a whole.

7.1.2 Net price calculation

Having addressed the consolidation of price information from multiple venues, the next step is to calculate the best price available, net of costs (the intermarket best net price). This involves a number of sub-tasks, and these calculations must be made in real time in order to be of any value. The first step has already been discussed – receiving the raw prices and storing them in a common location for processing. Next, the costs must be calculated for each. This would generally be done by applying rules based on fixed or semi-fixed costs which apply to specific information.

It is important to determine in advance which costs will be included in the rules and therefore the ultimate net price. Certain costs are clearly appropriate – exchange execution fees, taxes and duties, for example. These tend to be costs which are explicit, fixed (or assessed at a standard *ad valorem* rate) and knowable in advance of execution.

Commissions and mark-ups are also generally known in advance, and should normally be included in the net price calculations. In some cases, of course, these internal charges are somewhat discretionary, as the rate charged may be lowered for particularly valued customers. This would have no material impact on the prioritisation of orders, though, since the reduced rate would apply across the board for that customer, regardless of where or at what price the trade is executed.

There remains a more problematic category of fees, those which are difficult or impossible to know in advance of the trade. Chief amongst these, in the current environment, are clearing and settlement fees. While these costs can be standardised, the difficulty lies in the fact that a trader may not know in which depository the shares reside, through how many depositories they must be transferred and therefore how many intermediaries must be paid.

Two approaches to this problem have been proposed. The first option is to leave unknown costs out of the net price calculation. The advantage to such an approach is that it limits the calculation to those variables which are quantifiable in advance, and which therefore can be calculated with some degree of precision. The obvious limitation to the approach is that it leaves out costs which will in the end become part of the net cost or proceeds to the customer. The second approach, proposed by Hallam and Idelson,[5] is to programme the highest, "worst case" cost as the standard calculation. That is, the calculation would reflect the highest cost charged amongst the clearing and settlement organisations handling the security and question. Such an approach might also assume a standard number of transfers across settlement venues. As these are assumptions, they likely would not reflect the actual cost for any given trade. In contrast to the first approach, though, it would take these real costs into account. Hallam and Idelson also assert that this approach would put additional competitive pressure on clearing and settlement organisations to charge the lowest cost in order to have a lower standard calculation, and thus attract more business.

The presence of "unknowable" costs complicates matters, but should not be viewed as an insurmountable obstacle to the implementation of a consolidated net-price system. Even under current arrangements, not all costs are known. Moving to a consolidated net-price regime would thus not represent a step backwards. Moreover, the identification of these unknowable costs should be regarded as providing a basis for further rationalisation of the trading process. More specifically, the ambiguity of clearing and settlement costs provides an additional reason for the rationalisation of clearing and settlement from its current patchwork of arrangements. Work has already begun towards this goal, and the ultimate success of this project will make the net price calculations all the more precise in the future.

A further complication is posed by the current practice of paying "soft commissions", or "soft dollars" as they are sometimes known in the United States. The practice of paying soft commissions is as controversial as it is widespread. Used as an incentive for the receipt of order flow, they would tend to impede net price calculation in two ways: first, they tend to distort the decision-making process by introducing an incentive not directly related to the client's interest, and secondly, they complicate the calculation by introducing discounts which are not precisely quantifiable. Discussion regarding soft commissions tends to focus

---

[5]   Hallam and Idelson, p. 14.

on their use with regard to institutional investors, but the practice can and does apply to payment for retail order flow.

How should we account for soft commissions? The answer must be found by addressing the two ways in which it impedes best execution. First soft commissions potentially distort the trader's decision by providing an incentive to route an order to a given venue *without regard to* the best net price. This obviously runs contrary to the goal of finding and trading on the best net price, and for this reason we must conclude that soft commissions should not enter into the best execution calculation. The second difficulty in calculating their impact on the net price arises not only from the fact that soft commissions are generally services to which it is difficult to assign to a specific price, but quantification is also difficult because these services are not specific to a particular trade – that is, they are not assessed on a trade-by-trade basis. As such, they constitute part of the firm's general business and should therefore be excluded from the net price calculation in the same way as overhead costs are excluded.

Based on both of these difficulties, then, we must conclude that the potential impact of any soft commissions should be excluded from the net price calculation. It is worth noting, however, that reviews of the practice of paying soft commissions have been underway on both sides of the Atlantic, and restrictions to the practice will affect their proper treatment with respect to best execution.

The distinction between direct costs and overhead costs is an important one. Few would argue that overhead costs such as staff salaries, premises and the like should be included in the net price calculation. Such costs are spread across the entire business of the firm rather than to specific trades, and in any case they would affect each trade in the same way without regard to the execution price or venue. Less clear is the question of venue-specific costs which arise as the result of connecting to and executing on various execution venues. As the costs are not assessed on a trade-by-trade basis, it would be impossible to assign a specific portion of venue costs to each trade. In this sense, they are overhead. On the other hand, a firm might not do enough business on the venue in question to justify the cost, but finds itself required to pay these costs as a result of a mandated best net price execution policy. The treatment of these costs merits deeper consideration.

Take the case of a firm which chooses to belong only to a single exchange, the national exchange in the country in which the firm operates (the "home" exchange). This arrangement is permitted, and even common, in the present environment. When the firm receives an order from a client for a security traded on the home exchange, the firm might simply execute on that exchange at the prevailing best bid or offer. Current rules may not require the firm to look at other venues, within or outside that country, where the shares may be available. But what if a customer places an order for a security of whose home market the firm is not a member? Without membership and the necessary technical connections and settlement arrangements, the firm cannot deal directly with the "foreign" exchange. It must therefore go through an intermediary who is a member of the exchange or venue in question. This will result in an additional intermediation cost for the trade. The cost could be assessed to the customer as part of the trade, or the firm could absorb all intermediation costs as part of the cost of doing business – overhead – and recover the cost with the account charges it applies to customers across the board.

The case need not be radically different with a cross-market best execution obligation. Firms might still choose to limit membership to one or a small handful of execution venues.

Intermediation costs which apply to executions on other venues would constitute a cost which (assuming it is assessed to them on a trade-by-trade basis) could be entered into the standard calculation template as a cost applying to all executions on that venue. What of the alternative, requiring firms to absorb the costs rather than assess them to their customers? This approach would effectively impel firms to look at the amount of business they do on each venue, and assess whether it would be cheaper to join that venue than to continue to absorb the intermediation costs. This would reward those venues which frequently have the best net price, providing an incentive to those venues to keep their costs low. We see, then, two important incentives at work – for the firm to identify and join those venues on which it does significant business, and for venues to keep their costs low. However forceful the logic of these incentives may be, though, it has to be said that such an approach would be more appealing to regulators and theoreticians than to those firms which would find themselves absorbing these costs.

A third solution to the problem of venue access costs would be to regard all such costs as overhead, which would then be treated by firms in the same way as other overhead costs (i.e. by raising the rate of charges in general to the firm's customers). While this would be the simplest solution, it would also be the least desirable as it would increase the cost of investing to customers, run counter to the goal of making costs transparent, and would provide neither of the incentives discussed above.

In the long run, the best way to solve the venue access dilemma is to rationalise the costs to the point that they no longer need to be a serious concern. Possible routes to this goal are discussed in the section on affordability later in this chapter, but it is sufficient to say at this point that connectivity and related costs can be reduced substantially through "networking" arrangements which spread the costs amongst a number of firms.

7.1.3 *Order routing*

Once the various competing prices have been collected, adjusted to reflect costs and prioritised, the best net price has for all intents and purposes been identified. Now the system must follow through and send the customer's order for execution at that price wherever it may be available. This is the process of order routing, and it is not new. Rather, existing order routing mechanisms must be adapted to the requirements imposed by the cross-market nature of the best net price obligation.

It is worth pausing first to ask why orders must be routed to the market and firm offering the best price, if someone else is willing to match that price (for instance, the firm handling the order might be willing to internalise it, matching the best price itself). On the surface, there would seem to be no harm in price-matching as an alternative to order routing. The broader consequences, though, could be harmful to markets in general. If a firm assumes the risk of raising its bid (or lowering its offer) to the best price, it stands to reason that it should be rewarded with the business which that price attracts. It would seem perverse if the better price flushes out more investors willing to buy or sell, but then another firm steps in to take this business by matching the price against its own book. The long-term consequence would seem to be to diminish the incentive for firms to provide superior prices, and this can only be harmful to the operation of the markets. For the good of the overall market, order routing would appear to be preferable to price matching.

Order routing, like the best execution process itself, is often broken down into a series of tasks which must be performed in sequence. Some of the steps currently used in order routing algorithms would be performed by the net price calculation mechanisms discussed above, but other steps remain. These steps include:

- Classification of the order as market or limit, identification of the best price and venue. In practical terms, this would likely mean initiating the net price calculation sequence by feeding the security, quantity and relevant customer information into the algorithm.

- For limit orders, determination as to whether the order is "marketable" (a limit order whose limit price is within the currently available prices).

- For market and marketable limit orders, transmission to the appropriate venue.

- Determination as to whether the execution was successful, and whether execution was obtained in the full amount of the order. If some or all of the order remains unexecuted, repeating the previous steps or cancelling if appropriate.

This description is a simplified depiction of what occurs in the process; actual order routing algorithms tend to be more complex and customised. Nor is it the case that there is a single approach to order routing adopted by all firms. The TraderServe study identified four distinct methodologies – basic order routing, "execution strategy" and two kinds of "smart" order routing – generic and client specific.

Of these, basic order routing is the least applicable to cross-market situations since it involves the routing of orders to a predetermined, *designated* venue, rather than one determined on the basis of a net price calculation. Execution strategy algorithms are also of limited value in our discussion, since they tend to focus on the breaking up of large trades for execution on multiple exchanges according to predetermined strategic rules. While this could be of some relevance in best execution, the focus here is on mechanisms for the routing of smaller orders more typical of retail trading. For these trades, the "smart" order routing technologies are most relevant.

Whereas basic order routing technologies generally send the order to a predetermined destination, smart order routers make a determination as to which amongst many possible venues is the appropriate destination for the order. The rules upon which this determination is made can vary widely – from likelihood of execution (based on recent execution data) to displayed price to speed of execution. These rules can apply to all incoming orders, or they may differ. The use of static client data, as previously discussed, is just such an instance in which different rules (based on client status and preferences) may be applied to the smart routing algorithm.

The existence and widespread use of order routing technologies is an established fact. As pointed out even in the late 1990s, order handling had by then become a largely automated process, at least in the United States, amongst mid-size and larger firms.[6]

Taking but one example, many firms utilise "message switch" technologies to accomplish order routing tasks – they have been used for decades in the financial industry for purposes such as the routing of wire transfers.[7] Several broker-dealer firms in the United States have developed and operated their own message switches to send orders to markets which quote

---

[6] Wallman, Steven M.H. "Information Technology & the Securities Market: The Challenge for Regulators", in *Brookings Review*, Winter 1998, Vol. 16, No. 1, pp. 26–29.

[7] See Logica Plc. "Logica Announces New Open Financial Message Switch", Press Release, 9 January 1997.

most "aggressively", including best price and other factors (in this sense, they are no more complex than the "quote engines" employed by market makers and proprietary traders in all major markets).[8] Message switches were proposed by the SEC as early as 1978 as a means by which brokers could route orders to the best price on an order-by-order basis, but this proposal was rejected due to the practical limitations in the technology at the time.[9] The fact that brokerage firms are now using message switches for order-by-order routing demonstrates that these technical limitations have since been overcome. A technical discussion of message switches would be beyond the scope of this book. Their relevance lies in the fact that they constitute a technology which is already in use and which would allow order-by-order routing at the firm level to the best market based on price or on price-plus-other factors.

The increasing use of order routing technologies was also noted by the European Central Bank (ECB) in its study of euro-area equities markets.[10] Looking at the impact of fragmentation on the markets, it noted that:

> smart agents and order routing systems enable liquidity to be accessed at the best price, wherever that may be. Large asset managers interviewed confirmed that they were upgrading in-house dealing capacities, enabling them to participate in multiple platforms and to better execute trades (also in Asian and US markets).[11]

Portals

The need to consolidate and provide access to the prices on a number of exchanges has created a niche in the market which is being fastly filled by financial "portals" such as those provided by Instinet, TraderServe and Tradescape. These companies, and many others, provide a consolidation service not only to professional trading and brokerage firms, but even to individual investors who wish to trade actively (in this sense, the American rush to "day trading" in the 1990s, whatever its faults, provided a real benefit to the market).

Portals, generically, have become common in their use on the Internet. As the Internet consists of hundreds of thousands of separate and distinct sites, most with many separate pages, a way was needed to enable the user to search for and access all of the relevant sites and pages. From this requirement sprang such familiar portals as Yahoo, AOL and Compuserve. Portal technology was later adapted to provide "shopping bots" which help the user find the best price amongst several providers for a particular product, and then to send an order for the item to the merchant with the most favourable price.[12] The application of portal technology to shop for the best price for a stock was thus a matter of adapting existing technology rather than the creation of a new one from a blank sheet of paper.

This provides us with an important lesson – that the development of the requisite technological infrastructure for consolidated best execution policy (and for the integrated market itself) is primarily a matter of adapting and harnessing *existing* technologies rather

---

[8]   US Senate Banking Committee, Hearing on The Financial Marketplace of the Future, Testimony of Charles W. Schwab, 29 February 2000, p. 6.

[9]   Unger Report, p. 36.

[10] "The Euro Equity Markets", European Central Bank, 2001.

[11] *Ibid.*, p. 41.

[12] Patel, Simit. *Direct Access Execution: ECN's, SOES and Other Methods of Trading* (New York: McGraw-Hill), 2001, p. 33.

than inventing each and every sophisticated element from scratch. Viewed in this light, the task is far less daunting.

Integration

It is not enough that the technologies necessary for each of the component tasks are available, but they must also be integrated. This integration needs to occur at two levels. First, the component technologies – order and quote collection, net price calculation and order routing – must be able to work with each other to form a single system. Secondly, this system must be able to integrate into the market as a whole, including areas such as trade reporting and settlement systems.

The first level of integration has already become commonplace. A visit to a single website of a brokerage firm will provide concrete evidence not only of the availability of consolidation, cost calculating and order routing technology, but also of the ease with which it can be integrated into a single coherent service affordable not only to bulge-bracket investment banks but even to small individual investors.[13]

One of the largest retail firms offers its clients a choice between "direct access" trading (i.e. the ability to access multiple markets directly and in real time, and then decide on which to execute) and enhanced smart order routing which seeks the best price for the customer.[14] These services are integrated along with other investing tools (such as risk management and charting) to provide a comprehensive package for the investor.

Another prominent firm offers similar services, advertising direct, real-time single-point access to "every major source of liquidity" – some fourteen Electronic Trading Networks in addition to NASDAQ Level II (depth of book) data.[15] This direct access is complemented by "smart order routing technology" which serves to "scan the markets and automatically route orders to the best venue(s) for execution currently quoting within an order's price range".[16] The platform on which these technologies are provided includes a proprietary consolidated central order book presenting the best prices from all connected ECNs and NASDAQ market makers.

These two firms are by no means unique in their provision of integrated consolidation and order routing services. According to one industry source, direct access capabilities are so common that firms now compete on the value they *add to* direct access:

> More than ever before, technology is playing a "make-or-break" role in determin-
> ing success in the fast-paced world of online trading. Technology companies
> servicing this market have begun to move beyond the core direct-access capabil-
> ities and are now seeking to become "smart-order routers" for their clients.[17]

---

[13]   Not all such firms cater to individual investors. Firms such as NeoNet provide similar integrated services for institutional investor and broker-dealer clientele. See http://www.wallstreetandtech.com/story/wstWeek/WST20021121S0005.

[14]   Charles Schwab and Co., http://www.schwab.com, accessed 29 March 2003.

[15]   E*Trade, http://www.etradeprofessional.com, accessed 29 March 2003.

[16]   *Ibid.*

[17]   Bear Stearns, Inc. "Financial Technology", January 2001, quoted on E*Trade website, *op. cit.* See also Robertson Stephens, Inc., "Active Trading Report," 25 July 2000, quoted at the same location.

The examples presented here are meant only to provide concrete examples of the availability of consolidation, price calculation and order routing technology. While they may be more appropriate for better-informed (and less vulnerable) investors, the existence of these services clearly demonstrates both the availability and the affordability of the technology necessary to accomplish the tasks underlying cross-market net price executions. A comprehensive list of the systems now in operation and the firms employing them is not the aim of this discussion, and would in any case quickly fall out of date. Those wishing to satisfy themselves of the widespread availability of these technologies can easily do so by visiting the Internet or perusing many financial technology industry journals. The point should be clear, however, that the necessary technologies have been put in operation, have been integrated with one another and are widely available at prices low enough that even individual investors can make use of them. This does not imply that retail investors should be expected to use this technology instead of proper regulation. Rather, it leads us to question how technology available even to individual investors can be construed as beyond the reach of professional brokers and dealers.

Market-level integration may prove more of a challenge. When constructing a system within a single firm, the firm has the luxury of operating with identical formats on compatible IT platforms, without the cross-market headaches and competitive considerations inherent in constructing a market-wide infrastructure. It would therefore be instructive to examine previous and ongoing efforts to construct a cross-market infrastructure, and to consider how these obstacles were overcome. The earliest, and arguably most successful, such venture was the NMS in the United States.

7.1.4 *The National Market System*

The NMS traces its history as far back as the 1970s, when Congress passed amendments to the prevailing securities laws directing the SEC to facilitate the establishment of an NMS "linking...all markets for qualified securities through communication and data processing facilities".[18] Importantly, one of Congress' stated goals in doing so was to facilitate the achievement of best execution for investors. The history and regulatory aspects of the NMS are explored in Chapters 5 and 11. The focus of this section is on the infrastructure comprising the NMS itself.

CQS/CTS

Under Rule 11Ac1-1, the SEC mandated the creation of the Consolidated Quotation System (CQS). The CQS is essentially a quote montage incorporating all bids and offers for eligible securities, consolidating and distributing them to all participants. The participants in the CQS system are the NYSE, the American Stock Exchange (AMEX), the NASD and the various regional exchanges.

As currently established, the Securities Industry Automation Corporation (SIAC) acts as the single consolidator and redistributor of quotes for the CQS.[19] The significance of the CQS lies in two functions. First, it is a cross-market consolidated quote montage, demonstrating that such technology is (and in fact has been) available and for the most part reliable (at least as reliable as the exchanges themselves). Secondly, the best bid and offer on the CQS has

---

[18] Section 11A(a)(1)(D) of the Act, 15 U.S.C. 78k-1(a)(1)(D).

[19] Likewise, SIAC consolidates and redistributes trade reports for the Consolidated Transaction System (CTS), or "consolidated tape".

been recognised as the (National) Best Bid and Offer (NBBO or BBO). As such, the CQS has functioned for over two decades as the reference upon which best execution was based. In this regard, it has had a similar function as SETS in the United Kingdom, with the important difference that it was the best *intermarket* price which was the basis for best execution.[20] The CQS system (and its post-trade equivalent, the Consolidated Tape Service or "CTS") provides data for approximately 500 000 terminals on a global basis, in addition to feeds supplied to vendors for further transmission.[21]

In October 2000, the SEC's Division of Market Regulation established a public Advisory Committee on Market Information to review the way in which market data is collected, consolidated and provided to the public. The Advisory Committee met seven times over the ensuing nine months, during which the CQS was prominently discussed. Amongst the principal items of discussion was whether the provision of market data should continue to be provided by a single entity – SIAC – or by multiple, competing entities. The NASD took the position that " ... multiple consolidators would increase the potential for technological risk" by providing multiple points for potential failure.[22] The NYSE and other participants disagree that technological risks would necessarily increase with multiple consolidators.[23] It was also pointed out that any change to the existing system would have to take account of the fact that the exchanges and NASD generate a substantial portion of their revenues from the provision of market data to the system.[24] The NYSE indicated that approximately 17% of its costs are funded with market data revenues.[25] The figure for the NASD is even higher – according to its 1999 Annual Report, market data fees represent approximately 23% of the NASD's revenues.[26] Should any system akin to the CQS be established in Europe, the issue of market data revenues will need to be carefully examined to ensure that revenue streams from the system to the exchanges remain at approximately the same level as they are now.

ITS/CAES

In early 1978, the SEC called for the "prompt development of comprehensive market linkage and order routing systems to permit the efficient transmission of orders amongst the various markets".[27] Three months later, the SEC authorised participating exchanges and

---

[20]   It has been pointed out that legal decisions have weakened the basis of the NBBO as a safe harbour for best execution, holding that the best displayed price is not necessarily the best *available* price. Specifically, better prices could be available through (non-CQS) ECNs or through executing brokers guaranteeing price improvement over the NBBO. For that reason, the best price on the CQS is no longer referred to as the NBBO, but only as the BBO. (Lofchie, p. 273) Nonetheless, the (N)BBO's use as a minimum standard reflects its continuing importance in providing a price-based standard.

[21]   Thomas Haley, CQS/CTA Administrator, NYSE, in minutes of 12 April 2001 meeting of SEC Advisory Committee on Market Information.

[22]   Richard Ketchum (NASD), in minutes of 16 April 2001 meeting of SEC Advisory Committee on Market Information (Subcommittee on Alternative Models).

[23]   *Ibid.*

[24]   see Lofchie, Steven. *A Guide to Broker-Dealer Regulation* (Fairfield, NJ: Compliance International Inc.), 2000, p. 275.

[25]   Minutes of 16 April, 2001 Meeting of SEC Advisory Committee on Market Information (Subcommittee on Alternative Models); and New York Stock Exchange, 2000 Annual Report, p. 55.

[26]   NASD, 1999 Annual Report, p. 41.

[27]   SEC, Securities Exchange Act Release No. 14416 (26 January 1978) at 26 and 43 FR 4354, 4358.

self-regulatory organisations (SROs) to develop, plan and operate the Intermarket Trading System (ITS).[28] The NASD subsequently developed the Computer Assisted Execution Service (CAES) to enable exchange-listed securities to be accessed via market makers (i.e. "third market" linkages) on NASDAQ. The ITS/CAES system is the order routing and trading system which complements the CQS/CTS price display system.

Upon the direction of the SEC, an interface was established between the two systems. Once this was accomplished, the market-level integration of the technologies discussed in this chapter (with the exception of net price calculation) was effectively implemented.

The ITS/CAES facilitates intermarket trading of securities by allowing a broker-dealer in one market centre to send an order to another market centre for execution. Through the ITS/CAES link, orders normally routed to an exchange floor may be routed to the NASDAQ market for execution. Conversely, an NASDAQ market maker may route orders to the exchanges for execution through the ITS/CAES link.[29]

Two rules are particularly important to the operation of ITS/CAES.[30] First is the rule which prohibits firms from "trading through" a better price on another market (i.e. buy at a price higher than the lowest offer on another market). Secondly, a firm cannot "back away" from executing at its quoted price and size.[31]

Some twenty-five years on, ITS/CAES is now widely regarded as slow and inefficient.[32] Various proposals are under discussion with respect to improving, modernising or replacing the system. One potential replacement (at least for CAES) is the recently implemented NASDAQ Order Display Window, also known as NASDAQ SuperMontage®.

7.1.5 NASDAQ SuperMontage®

SuperMontage® is a proprietary system of the NASDAQ Stock Market, intended to be an improvement to the existing NASDAQ Workstation II (NWII)® and incorporating the Small Order Execution System (SOES) for retail orders, and Selectnet for institutional orders.[33] The system displays the aggregate size for the best price as well as for the next two best prices, thus displaying the depth of the market on both sides to three levels. Importantly, the price montage also includes the prices from some of the alternative trading systems which compete with NASDAQ. The introduction of the system required approval by the SEC, which put the proposal to the public for comment. The proposed system proved controversial, provoking 104 comments and nine amended submissions to reflect the concerns of market participants before a compromise was achieved some fifteen months later.[34]

The SuperMontage® system accommodates order execution either through directed execution to a specific participant or through a non-directed algorithm to the best price. The non-directed option functions along one of the three algorithms, which can be chosen

---

[28]   SEC, Securities Exchange Act Release No. 34-42212, 14 December 1999.
[29]   http://www.midnighttrader.com/markets-faq.htm.
[30]   Lofchie, p. 274.
[31]   *Ibid.*
[32]   SEC, Securities Exchange Act Release 34-42450, *Request for Comment on Issues Related to Market Fragmentation* ("Market Fragmentation Concept Release"), at IVA (3) (b), and testimony of Charles W. Schwab (*op. cit.*).
[33]   NASD, SuperMontage® Release 1.0 Functional Description, p. 4.
[34]   SEC Securities Exchange Act Release No. 34-43863.

by the executing participant. These algorithms find the best price based either on strict price/time priority, or price/size/time priority, or price/time priority net of access fees charged by any ECNs that may be in the queue.[35] The default process is the non-directed algorithm using the price/time priority.

The significance of the SuperMontage® with respect to this discussion is that it demonstrates in a concrete manner the feasibility of constructing order display and execution systems on a market-wide basis which (i) aggregate orders and quotes from a number of previously separate liquidity pools (e.g. ECNs and NASDAQ market makers); (ii) facilitate the use of order routing algorithms based on differently prioritised factors, including costs; and (iii) allow directed orders to accommodate customers with priorities not foreseen in the algorithms.

In sum, the integration of the necessary technologies appears to be achievable both at the firm level and on a market-wide basis. Future endeavours to create a system, especially across existing national markets, will not be without difficulty. Lack of standardisation, for instance with regard to data formats, will need to be addressed. Still, previous integration experiences seem to indicate that problems of this nature are not insurmountable.

The cost of implementation

Assessing the feasibility of technology is not a simple matter of balancing expenditures vs benefits. The cost of implementing a given technology will vary greatly depending, amongst other things, on the current systems used by the firm. Additionally, it must be recognised that firms, vendors and markets upgrade their technologies and implement systems in the normal course of their business, and "new" technologies can often be incorporated into previously planned upgrades.

Similarly, the value of the "benefit" is extremely difficult to measure. How does one measure investor protection? Whereas costs tend to be measured in precise monetary terms, benefits rarely lend themselves to the same measurement. Regulators cannot realistically be asked to judge the value of, for example, increased investor protection, market efficiency or regulatory clarity. For this reason, cost-benefit analyses are not clear comparative calculations, but involve judgement and opinions which will vary with the priorities and perspectives of those doing the assessment.

Still, a proposal which would drive a large number of firms out of business is unlikely to be to anyone's advantage, and so the question of cost must be addressed. At first, the cost of implementing the technologies discussed in this chapter might appear daunting, and especially so for small- and medium-sized firms. But it would not be necessary for these firms to develop systems from a blank sheet of paper, since the development of the technologies has already largely been done. Instead it may be more a question of *applying* available technologies and ensuring access to the appropriate venues. Small- and medium-sized firms already operate in a highly technological marketplace, and the same methods used to reduce technology costs for other systems could be applied usefully for best execution technologies.

While some large firms choose to build their own systems, many small- and medium-sized firms purchase or lease systems from vendors. These vendors have in fact come into existence precisely because they fill a niche, that of providing technology, systems and

---

[35]   *Ibid.*

access on a more cost-effective basis. In some cases, vendors operate service bureaus for their client firms, in which the systems are run on the vendor's computers, and the vendor manages the software for the client firm.[36] Outsourcing not only eliminates development costs, it allows the client firm to save on related expenses such as data processing and system development personnel, and maintaining the physical computer facility.[37]

The TraderServe study provides a detailed analysis of the cost to a firm implementing the technology necessary for best execution, breaking the costs down into three major areas: connectivity costs, support costs and the price of processing power.[38] It concludes that costs can be reduced substantially through third-party outsourcing, and that in fact several large and small institutions already use this type of structure for equities trading order management. It also notes that the world wide web can be used to simplify this process (through a "web-native application service provider" configuration), using browsers and eliminating the need for dedicated telecommunication links to clients.[39] This system would allow the client firm to enter the equity and desired quantity of the order via a web page, along with any preferences such as limit prices or one of the non-price priority factors mentioned in Chapters 3 and 4. This type of technology, according to the study, would not only be cost effective, but it would retain considerable flexibility (users could easily modify their costs for the net cost calculation, for instance) and dependability. Certain internal costs would remain for the client firms (interface with the back office, for example), but the study's authors conclude that this approach permits the deployment of the necessary technology at a cost affordable to all sizes of firms.

The cost to implement an effective cross-market best execution policy may involve infrastructure costs above and beyond the direct costs falling on the individual firms. Whether additional infrastructure costs would be involved is as yet an open question, since it would depend greatly on how it is accomplished. If the market sees a business case for creating consolidated price montages, as they evidently have, then the market will fill this void of its own volition. The same would presumably be the case for any post-trade consolidated montages. If policy makers were to decide to follow the course taken in the United States with the NMS, some sort of governance and financial structure would need to be arranged. Since the Seligman report found that the present structure is almost universally disliked,[40] alternatives would need to be explored as is being done now with respect to the NMS.

7.1.6 *The role of regulation*

Regulators have a number of tools in their toolbox to achieve their goals. The more intrusive tools, such as mandating actions through rules and directives, are not always necessary or appropriate. A useful, and less intrusive, role for the regulatory authorities in facilitating the use of technology would be to create standards and to co-ordinate efforts so that sufficient critical mass is achieved to help make the use of the necessary systems and procedures commonplace. Just as regulation must always consider the capabilities and constraints posed by technology, the direction technology takes must sometimes be driven by the regulator.

---

[36] SEC Technology Report at IV.A, IV.C.5.
[37] SEC Technology Report at IV.C.6.
[38] Hallam and Idelson, p. 22.
[39] Hallam and Idelson, p. 24.
[40] Seligman Report, Introduction.

Indeed, the lack of clear and defined standards often makes it difficult for firms to proceed with software upgrades, due to the risk that formats and protocols might conflict with other software used for a different purpose. Moreover, a firm which has invested substantially in the software necessary to interface with one system could find it difficult to switch over to a competing vendor which uses different standards.

There have of course been important instances where the market has developed its own standard protocols and formats, such as the FIX protocol, the MDDL market data language or even those responsible for the explosive growth of the internet. Yet the universality of these standards depends on a certain critical mass being achieved, whereby all firms use the standard because all other firms use it. This is where regulatory authorities are able to use their powers of co-ordination, persuasion and direction to ensure that the market develops appropriate standards. This does not need to mean favouring a single standard and mandating its use (with the attendant anti-competitive side effects), but it could mean requiring the industry to co-ordinate with itself for the use of single or compatible standards. This method has been used successfully in a number of industries. It has been used in the financial services industry with some success in the United States, and serious consideration is being given within the European Union for using this method to reduce the Tower of Babel of exchange data feeds which constitutes a hindrance to consolidated price montages.

The co-ordinating role of the regulator is discussed further in Chapter 12, with specific reference to the broader issue of integrating markets.

Conclusion

The capability of available technology is of critical importance to the issue of best execution. Key concepts such as "reasonably available" and practicality hinge upon these technical capabilities. The brief survey of technology in this chapter is not meant to be exhaustive, but rather representative, of the technology in operation or under development. It demonstrates that quote montages are already widely available. Likewise, the other two main technologies – real-time net price calculation and sophisticated order routing technologies accommodating variable priorities – are available and under further development, both at the market level and at the level of the firm. Given the technologies currently available, it is difficult to justify a continued assumption that it is impractical to make direct, immediate comparison of prices across markets or to access the best available price.

A point explored earlier was that regulatory intervention is not always necessary, as market-driven solutions may be developed without regulatory direction. In the United States, the development of the NMS was, in the end, the result of specific intervention of the SEC, but only when it appeared that satisfactory solutions were not being produced by the markets themselves. The appearance of consolidated quote montages and Pan-European exchanges provides early (though inconclusive) evidence that the level of regulatory intervention required in the United Kingdom and Europe may be substantially lower than that required in the United States.

Trading is no longer done by gentlemen meeting for a few hours a day under a tree or in a coffeehouse. It has become highly dependent on technology. Indeed, more than most industries, there is a direct link in financial services between the technology employed and the profits enjoyed, and this is reflected in the level of market-driven innovation. Increasingly, trading is becoming a process of interaction amongst the automated systems of different firms and organisations, with human intervention necessary at certain points in the process. Futurists may even see a day when firms' daily trading activities essentially pit their systems against the other firms' systems, rather than the talent of their traders.

To be useful, financial technology must meet the "Three A's" test – what is available, appropriate and affordable. It is clear that the technology meeting these three criteria already exists and can be integrated into a coherent and affordable system. This brings us back to the premise of this chapter – the question of what is reasonably available to firms with respect to discovering better overall prices for their customers. The answer would seem to be that the tools are already available to check multiple markets simultaneously for the best price, net of costs and to route the order to the venue where that price resides.

In short, technological constraints should not be assumed to be a "show stopper" when deciding whether to implement a cross-market, net-price-based best execution policy.

Best Execution: Conclusions

At the beginning of this book, it was pointed out that the idea of best execution seems rather simple and straightforward. A customer should receive the best available price when buying or selling shares. The preceding chapters have shown that it is a far more complex concept in its operation and application. This does not mean that it is impossible or impractical, or that the problem should just be ignored. As a core investor protection measure, it is too important to neglect. The question is how best to construct a best execution policy.

Regulation is appropriate and necessary for ensuring best execution. Retail investors generally do not have sufficient real-time access to data, nor the expertise, to make an accurate analysis of best execution themselves. Since they rarely have sufficient knowledge to know whether they have been wronged, they cannot rely on legal redress in the civil courts. Similarly, the power of reputation cannot be relied upon to guard against poor executions if investors generally do not know when executions have been poor.

Additionally, surveillance and enforcement of best execution relies upon access to trading information which markets are not likely to share with one another. Lastly, the immobility of liquidity constitutes a market failure for which regulatory remedies are appropriate.

Much of the complexity in devising a best execution policy arises from the fact that investors have different priorities with regard to execution, and so no single measure captures the notion of "best" for all investors all the time. Yet, as pointed out earlier, it becomes apparent on closer examination that the lion's share of these differences fall along the retail/institutional divide. Moreover, the priorities of retail investors are fairly homogenous, in that the net price is most commonly the bottom line priority, and expectation, when it comes to the execution of their orders. These retail investors also happen to be the presumed focus of investor protection policies such as best execution. It therefore makes sense to pursue a differentiated policy, in which the core standard focuses on retail investors, and a more flexible, conceptual standard is employed for the complex needs of sophisticated institutional investors, who are presumably less in need of regulatory protection anyway.

The core retail standard, like any investor protection measure, must be clearly defined in order to be enforceable. This also serves the interests of the firms who execute these orders, since it provides regulatory clarity and reduces their risk of litigation. To provide this clarity, it is appropriate to use the net price to the investor as the benchmark against which retail executions should be judged. It is no longer appropriate to limit the benchmark to the prices on a single market, though, since market structure has evolved to the point where ignoring prices on other venues can no longer be justified.

Though the core standard must be clear, its application should be flexible by allowing investors to opt up to the more flexible institutional standard. It is important, though, that the presumed standard for non-institutional investors be the core retail standard, in order to ensure that those entitled to this protection receive it. For institutions, a well-defined set of exemptions, waivers and safe harbours is appropriate.

Public disclosure of execution procedures will help to contribute to investor eduction and therefore protection, but it is not sufficient in itself to ensure best execution. It should be considered a supplement to a rigorous best execution policy rather than a substitute. The disclosure of execution quality *statistics*, on the other hand, may be misleading and confusing, and therefore counterproductive.

The implementation of the core retail standards requires the use of sophisticated technology to collect price information from a number of venues, to calculate net prices in real time and to route orders to the appropriate venue. At one time, this level of technological sophistication was out of reach, justifying the rejection of the cross-market approach. Today, however, the technology already exists and can be implemented in an affordable way, so that technological concerns are no longer a valid justification for avoiding an intermarket best net price approach for retail investors. The approach for non-retail investors is more conceptual and does not rely on a benchmark, and is therefore not subject to the same technological concerns.

This is the situation as it exists today, but it is a snapshot of a moment in time. Periodic surveys and reviews by regulators of relevant technologies would be a useful means of establishing the technical state of the industry and in reducing the "regulatory lag" which can arise from regulation failing to keep pace with the state of the markets.

It seems appropriate at this point to examine the policy put forward in these chapters with respect to the elements proposed as necessary for a sound best execution policy. The use of a benchmark was deemed to be critical to the enforceability necessary for an investor protection measure such as best execution. For this reason, a benchmark was identified which focuses on the needs of retail investors (net price) and entitles them to executions at prices available outside the dominant market or the executing firm. Flexibility is afforded by the ability of investors to waive the retail protections on an ongoing or trade-by-trade basis. Investors need not be straightjacketed by unwanted or unneeded protections.

The practicality of the proposals lies largely with this flexibility, but also with the technology used to put it into practice. Whereas it once was impractical to expect traders to check multiple markets, let alone to compare net prices in real time, it is clear that the time has come when this is no longer the case.

Perhaps the most important element of this policy, though, is the use of a "core standard" approach to arrive at a differentiated policy, separating the core benchmark standard for retail investors from the more conceptual standard for institutions, which permits consideration of non-price factors appropriate to the type of trading they do. This differentiated approach gets around one of the most difficult obstacles which has arisen in the best execution debate – the impossibility of accommodating the wide range of investors within a single standard.

In the debate on best execution, the argument against benchmarks is often that "institutions are different from retail" and therefore should be treated differently. But then the reverse is also true – retail is different from institutions and should not be treated in the same way.

The differentiated approach provides a high level of protection where it is needed, but a less prescriptive approach where this is appropriate. It is made possible by three often overlooked, but critical, facts:

1. A one-size-fits-all approach cannot accommodate the whole range of investors' needs, but the differences fall mostly along a retail/institutional divide.

2. The priorities of retail investors are relatively homogenous, that is, concern for the net price.

3. This focus on net price permits the use of a benchmark, thereby providing necessary enforceability.

The result is a policy which is appropriate to the type of investor involved, strikes an appropriate balance between enforceability and flexibility, and is in the end practical to implement if the regulators and market participants have the desire to do so.

Some observers will disagree with parts or all of this approach, and they should make their views known. The quality of the best execution debate is improved substantially when the merits and drawbacks of a specific proposal can be used as serve as the focus for discussion, and so it is hoped that this approach will serve a purpose whether its premises are accepted or not.

Best execution is universally regarded as an investor protection measure. But a policy which requires orders to flow across markets to execute on other venues also acts to drive the integration of markets, by ensuring that capital actually moves to where it can be employed most efficiently. The ensuing chapters of this book deal more broadly with this issue of market integration, but the subject of best execution returns in the course of that discussion. As we shall see, effective best execution requires well-integrated markets, and market integration requires a cross-market best execution policy.

Best execution – Conclusions

1. Regulation is necessary in order to provide for best execution.

2. A differentiated approach is necessary to distinguish between retail and non-retail investors.

3. The core standard should be that which focuses on retail investors.

4. Best execution for retail investors requires a clear, enforceable standard.

5. Best execution also requires flexibility and practical application.

6. Disclosure of execution-related data is helpful, but not sufficient and probably not cost-effective in providing best execution.

7. The proposed best execution policy should be applied across markets.

8. Current technology allows the implementation of this policy in an effective and affordable manner.

9. Periodic reviews of market structure and technology should be undertaken to reduce the impact of regulatory lag.

Part II
Market Integration

Introduction

As markets evolve, they strive for efficiency. As a result, there is an inexorable underlying trend for markets to integrate, because it is through integration that markets optimise their efficiency by maximising order interaction and the effectiveness of price discovery. Just as nature abhors vacuum, markets abhor isolation.

The instinctive imperative to integrate markets is generally accepted as a principle of financial markets. The need was so clear in the United States in the 1970s that Congress took the rare step of amending the existing legislation, largely unchanged for four decades, to direct the creation of a national market infrastructure to integrate the existing exchanges and the nascent NASDAQ market. The necessity of market integration in the United States, then, has been a settled matter for nearly thirty years.

Nor has this necessity been particularly controversial in Europe. The Treaty of Rome, which established the European Economic Community in 1957, enumerated the free movement of capital as one of the four fundamental freedoms necessary for the integration of Europe.[1] The free movement of capital cannot be achieved while that capital is trapped in isolated pools within each country. Exactly how to go about creating an integrated securities market in Europe is now a matter of high priority within the institutions of the European Union, as well as the national authorities and (not least) the market participants who suffer from the current isolation of the European markets.

The following chapters will discuss the fundamental issues involved in market integration – chiefly, the concepts of liquidity, fragmentation and the interaction of orders. They will also examine the historical roots of market integration. This historical view will focus particularly on the European Union, as it is in Europe that the process is most visibly unfolding.

---

[1]   Articles 67-73, Treaty Establishing the European Economic Community, 1957.

8 Liquidity, Market Fragmentation and Price Formation

In one sense, market integration is not so much an issue in itself, but the goal of a number of closely related issues. As policy makers grapple with issues such as best execution, internalisation and provision of market data, it becomes clear that they cannot be addressed in isolation from each other. The policy taken on any one issue affects, and is affected by, the policy on one or more of the others and ultimately affects the integration of the markets. The Seligman Committee, when calling for a broad review of market structure and technology, acknowledged this "inevitable interconnectedness"[1] between securities market structure issues and issues such as order execution and competition. To examine the integration of securities markets, then, it is necessary to examine the nature of these related issues and how they fit together to advance or hinder market integration.

It has become accepted wisdom that the simultaneous trading of securities in separate markets is contrary to the interests of an orderly market, because it fragments the liquidity necessary for efficient price formation and discovery. This chapter will introduce the key concepts of liquidity, price formation and fragmentation. It will then argue that the accepted wisdom is only half right. The key ingredient to efficient price formation is not liquidity per se, but rather something else – order interaction.

8.1 What is liquidity?

Most people are familiar with the term "liquid assets". These are the assets which can be sold easily in order to raise cash. The more easily and quickly an asset can be sold, the more "liquid" it is considered to be. This concept applies also to markets; a liquid market is one in which assets can be brought and sold with relative ease. Put differently, liquidity is a reflection of the size of the market for an asset.

Some classes of assets, such as limited partnerships, are difficult to trade because they do not have a large population of buyers and sellers. The owners of these assets may need to wait a long period of time to sell them and accept whatever offer comes along. The "spread" between the prices of buyers and sellers tends to be widely divergent, reflecting the inefficiency of the market for the asset.

At the other end of the spectrum, shares of stock are generally considered to be very liquid. There are, at any given time, sufficient buyers and sellers to make the market for the stock efficient – the buying and selling prices tend to be close to each other, and orders are executed quickly. Yet not all shares are equally liquid. The largest, most well-known stocks – the "blue chips" – tend to be very liquid, while smaller stocks tend to be far less so. This is generally reflected in the narrower price spreads of the blue chips, since a larger population

---

[1] Seligman Report, Introduction.

is competing to offer the best price (in the same sense that an art auction tends to be more active when there are more bidders).

Liquidity, then, tends to lead to an increase in the efficiency of the market, and is a function of the number and size of the buy and sell orders (also known as the "depth of the market") for the security in question.

8.2   Liquidity begets liquidity

Consider an illiquid stock, in which the highest bid is €3, and the lowest offer is €6. There is not likely to be much interest in purchasing this stock, since the purchaser would buy the stock at €6 (plus fees), but could only sell at €3 (less fees), unless the market for the stock were to rise between the purchase and the sale. This means the market would need to double – the bid would need to rise from €3 to €6 – before the investor would even break even (not considering the fees). Nor will there be much selling interest in the stock, since most holders of the stock would likely have bought it at an offer price significantly higher than the current best bid of €3. The difficulty of selling at a profit would likely be a significant factor to be considered by the potential investor. For this reason, orders do not tend to flow to stocks that do not already have significant buying and selling interest. A lack of liquidity becomes a major obstacle to attracting liquidity.

In contrast, a highly liquid stock with a "tight" spread would represent a more reasonable investment for most people. With a spread of, for instance, €20.10 bid/€20.12 offer, the investment would be profitable even with a modest increase in the market (i.e. the bid rises from €20.10 to €20.12). Lack of liquidity is not a factor in the investment decision in the way it would be in the case of the stock in the previous example. Orders to buy and sell will tend to flow towards the stock, as investors compete with one another to have the highest bid or the lowest offer for the stock. In the same way that the number of pixels on a screen increases the clarity of a picture, the number of orders can increase the efficiency of the price formation process.

8.2.1   *The price formation process*

The competition for best price is the foundation of the price formation process. Another element is the volume, or number of shares bid and offered. An investor wishing to buy or sell a large number of shares obviously would prefer to do the entire transaction at the best bid or offer. If the number of shares at the best price is too small, however, the investor will need to continue through the remaining orders, at progressively inferior prices, to fill the entire order. A low level of liquidity makes it difficult to fill orders and can result in price volatility as well. Consider the hypothetical order book depicted in Figure 8.1.

A potential investor wishing to purchase 2000 shares of XYZ Ltd could enter an order to buy the shares at a price higher than the current best bid of €20.10, becoming the most competitive bid on the market. In order to attract selling interest, the order will likely need to be closer to the best offer than the current best bid. He knows that a bid of €20.10 will not get executed (since a bid already exists at that price), and he knows that a bid of €20.20 will be accepted (since there is already selling interest displayed at this price). What he does *not* know is where, if anywhere, in between €20.10 and €20.20 he can place a bid and still get an execution. If his bid is too low, it may never attract a seller and it could remain unexecuted (and the market could rise while the order remains unexecuted). The alternative, of course,

Offers	Size	Price	Price	Size
	1000	20.27		
	1000	20.23		
	500	20.20		
			20.10	1500
			20.05	250
			20.00	1000
				Bids

Figure 8.1: Order Book for XYZ Ltd.

would be to take the lowest offer, buying the 500 shares available at €20.20. This would have the virtue of speedy and certain execution, even though it is more expensive than that the rest of the market is willing to pay. However, only part of the order could be executed at this price. The remaining shares will need to be purchased at €20.23 (1000 shares) and €20.27 (the final 500 shares). Because of the low volumes on the offer side, and the large gaps between offer prices, the average price paid by the investor (not including transaction costs) would be just over €20.23. The investor would need the best bid to rise by thirteen cents just to break even when he sells. Moreover, when it is time to sell, he will not be able to unload all 2000 shares even at the best two bids, unless the character of the market were to change. Though the market in this example uses an order book, the same principles apply in a quote-driven market, in which professional market makers enter the prices and volumes at which they are prepared to deal.

It is also worth noting that in purchasing his 2000 shares, the investor has "taken out" nearly all of the displayed selling interest in XYZ. After his purchase, the "inside spread" is €20.10 bid and €20.27 offer, with only 500 shares offered at €20.27. This would inhibit the price formation process by making it even more difficult for the next potential buyer.

Now consider a more liquid market for the same security, depicted in Figure 8.2. The increased liquidity of the stock is manifested in the higher number of orders and the larger size of the orders. As investors compete for the highest bid and lowest offer, the "gaps" between prices tend to be filled, resulting both in a tighter inside spread and in smaller price increments between orders. In this order book, the investor could place his order in between the best bid and offer, at €20.13, and stand a reasonable chance of attracting a seller willing to come down one cent from the best displayed offer. Alternatively, he can fill his order immediately by taking 2000 shares of the 3500 offered at €20.14. If he does so, there would remain 1500 shares at €20.14, and additional shares available at close intervals. This market can absorb more buying and selling without causing the volatility of the previous example.

When the trade of 2000 shares at €20.14 is published (in real time), the €20.14 price is "validated", meaning that the other market participants see that €20.14 is a valid price at which both buying and selling interest exist (hence the role of a consolidated tape, as discussed in other chapters).

Clearly, the price formation process can be more efficient, reliable and attractive when there are more orders – more liquidity – interacting in the order book. This example

Offers	Size	Price	Price	Size
	1000	20.27		
	1000	20.23		
	4000	20.21		
	5500	20.20		
	10000	20.17		
	1250	20.15		
	3500	20.14		
			20.12	1500
			20.10	1250
			20.09	10000
			20.07	7500
				Bids

Figure 8.2: Order Book for XYZ Ltd.

demonstrates why it is axiomatic that *price formation efficiency is directly related to the liquidity of the market for the security.*

8.2.2 *Fragmentation*

The last example makes certain simplifying assumptions for clarity's sake. One of the key assumptions is that the security only trades on one exchange, so all the orders are displayed in a single order book. What would happen, though, if XYZ were to trade simultaneously on two different exchanges? Theoretically, some of the orders displayed in Figure 8.2 would be displayed instead in another order book. In fact, if enough of the orders were displayed on the other exchange, both order books could well end up looking like the less liquid market in Figure 8.1. Instead of one liquid market, there would be two illiquid markets. With liquidity thus divided between the two exchanges, the price formation process on each would be less efficient, and the stock could even trade at different prices on the two markets.

8.2.3 *Breaking the law of one price*

In theory, a security should not trade at different prices on different markets. The "law of one price" dictates that fungible securities trading simultaneously should do so at the same price on all markets. Any price difference in a tradeable instrument would present a profit opportunity to arbitrageurs, who could buy the instrument on the market with the lower price and sell it in the market with the higher price. This arbitrage activity would narrow the price difference, and in theory would continue until the prices are the same on both markets. The law of one price would seem to imply that securities (which are generally fungible) should trade at the same price on all markets. Best execution would not require a cross-market standard, since there would never be a better price on another market.

Yet prices do differ from market to market, even after accounting for cost differentials. In practice, liquidity tends to be price inelastic (i.e. immobile), remaining on the dominant market as traders continue to trade there regardless of the potentially superior prices on other markets.

The immobility of liquidity has been substantiated by policy makers in the European Union. In 2000, the ECB undertook a study conducted to assess the level of integration and efficiency in the equity markets of those countries which had adopted the Euro (the "Euro zone").[2] The study was based on internal research, and on interviews of market participants and exchanges in Europe. The report found that the European market is not substantially integrated, and instead is characterised by a significant level of fragmentation. Amongst the causes cited for this fragmentation, according to the ECB, was that "market liquidity tends to be 'sticky', meaning that turnover for stocks ... still tends to be concentrated on the first market of listing".[3]

The ECB's findings are reinforced by those of an independent study conducted in 2001.[4] Having surveyed a number of industry leaders, the study found a number of possible explanations for the immobility of liquidity. Amongst these reasons, according to the survey, was the fact that many firms pass on the cost of market inefficiencies to their customers, at a mark-up. That is, an inefficient market is a revenue-generator for these firms. Another explanation lies with the way in which compensation within a firm is structured. In many firms, traders' bonuses are biased towards trading on the dominant market. Firms which seek to attract investment banking business often promote themselves on the basis of their market share in these dominant markets, implying a greater ability to maintain liquidity in the secondary market for a potential client's shares. To maintain their market share, many firms reward traders for their activity in these markets (and, according to the Charteris study, firms' accounting systems do not attribute the cost of capital to individual traders' profit and loss). Under such an arrangement, there is a strong personal incentive for the trader to execute his trades on the dominant market, and in fact he would potentially reduce his own remuneration by trading anywhere else.

Viewed in the perspective of best execution obligations discussed in the preceding chapters, these practices and other practices of this nature would not only reduce integration, they would also constitute a conflict of interest which has the potential to distort best execution determinations by the conflicted trader.

Another potential explanation for the immobility is that there is *no* particular explanation – people are creatures of habit, and "inertia" drives them to do things the way they always have.

Whatever the reason for the immobility of liquidity, there is little dispute over the fact that orders frequently fail to execute across markets when they could do so at a superior price. That is, the law of one price does not always hold in actual practice. In the presence of such market failures, the "invisible hand" does not operate to maximise efficiency. This

---

[2]   European Central Bank, p. 7.
[3]   *Ibid.*, p. 39.
[4]   European Financial Markets 2001: Revolution or Evolution?, Charteris Plc, 2001.

brings us to the question of what should be done to ensure that order flows do in fact move freely to the best price. The use of regulatory measures – the visible hand – to correct market failures is generally accepted as legitimate and necessary. It is here that best execution and market integration meet, since a requirement to execute trades on the venue at which the best price resides would overcome the immobility of liquidity and allow capital to move to its most efficient use. The approach of the European Commission takes note of this regulatory symbiosis of market linkages, order interaction, market efficiency and best execution. Amongst its "Guiding Principles for Revised ISD Orientations",[5] it included

> Promote overall market efficiency by allowing interaction of EU-wide buy and sell interest across trading systems. Transparency and "best execution" are mechanisms for interlinking markets and trading systems.

8.2.4 *A challenge to the assumption*

The "fragmentation" of liquidity is of great concern to regulators and market participants alike, since it tends to inhibit efficient price formation and discovery by reducing liquidity. This has led to a common assumption that "market fragmentation" – the simultaneous trading of securities on multiple markets – is inimical to efficient price formation, because it results in the fragmentation of liquidity.

This assumption confuses simultaneous trading, on the one hand, with fragmentation of liquidity, on the other. It confuses separate pools of liquidity with *isolated* pools of liquidity. The two are not necessarily the same, and the distinction is subtle but crucial in under-standing market integration. As explained above, the existence of two simultaneous markets could mean that each has only a portion of the total liquidity for the security. But what if the markets are not *isolated* from each other, but could actually interact?

If the markets were linked in such a way that the buy orders from one market could match the sell orders from the other (and vice versa), the *liquidity* would not be fragmented even if the "market" was. An order placed on one market could interact with the best order from any other market, regardless of whether that order was entered in Milan, London or any other market in the network. In short, competing markets can trade simultaneously without fragmenting the pool of liquidity, as long as they are adequately linked so that their orders can interact with each other. It is an absence of order interaction, rather than the existence of separate markets, which fragments liquidity and inhibits market integration.

Contrary to the common assumption, then, market fragmentation – the simultaneous trading of a security on more than one market – is not the same as liquidity fragmentation. As such, market fragmentation *per se* does not inhibit price formation. Rather, it is the lack of order interaction arising from *liquidity fragmentation* which inhibits the process. The crucial difference is whether the competing pools of liquidity are linked to each other, into a network of liquidity.

This has important implications for competition as well as for integration. In recent debates on market structure, discussion has frequently been framed in terms of two presumed and contradictory alternatives. On one hand, regulators could impose "concentration" rules requiring all orders for a given security to flow to a single market,

---

[5]   Presented at the European Commission's Open Hearing on the Revised ISD, April 2002.

thus maximising order interaction – but at the expense of competition, since that market would have a natural monopoly on trading in that security. The alternative, it was suggested, would be to allow multiple markets to trade the security, competing with one another for order flow but at the expense of efficiency, since order interaction would be diminished. Yet we see that these are not in fact the only alternatives. If competing markets are linked to enable cross-market order interaction, the benefits of competition amongst markets can be preserved without sacrificing the efficiency of the price formation process.

Conclusion

If a framework is developed by which orders in separate markets can interact with each other *across* markets, an integrated market can be created without creating a single monopolistic "super exchange" on which all orders must trade. There would no longer need to be a choice between market efficiency (concentrating liquidity in a single pool) and competition (multiple competing markets). The development of such a framework is an important theme of this book.

This is not a radical new assumption, but rather a slightly different view of an old one. All markets, after all, are networks[6] and networks are more efficient when there are more participants in the network. It is the emphasis on order interaction rather than "market fragmentation" which is perhaps a different perspective.

Nor is the pooling of liquidity new in practice, since the NMS has accomplished this task more or less effectively for some two decades. The pooling of pre- and post-trade information is viewed in the United States as critical to the effectiveness of both market integration and best execution. According to one SEC market regulation official:

> A regulatory framework that promotes transparency helps ensure that prices across our national market system are available to all market participants, and this, in turn, contributes to the efficient price discovery and the best execution of customer orders.[7]

The important relationship between fragmentation and best execution is further developed in the following chapters.

---

[6]   Schwartz, Robert A., Wood, Robert A. and Deniz. Ozenbas, "Volatility in U.S. and European Equity Markets: An Assessment of Market Quality", in *International Finance*, Vol. 5, No. 3, pp. 437–461.

[7]   Minutes of 10 October 2000 meeting of Advisory Committee on Market Information, 10 October 2000.

9 Fragmentation and Concentration

In practice, fragmentation has arisen from three market structure developments – internalisation of customer orders, the use of Alternative Trading Systems (ATSs), and the simultaneous trading of shares on multiple exchanges. The latter needs little additional explanation beyond what has already been pointed out in this book – that many securities, and certainly most blue-chip equities, today trade simultaneously on more than one market. The other two phenomena, however, are both more complex and more controversial. This chapter will aim to provide an overview of how each affects liquidity and market structure.

In a sense, the controversy over the impact of ATSs and internalisation is an extension of the arguments on fragmentation raised in the previous chapter. As will be seen in the pages that follow, the central issue raised by these practices is whether their consequent diversion of liquidity is harmful to the market. Opponents point to the iron logic of the price formation process – reduced liquidity leads to less order interaction, which in turn degrades the price formation process. The remedy, according to some in this school, is to require orders to be concentrated in a single market, maximising order interaction (and for all intents and purposes prohibiting internalisation and alternative venues in the process). Others question the validity of concentration rules, claiming that the increased competition resulting from a greater number of competing venues will inevitably reduce overall market costs.

9.1 Concentration rules in Europe and the United States

The concentration debate has been important in varying degrees in most developed markets. It is worth looking briefly at the European experience in particular, though, since the debate there is recent and the arguments for and against have been marshalled in particularly clear, if sometimes fiery, terms.

The concentration principle made its first significant appearance in the negotiations for the first (1993) Investment Services Directive. In late 1990, the French proposed a measure which would permit Member States to require transactions to be carried out on a "regulated market", which in effect meant the established stock exchanges. Given the definition of "regulated market" and the insignificant level of cross-border activity at the time, this meant for all intents and purposes that transactions would have to be effected on the home market, rather than over-the-counter (OTC) (off-exchange). The French were supported in this proposal by Italy, Spain, Belgium, Portugal and Greece – the so-called Club Med – and opposed by the United Kingdom, Ireland, Germany and the Netherlands.[1] Amongst the reasons put forward for the adoption of the concentration rule were the need to concentrate liquidity for the sake of market efficiency and the need to ensure adequate investor

---

[1] Underhill, Geoffrey (ed.) *The New World Order in International Finance* (New York: St. Martin's Press), 1997, p. 114.

protection. Opposing arguments were not so much against concentration as they were in favour of OTC dealing. The virtues of OTC dealing, so the argument went, included competition between exchange and OTC products and the ability of OTC markets to tailor products to particular classes of investors.[2]

Underlying the debate was a more raw form of competition – that of Member States seeking to protect the position of their own markets and preserve business practices to which they were accustomed.[3] The intrusion of national protectionism comes as no surprise to anyone acquainted with the policy-making process in the European Union, as it has become a more or less accepted reality over the decades. In the end, Club Med won the battle on concentration with its inclusion in Article 14 of the 1993 ISD.

The commitment to revise the ISD meant the opportunity for a second round, and opponents were keen to do away with concentration rules once and for all. Though a concentration rule was proposed early in the drafting stage of the revised ISD, opposition was vocal, fervent and well organised, and the provision fell out in subsequent drafts. At the last minute – almost literally – a concentration rule reappeared in the Commission's final text for review by the European Parliament and Council. The late insertion of the text was done without the customary prior consultation with the market, and its inclusion was widely attributed to the invisible hand of the Italian president of the Commission. Not surprisingly, opposition to the new article was especially strong, and the proposal became the most controversial article in the draft ISD.

The final fate of a European concentration rule is as yet undetermined, but its tumultuous history illustrates the importance placed on this issue of market structure by regulators and market participants alike. The concentration vs fragmentation issue also provides the context in which to examine the issues of internalisation and alternative trading systems. Whatever their other implications, the increased prominence of these two phenomena raises the level of debate as to the need for rules to consolidate liquidity.

In the United States, the debate on concentration has revolved largely around the NYSE's controversial Rule 390, which for all intents and purposes prevented NYSE member firms from trading NYSE-listed shares anywhere except on the NYSE. While the NYSE defended the use of such a concentration rule on the grounds that it helped to centralise liquidity, opponents saw it as fundamentally anti-competitive. The SEC made no secret of its discomfort with the Rule, and actions such as the establishment of Unlisted Trading Privileges and the Intermarket Trading System (see Chapter 11) helped to dilute the effect of the Rule. Rule 390 made its last stand in December 1999, when the NYSE proposed to eliminate it, though the proposal was coupled with the proposed introduction by the NYSE of rules to limit the use of internalisation. The SEC separated the two issues, and approved the repeal of Rule 390 shortly thereafter.

9.1.1 *Internalisation*

Simply put, "internalisation" is the process in which a firm which has received customer buy and sell orders either matches them against each other (assuming the price parameters

---

[2]   Underhill, p. 115.
[3]   *Ibid.*

permit this) or executes the trades against the firm's own trading account. In either case, the trades are executed *internally*, without going to a market prior to execution.

If orders are internalised, they are not included in the overall (consolidated) market, and therefore neither contribute to nor benefit from the liquidity of the rest of the market. In other words, internalisation fragments liquidity by creating a "micro-market" within each internalising firm. Unlike the linked markets described in the previous chapter, internalisation by its nature involves an isolated pool of liquidity which does not interact with the other markets for the security in question.

This is harmful in two ways. First, by reducing the number of orders interacting in the consolidated market, internalisation lowers the degree of order interaction for the security. This diminished interaction reduces the efficiency of the price formation process, and is normally reflected in wider spreads on the consolidated market. Secondly, the price formation process within the internalising firm is itself inhibited by the fact that the orders only interact with each other, not with the (usually larger) pool of orders in the broader market. In theory, at least, internalisation results in two or more markets which are inherently less efficient and therefore provide prices inferior to what could be expected with full interaction.

Take, for instance, the example of a firm which is fairly dominant in the trading of a particular security. If this firm were typically responsible for 30% of the orders in the security and were then to decide to internalise these orders, the impact of the withdrawal of these trades from the price formation process would be profound and immediately apparent in the price spread on the consolidated market (recall the order book examples in Chapter 8). This would be to the disadvantage of the investors whose orders are attempting to find a counterparty on the consolidated market. At the same time, the internalised orders are now attempting to match against orders in a pool less than one-third the size of the previous consolidated market. Even taking into account any savings resulting from lesser fees, these investors would be harmed by the wider spreads resulting from the smaller pool of orders. They might be paying lower costs, but on a wider spread (roughly analogous to paying a lower commission for a house but a higher price). This result would be, quite literally, penny-wise but pound-foolish.

Those in favour of internalisation argue that the practice could reduce the cost of executing the customer's order by eliminating the need to pay certain fees to exchanges, clearing houses and other organisations whose services are not necessary for trades executed in-house. Assuming these cost reductions are passed on, this could result in a lower net cost or proceeds to the customer. Firms also stand to benefit from internalisation in that they generate additional income from the spread, as opposed to merely making a commission when acting as broker to a trade done on an exchange.[4] That is, internalising firms executing against themselves rather than merely matching incoming orders to each other would pay the bid price and receive the offer price, keeping the difference (the spread) as profit.

As noted above, the first (1993) ISD permitted Member States to establish concentration rules for their markets (France and Italy, amongst others, did so), severely limiting the potential for internalisation in these markets. The Commission addressed internalisation more specifically in its initial draft of the second (2003) ISD, with proposed rules that would

---

4   "Internalisation", Euronext Amsterdam, January 2002, p. 4.

require post-trade transparency only, and would differentiate between "incidental" and "systematic" internalisers. Those firms for whom internalised orders account for more than 10% of total business would be deemed "systematic", and would be required to report those trades to the "lead" regulated market (most liquid or market of first listing). Incidental internalisers would be required to report their internalised trades to any regulated market. Not surprisingly, most exchanges were against these proposals (though not all exchanges felt the threat from internalisation was significant).

Is post-trade transparency enough? The debate surrounding internalisation centres on the degree to which it impedes the order interaction necessary for efficient price formation, and order interaction is by its nature a pre-trade phenomenon. Post-trade transparency does nothing to facilitate order interaction, since it occurs after the trade. Without public pre-trade transparency, each internaliser would therefore operate their own isolated pool of liquidity, and the rest of the market would become aware of orders at the firm only after they had already been executed. This is diametrically opposed to the general view that order interaction is necessary to efficient markets.[5]

It may be politically unrealistic, though, to expect a regulator to establish a rule which effectively eliminates internalisation. One compromise approach has been the US' Limit Order Handling Rule, which requires customer orders superior to those of the firm's own orders or quotes to be exposed to the market for a period of time before they can be executed internally. This, along with a best execution rule, would likely bring the bulk of executable orders to the outside (consolidated) market and still enable firms to internalise under some circumstances.

Internalisation is generally viewed as the antithesis of concentration rules. In this perspective, the debate on internalisation takes on the competition vs concentration theme described in Chapter 8. Opponents of internalisation believe that it drains liquidity from the broader market, inhibiting order interaction and degrading the efficiency of the price formation process. Conversely, proponents of internalisation (and of ATSs) assert that the practice promotes healthy competition between firms and exchanges. In Chapter 8, it was suggested that the linking of disparate markets would permit both concentration and competition, but this raises issues with respect to internalisation. If internalising pools of liquidity are linked to the broader market, and the orders interact across this network, can it really be said that internalisation still occurs?

If internalisation drains a high level of liquidity from the marketplace, it has been argued, it could lead to a vicious cycle of decreased efficiency on the central market leading to more and more internalisation.[6] In the end, a high level of internalisation promotes fragmentation of liquidity, inhibits order interaction and is the antithesis of market integration.

Recent studies
In July 2002, a paper was published by the Autoriteit Financiële Markten (AFM), the Dutch securities regulator, which examined the regulatory challenges posed by internalisation.[7]

---

[5] It should be said that some exceptions to the need for pre-trade transparency have been recognised, such as very large orders whose execution would be prejudiced by their market impact should they be fully transparent before execution.

[6] Euronext Amsterdam, p. 5.

[7] "Position Paper: In-House Matching", Autoriteit Financiële Markten, July 2002.

It provided a useful line of analysis along two "relevant regulatory objectives": the adequate functioning of the markets and best execution.

The question of whether internalisation diminishes the efficiency of markets depends on the amount of internalisation occurring within the market. If large proportions of liquidity – say, 30% or more – were effected through internalisation, then the price formation process would likely be profoundly diminished. Further, the problem is exacerbated if that 30% is itself fragmented amongst a number of internalising firms, for instance each with 5% of the total volume. These micropools would themselves be less efficient than if the entire 30% slice were interacting as a single internalised pool. The problem is that no one knows exactly how much off-market activity can occur before the price formation process is significantly degraded. Further, the proportion executed off the market could vary greatly over time. As the internalisation debate in Europe has shown, the issue will not be resolved on the basis of a definitive answer to the effect of internalisation on overall market efficiency.

The picture may be different when viewed from a customer protection angle rather than as a matter of market efficiency. The danger to the customer of having an order executed internally lies in how best execution is determined for that order. If best execution is considered to be the best available price *within* the internalised pool of liquidity (the equivalent of the old single-market standards), the investor may lose out on a better price elsewhere. For this reason, cross-market best execution must be strictly applied in order to protect the customer from being disadvantaged.

Moreover, this best execution standard must be clearly based on the net price, since a more amorphous standard such as "best interests" could be used by some internalising firms to justify an inferior internal price, based on a broad interpretation of the customer's interests.

In January 2002, a paper on internalisation was published by Euronext, the stock market created by the merger of the French, Dutch and Belgian markets.[8] The paper took a strong position against internalisation, on several grounds. The principal arguments in the Euronext paper fell along similar lines as the AFM's position paper, namely, concerns over customer protection (best execution) and fragmentation resulting in reduced efficiency of the market's price mechanism. The report concluded that internalisation is potentially harmful in its effect on best execution, and harmful to the adequate functioning of the market due to its fragmenting effect on liquidity.[9]

A third view was provided in April 2002, in an internal study sponsored by the Federation of European Securities Exchanges (FESE).[10] This study identified two fundamental reasons for the increased focus in Europe on internalisation. First was the increase (through the time of the study's publication) of trading in volumes in general, and of retail trading in particular.[11] Since it is primarily retail orders which are internalised, the substantial increase in the retail equity culture in Europe made internalisation matter. The second impetus, occurring at roughly the same time, was the European Union's review of the existing ISD, and more particularly the proposal to remove the clause which permitted the establishment of

---

[8]   Euronext Amsterdam, January 2002.

[9]   *Ibid.*, pp. 4–5, 12–13.

[10] Davydoff, Didier, Gresse, Carole and Grillet-Aubert, Laruent. *Internalisation of the order Flow*, April 2002. (On file with author.)

[11] *Ibid.*, p. 6.

concentration rules.[12] The internal study concluded that internalisation was as yet limited in Europe, but that the practice could increase substantially if regulatory changes precipitated a less restrictive environment.[13] Like the Euronext and AFM studies, it found the risk of fragmentation posed by internalisation to be potentially harmful to the price discovery process.[14] Importantly, it points out the danger of "massive" or "large-scale" internalisation,[15] implicitly highlighting an important issue – the *proportion* of total liquidity drained from the central market into internalised pools.

Not all market participants agree that internalisation poses a danger to the marketplace. APCIMS-EASD,[16] a European organisation representing the interests of stockbrokers, private banks and investment managers opposed restrictions on the practice, questioning the validity and motives of the customer protection concerns raised in other studies.[17] According to the organisation's Chief Executive, "Consumer protection is being used as an excuse by many of those, including exchanges, who are commenting on the Directive. Stock exchanges are trying to ensure that all trading is done on their markets by seeking substantial increases in regulation and costs on other cost-effective trading methods."[18] In claiming that consumers can be adequately protected even when their orders are executed internally, APCIMS-EASD made specific reference to the best execution obligations which apply to the internalising firm. Significantly, the best execution provisions described were those in force at the time, in which the LSE price was used as a concrete benchmark and in which assessments were done on a trade-by-trade basis. Of more concern to APCIMS-EASD, though, was the stifling effect on competition it saw arising from exchanges attempting to preclude firms from executing orders internally.

Attempts have been made to find a middle ground on internalisation. Deutsche Börse has proposed a "default" measure, in which retail clients must grant specific authorisation for a trade to be executed anywhere other than a regulated market. Other possibilities include requiring clients to be advised in advance that their trades may be internalised, with appropriate risk disclosure provisions, or order handling rules akin to those enacted in the United States (see Chapter 5).

The polarisation of views on internalisation has made it extremely controversial and perhaps even intractable. On its face, it is a commercial issue and one would expect to see the battle lines drawn between opposing business interests (as in the United States, for instance). In Europe, these commercial interests have become entangled with supposedly extinct national protectionist imperatives, raising the stakes and making compromise both more important and more difficult. This was made especially manifest with the last-minute inclusion of a transparency (anti-internalisation) rule into European Commission's final draft of ISD proposal in November 2002, much to the surprise and chagrin of market participants who had not been given the normal opportunity to consult on the measure.

---

12   *Ibid.*, p. 6.
13   *Ibid.*, p. 70.
14   *Ibid.*
15   *Ibid.*, p. 6.
16   Association of Private Client Investment Managers and Stockbrokers – European Association of Securities Dealers.
17   APCIMS-EASD, press release, 31 May 2002.
18   *Ibid.*

Market reaction in nations against concentration rules (such as the UK), was swift, brutal and public, alleging that its inclusion was due to the personal intervention of the Commission's President, who was from a pro-concentration nation.

The friction arising from this level of controversy has largely generated more heat than light. At its core, the question of how internalisation should be regulated comes down to the two issues identified earlier – investor protection and market efficiency. If best execution is interpreted in such a way as to prohibit internalisation at prices inferior to those on the central market, customers are in all likelihood not disadvantaged by internalisation – their orders would simply not be internalised if a better price resides elsewhere. The question of market efficiency in the end comes down to the *level* of internalisation in the market. If internalised pools are in fact isolated from the outside market place – that is, they do not have any opportunity to interact outside the executing firm – then liquidity is indeed fragmented. The question then becomes how much order flow can be internalised before it begins to harm the efficiency of the market.

There are valid arguments both in favour of and against internalisation, though many of the arguments on both sides are unproven and dependent on interpretation. Are investors at risk, or does internalisation actually provide them what they want? Does it fatally harm the price formation process? Are concentration rules anti-competitive? The answer to each of these questions, at least for now, is "it depends". A proper treatment of the issue would fill a book on its own, but it is important here at least to recognise the *potential* impact of the practice on the consolidation of liquidity and the facilitation of order interaction, and that any eventual policy on internalisation must either address the fragmentation issue or conclude that the degree of fragmentation is immaterial to the level of order interaction and the efficiency of the price formation process.

9.2 Alternative Trading Systems (ATSs)

Alternative trading systems are in large part a product of the advance of technology in financial markets over the years. The term is commonly used to describe a non-exchange trading system which operates electronically and according to set rules to match orders in such a way as to result in a contract.[19] Many of the issues related to ATSs are the same as those which arise with regard to internalisation. Do they fragment liquidity? Does this harm the efficiency of the market? Do the benefits arising from increased competition outweigh the potential harm arising from this fragmentation?

Also like internalisation, the execution of orders on ATSs raises investor protection issues, since the orders are done away from the putative protection of a regulated market. The problem is a bit more complex, though, because ATSs are often neither fish nor fowl – not really a broker-dealer firm, but not an exchange either. Regulating ATSs as broker-dealers is often inappropriate since much of that regulation focuses on areas not relevant to the business of an ATS. On the other hand, regulation as an exchange may be too heavy handed. An alternative regulation was needed for these alternative systems.

The first jurisdiction to attempt this exercise was the United States, where ATSs first came to prominence. The ATSs such as Instinet have existed, even if in primitive form, since the

---

[19]   CESR, *Standards for Alternative Trading Systems* ("CESR ATS Standards"), CESR/02-086b, p. 4.

1980s. At first the SEC took a "light touch" approach to ATS regulation, ruling for instance that ATSs could operate as brokers (handling others' orders) rather than as exchanges.[20] Over time, additional regulation was imposed incrementally. Towards the end of the 1980s ATSs were required to provide more information to the SEC as to their activities (with a view that providing information would be the foundation for more detailed regulation), on the assumption that further regulation would be appropriate should ATSs begin to account for a larger share of the overall liquidity of the market.[21] A significant step forward was taken in 1996, when the SEC's new Order Handling Rules required NASDAQ market makers placing orders on an ATS to equal or better that quote on the (public) NASDAQ market.[22] Shortly thereafter, the SEC issued a Concept Release seeking public comment on the proper way to regulate ATSs, followed in late 1998 by the adoption of the imaginatively named Regulation ATS.

Regulation ATS sought to address the supervision of ATSs operating within the United States by more closely defining what an exchange is, by permitting ATSs to decide whether they wish to be regulated as an exchange or as a broker-dealer and by providing specific regulation based on whether the ATS was acting as an exchange or as a broker-dealer.

Significantly in the light of subsequent European proposals, Regulation ATS defined an exchange as an organisation which brings together multiple buyers and multiple sellers. This effectively excludes from Regulation ATS internalising firms which trade bilaterally, acting as the counterparty to all internalised client orders. This distinction was raised again in the European debate, where "bilateral" systems (e.g. internalisers) were at first included, and then excluded, from ATS regulation.

For those ATSs which choose under Regulation ATS to be regulated as broker-dealer firms rather than as exchanges, a three-tier system of regulation was established. Under this system, additional levels of regulation were imposed on the ATS compared to "normal" broker-dealers in terms of regulatory reporting, safeguards, transparency and fair access. The level of regulation is determined by the amount of activity done on the ATS. Transparency levels are determined on a security-by-security basis, so that an ATS may be required to provide its best orders to the CQS (via a registered market) on some securities but not others. Other regulatory requirements (e.g. fair access requirements) are triggered if the ATS reaches the prescribed activity level on any security.

Alternative Trading Systems which do enough business to be brought under the third (highest) tier of regulation assume regulatory burdens close to those of exchanges without necessarily receiving the benefits of an official exchange status. For this reason, ATSs are given the option of being regulated as exchanges, with all the rights and responsibilities accruing to this status. Importantly, this includes mandatory participation in the NMS and the right to participate in the pro rata revenues of the NMS. The ATSs registering as exchanges also acquire the responsibility to enforce compliance not only with their own rules, but also with the federal securities laws (this responsibility, though, can be outsourced to another self-regulatory organisation). Additionally, as exchanges ATSs would be required to limit membership to

---

[20]   SEC, No-Action Letters to Instinet, 8 September 1986 and 6 December 1991, cited in Lofchie, p. 257.
[21]   See Lofchie, p. 257, SEC Rule 17a-23, and SEC Release No. 33-27611 (12 January 1990).
[22]   Certain exemptions were provided, such as when the ATS in question only executes against its own account and for crossing systems.

registered broker-dealers, and thus would not be able to provide direct access to institutional investors.

Shortly after the adoption of Regulation ATS, European regulators established an Expert Group to study the issues raised by ATSs. The Expert Group produced a paper discussing the broad options available for regulating ATSs in the context of EU legislation; this paper was adopted in September 2000 by FESCO, forerunner of the present CESR. The FESCO then instructed the Expert Group to develop specific proposals to address the risks posed by ATSs to investor protection and market integrity (fragmentation). The proposed standards were published for consultation the following June. These standards were the subject of considerable attention and discussion amongst market players, and the standards were revised for another public consultation in January 2002. In response to concern that the definition of ATS would be overly broad and that too much transparency would be required under the standards, CESR issued a third iteration of the proposed standards in mid-2002.

The concern over the scope of the definition of a qualifying ATS likely arose from the fact that the CESR standards, unlike those of Regulation ATS, do not give the ATS the choice of how to be regulated. Instead, CESR opted for a "functional" approach – if a system performs the functions of a regulated market, it should be subject to the same or equivalent regulation. The rewritten definition covered any "multilateral system ... which ... brings together multiple buying and selling interests in financial instruments – in the system and according to non-discretionary rules set by the system's operator – in a way which results in a contract".[23] This definition excluded "bilateral systems" – essentially, internalisers – in which the orders are executed against a single counterparty. It also excluded "crossing networks" which periodically execute buy and sell orders at the current price of a regulated market.

The CESR standards focused on four areas: notification, transparency, reporting rules and the prevention of market abuse. Notification required ATSs to provide to their national regulator information concerning the operation of the system – the price formation process, market rules, types of instruments traded and similar types of information. The transparency requirement mandated that ATSs make public "on a reasonable commercial basis" information on orders and quotes in the system (pre-trade transparency) and completed transactions (post-trade transparency). This information did not necessarily need to be sent to a (competing) regulated market, as it could instead be sent to a website, an information vendor or any CQS which might exist. The standards concerning reporting rules were aimed to require ATSs to provide sufficient information to their regulators to enable those authorities to monitor their compliance with their responsibilities to prevent market abuse and to monitor their market share. The standards on the prevention of market abuse required ATSs to establish and enforce rules in the same way in which regulated markets are required (as broker-dealer firms, they would have no such specific requirement).

It is worth noting that CESR made a specific distinction between retail and professional users in its discussion of ATSs – a distinction, as noted earlier in this book, which was fatally absent from its subsequent best execution standard. In its discussion regarding the requirement for an ATS to provide a "fair and orderly" trading environment, CESR said that ATS operators should be prepared to demonstrate that the system "enables users to obtain the

---

[23]   CESR ATS Standards, p. 4.

best price available on the system, at that time and for their size of order". This passing reference to best execution is worth a brief mention for its insight into the extent to which conflicting views of the concept have taken root amongst European policy makers. First, the reference in the ATS standards made specific reference to price, rather than conceptual standards such as "best overall result". While this would establish a useful benchmark for the policy, the reference to "available on the system" would critically undermine the policy by ignoring potentially better prices off the system (i.e. on the regulated markets). The conflict between the "ISD"and the "ATS" interpretations of best execution is noteworthy not only because they came so close in time to one another, but also because the groups working on the ATS (CESR) and the ISD (the European Commission) claimed to be in discussions with each other throughout the process.[24]

In both the United States and Europe, and indeed other jurisdictions, the regulation of ATSs will likely continue to evolve and will be the subject of considerable debate for many years.

Conclusion

Internalisation and the regulation of ATSs have been amongst the most controversial topics of discussion in the financial markets for the past several years. This is perhaps because they touch on a number of "hot-button" issues. On one level, the debate is about fair competition amongst order execution venues. Those in favour of internalisation and of loose regulation of ATSs believe restrictions would be anti-competitive, while existing regulated markets believe failure to provide equivalent regulation to those under which the markets operate would give unfair advantage to ATSs and internalisers. On a second level, the debate is about investor protection: ensuring that investors, or at least retail investors, are not disadvantaged by the fact that their order – or someone else's order – was executed away from the central market. Lastly, the debate also centres on the problem of market structure – concentration vs fragmentation. The key issue here is whether the liquidity which does not interact with the central market is significant enough to undermine the price formation process. The answer to this question likely depends on the amount of liquidity drained from the interacting pool – a few orders may not materially affect the price formation process, but the draining of a large proportion of liquidity can only be detrimental to the process. This leaves regulators with the rather formidable task of establishing the thresholds at which the resulting fragmentation becomes a concern (as in the three levels established by Regulation ATS).

The question of whether the orders are able to interact, is more important than where they reside. Orders may be located in fifty different pools of liquidity, but if they are able to interact with each other the price formation process is not undermined. And this brings the discussion back around to an earlier point. By linking markets – using the infrastructure discussed in Chapter 7, for instance – competing markets can operate independent of each other but not in harmful isolation from each other.

---

[24]   *Ibid.*, p. 3.

10 Clearing and Settlement

The integration of securities markets is not simply a matter of bringing prices and orders together. What happens after the trade – the confirmation, clearing and settlement of the trades – is equally important and, alas, no less daunting in its complexity. In terms of market structure, the fragmentation of clearing and settlement arrangements can be as injurious to financial market integration as the fragmentation of liquidity itself.

In Europe, clearing and settlement organisations historically have been established locally to meet the demands of trading on the various national markets. They have consequently developed into the same patchwork as the exchanges they are meant to serve. While there has been considerable consolidation amongst clearing and settlement houses, and even the creation of "International Central Securities Depositories", the fragmented nature of clearing and settlement arrangements nonetheless presents a significant obstacle to the integration of the securities markets. This chapter will look at the nature of cross-border clearing and settlement, the impediments posed by the present arrangements, and the ways in which these impediments are being addressed.

As is the case with the "front-end" infrastructure of trading systems, the clearing and settlement arrangements in the United States are, for largely historical reasons, far less fragmented than those in Europe. The consolidation of clearing and settlement structures in the United States dates back to 1976, when the clearing organisations of the NYSE, the AMEX and the NASD combined into what is now the National Securities Clearing Corporation (NSCC). It is no coincidence that this was the same year that Congress enacted the amendments to the Securities Exchange Act which mandated the creation of the NMS, for, as we shall see, the consolidation of back office operations is necessary for the success of market integration.

10.1 The nature of clearing and settlement arrangements

Viewed at its most elementary level, the clearing and settlement process involves those back office operations which occur after the trade is agreed, and which turn it from a deal between traders to a deal between the counterparties (the firms).

The first step is trade confirmation, in which the details of the transaction (which security, the number of shares, the price, and so forth) are verified and submitted to the clearing party for further processing. This is done in the form of standardised clearing instructions, which also contain static data with regard to the firms reporting the transaction.

Once these instructions are received, the clearing organisation calculates the "position" or number of shares, long or short, for each party in the security in question. The result is an instruction to the settlement organisation to transfer securities from the selling firm's account to that of the buying firm, and to send the appropriate funds in the reverse direction. This can be done on a trade-by-trade basis, or at the end of the day on a "net" basis.

Of course, this simplified model assumes that both firms involved in the transaction – and therefore, all firms in the larger picture – belong to the same clearing and settlement organisations and that these organisations also accommodate the security in question.

This is not always the case, and it is from this complication that many of the problems involved in cross-border clearing and settlement arise. A number of ways around this dilemma have been constructed, particularly in Europe where the problem is most acute.[1] These arrangements each have their limitations, however, with the result that cross-market settlement remains more complex, more costly and more risky than domestic arrangements, resulting in a structural impediment to cross-market trading.

Starting at the most basic level, a firm might employ another firm as an intermediary (a "correspondent firm") which is a member of the clearing or settlement depository in which the first firm wishes to do business. This practice is often done domestically, where small firms may find it more efficient to hire a correspondent firm to handle their clearing and settlement arrangements. Efficiency and cost also drive the logic behind hiring a foreign correspondent firm. Firms may not do enough business in the securities of a particular market to justify the expense of membership, but they still need to be able to settle the occasional trade which does occur.

Just as trading firms may act as intermediaries for other firms, so too can settlement organisations act as intermediaries for other settlement organisations. A common settlement arrangement is for the Central Settlement Depository (CSD) serving one market to become a member of other CSDs, acting as intermediary for its own members when they do business on those markets. This is one form of bilateral, CSD-to-CSD linkage, which facilitates cross-border trading but falls short of creating the kind of low cost, market-wide solution necessary to facilitate seamless cross-border trading. Bilateral solutions such as cross-membership represent temporary patches to enable the limited level of cross-border trading already occurring. To remove the clearing and settlement bottleneck, an efficient market-wide solution is necessary. This is already the case in the United States and is not presently a priority in Asia,[2] but has been elevated to a high priority in Europe both by market participants and by regulators.

Perhaps the ideal solution is the creation of a single Central Counterparty, or CCP, interposed between buyers and sellers and clearing all transactions. In a CCP model, the CCP acts as the buyer for all sellers and the seller for all buyers, and in some models actually takes on legal responsibility for the trade, eliminating counterparty default risk. In addition to this risk management function, CCPs enable trading to be done with complete anonymity since the parties to a trade need only to settle with the CCP. This anonymity is of particular importance to institutions who wish to conceal their intentions from their competitors. It also permits the "netting" of trades between parties, vastly reducing the number of trades which must be settled for each firm.

There are two principal models to achieving this goal. The first involves a "hub" structure, in which participating (domestic) CSDs maintain accounts with the central CSD, where all cross-market transactions are settled (purely domestic transactions would continue to be settled within the domestic CSD). In order to attract the domestic CSDs to

---

[1]   For an excellent summary of the problems facing cross-border clearing and settlement, particularly in respect of Europe, see "Achieving Cross-Border Trade Processing Goals" in the March and April 2001(Vol. 2, Nos. 3 and 4), Research Reports of the Securities Industry Association, available at http://www.sia.com.

[2]   SIA, "Achieving Cross-Border Trade Processing Goals", Research Reports, Vol. 2 No. 3, p. 11.

this model, though, some incentive would need to be provided to compensate for the loss of their existing profitable, though inefficient, cross-border business.

A variation of this model was put into place by virt-x, the Pan-European stock exchange based in London which serves as the home market for Swiss blue chip securities. This model involves two settlement organisations, x-clear for Swiss securities, and London Clearing House (LCH) for United Kingdom and other non-Swiss securities. Under this arrangement, x-clear is a "sub-CCP" in LCH, in addition to being the CCP for its own members. When a trade involves one party which is a member of LCH and the other is a member of x-clear, x-clear acts in its capacity as sub-CCP, that is, as the party to trade on behalf of its member, while LCH acts as the CCP. For trades in which both parties are members of x-clear, x-clear would act as the CCP and LCH would not be involved. Similarly, LCH would act as CCP to any trade in which both parties are members of LCH. The end result is a CCP arrangement which helps to remove the inefficiencies inherent in dealing with isolated clearing and settlement organisations, and provides the anonymity, elimination of counterparty risk and netting which are the main benefits of CCPs.

The construction of this type of CCP requires the resolution of a number of contractual and other legal questions. After all, the transfer of ownership of a security is as much a legal matter as a technical one. Arrangements must determine the responsibilities in the event a member (or even one of the CSDs) cannot meet its obligations and is declared in default. All of these legal questions are further complicated by the potential conflict of the domestic laws governing each of the CSDs.

The alternative model involves consolidating, rather than linking, existing CSDs. The result would be a single settlement agency serving all markets, as is the case in the United States. A degree of consolidation has already occurred in Europe, with the merger of Cedel International with Deutsche Börse Clearing. The consolidation of settlement organisations would be a logical follow-up to any merger of the markets they serve.

10.1.1 *Horizontal and vertical models*

It is apparent that clearing and settlement organisations must be integrated into the overall market structure, yet the way in which this integration is implemented is also a point of contention. Some of the larger European markets (such as Deutsche Börse), favour the "vertical" integration model characteristic of the large industrial organisations of the nineteenth century. Under a vertical integration model, the market itself and the clearing and settlement organisation are owned and operated by the same parent company. In the alternative, "horizontal", structure, the market and the clearing and settlement organisations are owned separately. Arguments in favour of vertical integration centre on the presumed cost savings derived from in-house ownership, while opponents of this structure say that it removes the competitive pressures which normally drive prices down and promote innovation. Vertical silos also lead to potential access and discriminatory pricing concerns. Exchanges which own (or are under shared ownership with) clearing and settlement organisations could prevent other exchanges from dealing in their shares by blocking access to the settlement depository, for instance, or by charging higher rates for this access. Practices of this nature are contrary to the operation of an integrated market based on cross-market trading.

One way or the other, the fragmentation of clearing and settlement arrangements must be addressed in order for the rest of the market structure to be integrated. If trades are done across borders but cannot be settled cheaply or efficiently, the integration of the market is seriously undermined. The high costs of cross-border settlement in comparison to domestic trading increase the net cost of a cross-border trade. Not only does this make cross-border trading more expensive for firms and for their customers, it also inhibits the integrating function of best execution, since cross-border trades will tend to be more expensive on a net basis once the clearing and settlement costs are factored in. The European Commission has recognised the role of clearing and settlement in market integration, and established an Expert Group – the "Giovannini Group" – to propose measures to remove barriers to the integration of European clearing and settlement. The Giovannini Group identified fifteen individual obstacles to efficient cross-border clearing and settlement, including tax, legal and information technology conflicts. It has proposed measures to eliminate these barriers by the time the European Union's other market integration measures are in place, in 2005 (giving the European Commission less than three years to accomplish this Herculean task).

Conclusion

Clearing and settlement is a particularly complex and specialised field, and a detailed discussion of the full range of these issues is beyond the scope of this book. This brief chapter has aimed instead to highlight the ways in which clearing and settlement arrangements can facilitate or impede the integration of markets. It is clear even from this cursory examination that the rationalisation of clearing and settlement arrangements is a necessary condition to market integration, and regulatory efforts in this regard deserve to be watched closely.

11 Old Solutions to New Problems: *Historical Attempts to Integrate Markets*

The previous chapters have looked at some of the critical issues involved in the integration of markets – concentration, order interaction, competition, clearing and settlement, and the like. These are contemporary issues which will likely continue to occupy policy makers for years to come. Yet efforts to integrate markets stretch back for decades, and valuable lessons can be drawn from the successes and frustrations of these previous endeavours. This chapter will in particular examine and contrast the ongoing integration of the US markets with the efforts to create a single European market.

11.1 The integration of the US markets

Like Europe, but unlike most European countries, the United States securities environment has long been characterised by the existence of multiple, competing markets. In addition to the NYSE and the AMEX, OTC markets grew in the 1970s into the formidable NASDAQ market. Additionally, regional exchanges in a number of cities have served the markets for over a hundred and fifty years. The markets were supplemented by competing ATSs in the 1980s and 1990s.

The SEC has long recognised the role technology could play in promoting innovation in the markets. As early as 1963, the SEC noted that "[w]ith an already strong communications network, there is on the horizon the likelihood of a computer system that would assemble all interdealer quotations for particular securities at any given time", and urged the NASD to create an electronic display of this kind.[1] In 1972, an SEC report on the future of the securities markets called for "a comprehensive system to make information on securities sizes, volumes and prices available to all investors".[2] In 1975, Congress enacted legislation requiring the SEC to facilitate the establishment of the NMS,[3] linking the exchanges and NASDAQ. In doing so, it established three elements of the infrastructure for market integration – pre-trade transparency, post-trade transparency and order routing.

By 1978, the main elements of the NMS were in place. Pre-trade and post-trade information was sent via the CQS and Consolidated Transaction System (CTS), respectively, to a central processor, the SIAC, which processed the information and then broadcast it in real time to the various market data vendors. The ITS enabled traders on one market to execute trades (for exchange-traded securities) easily at better prices on other markets.

---

[1] SEC Technology Study, at IV.C.1, citing SEC, Report of the Special Study of the Securities Markets, reprinted in H.R. Doc. No. 95, 88th Cong., 1st Sess. 41-42 (1963).
[2] SEC Technology Study at IV.C.1, citing Statement of the Securities and Exchange Commission on the Future Structure of the Securities Markets, Exchange Act Release No. 9484 (February 1972).
[3] Securities Acts Amendments of 1975, HR Rep. 94-229 (1975).

The infrastructure provided a place for integration to occur, but this by itself was not the end of the story. In mandating the establishment of the NMS, Congress set specific goals for the SEC to achieve, which were aimed at ensuring that integration actually came to be. Amongst these were to assure fair competition amongst the markets and amongst broker-dealers, investor protection (specifically the facilitation of intermarket best execution), and the maintenance of fair and orderly markets.[4] Specific provisions were added to the amendments which directed the exchanges and non-exchange markets to "design rules to remove impediments to, and perfect the mechanism of, a free and open... national market".[5]

The multiple goals enumerated in the legislation demonstrate Congress's view that the problems of fragmentation, transparency and best execution were different aspects of a single issue. Moreover, they demonstrate the view that the networking of liquidity through linked markets and the facilitation of cross-market access are the best ways to address these issues. One SEC official later confirmed this in describing the goals of an NMS:

> To achieve the goals of efficient price discovery and best execution, not only must quotation and transaction information from each market be accessible to investors, but that information must be available in one place.[6]

11.2 Rules

The establishment of the necessary NMS infrastructure did not by itself, as it has been noted, integrate the markets. While the infrastructure enables trading to occur across markets, market inefficiencies such as those discussed in Chapters 4 and 5 needed to be overcome through the establishment of appropriate rules. For instance, the SEC mandated the admission to trading of securities on competing markets through "unlisted trading privileges" amongst the exchanges (similar provisions allow the trading of exchange-traded securities on NASDAQ, and vice versa). These provisions undermined the existing concentration rules such as NYSE Rule 390 (see Chapter 9), permitting the simultaneous trading of securities in multiple locations which underlies the integration of markets.

Further, the SEC promulgated rules which essentially require broker-dealers and the markets to use the NMS effectively. The Quote Rule required the exchanges and NASDAQ to devise procedures for providing publication of price and size information on the securities traded on their respective markets, and required member firms to comply with these procedures. The Quote Rule also required, with certain exceptions, that these quotes be "firm", that is, that members honour the prices and sizes published through the system. A similar Transaction Reporting Rule was adopted at the same time to require post-trade transparency. The Display Rule[7] required market makers to display publicly the best prices at which they are willing to buy and sell a security. Further, data vendors were required to publish intermarket data (either the

---

4   See Section 11A(a)(1) and Section 11A(a)(2), Securities Exchange Act.
5   Letter from the National Association of Securities Dealers to the SEC, 6 January 1998.
6   Minutes of 10 October 2000 meeting of Advisory Committee on Market Information.
7   Rule 11Ac1-2.

intermarket best bid and offer, or a montage of prices from all NMS markets), rather than favouring the dominant markets in their public displays. Many vendors were already amenable to doing so, but for competitive reasons did not wish to be first and so favoured action by the SEC to make intermarket display mandatory.[8]

In 1996, further rules were enacted governing the fair and equitable handling of customer orders and the proper use of a firm's quotations. Like best execution rules, these Order Handling Rules[9] were primarily aimed at investor protection but also were important in their effect on market integration (more specifically in this case, the operation of the NMS). Amongst other provisions, these rules required market makers on NASDAQ and specialists on the exchanges to reflect in their public quotes any customer limit order which was equal or superior to the firm's existing best price. The rules also required firms to reflect in their public prices any superior price displayed on an ATS. The effect of these rules was to bring more orders to the centralised pool of liquidity by requiring publication of orders and quotes which would previously have been the exclusive domain of internalising firms or ATSs.

With the infrastructure in place and the rules established requiring its use, one might well wonder to what extent liquidity in US markets remain fragmented. In February 2000, the SEC published its Concept Release on market fragmentation.[10] The release discusses a number of issues related to the possible fragmentation of the US market, soliciting comments on each. The topics, not surprisingly, included competition between market centres, the need for linkages between markets (or lack thereof), the effects of internalisation and payment for order flow, and best execution.

The Concept Release asserted that fragmentation is far less evident for exchange-listed securities than for NASDAQ-traded securities. It pointed out that, as of September 1999, some 74.4% trades in NYSE-listed shares were effected on the NYSE, and 68.7% of trades in AMEX-listed shares were done on the AMEX.[11] The report contended that NASDAQ-traded shares experienced significantly more fragmentation, as there were on average over eleven market makers quoting each share at any given time. This comparison is not entirely consistent, since the orders and quotations of all market makers in a security are displayed together and compete in one location on the NASDAQ workstation. In fact, they are exactly the type of linked pools of liquidity to which the discussion in earlier chapters has alluded. Similarly, it is a mistake to regard exchange-listed securities traded on other NMS markets such as NASDAQ as fragmentation since these other markets, unlike ATSs at the time, are linked via the NMS. An NYSE-listed share traded on NASDAQ via the NMS does not really represent fragmentation, but rather it demonstrates the interaction of order via market linkages.

More importantly, the Concept Release pointed to the fact that nine of the largest ATSs accounted for 28% of trades in NASDAQ-traded shares.[12] If one then considers the proportion of trades done on NASDAQ as opposed to the ATSs, the resulting figure of

---

[8]   Seligman Report at VII.B.1.
[9]   Rule 11Ac1-4 and amendments to Rule 11Ac1-1.
[10] Commission Request for Comment on Issues Related to Market Fragmentation, Release No. 34-42450 ("Market Fragmentation Concept Release").
[11] *Ibid.*, p. 3.
[12] *Ibid.*, p. 7.

approximately 72% is comparable to the level of concentration the study found on the NYSE and AMEX. The 28% of NASDAQ shares traded away from NASDAQ are significant, since at the time the study was conducted these trades would have been negotiated and executed outside the NMS system. As such, they represent true fragmentation of the liquidity. With the implementation of Regulation ATS (see Chapter 9), though, the larger ATSs were brought within the scope of the NMS and much of the problem was thereby ameliorated.

The principal concern raised in the Concept Release with respect to fragmentation was whether "the existence of multiple market centers competing for order flow in the same security may isolate orders and hence reduce the opportunity for interaction of all buying and selling interest in that security".[13] One potential problem, according to the release, was the fact that the existing NMS did not require orders to be routed to the market centre which was actually displaying the best price, but allowed firms instead to match the price themselves.[14] As a result, the firm displaying the best price might take the risk of doing so without receiving the reward of attracting the order flow.

After discussing the current state of the NMS and potential issues related to fragmentation, the release requested comments on the issues. Broadly, it asked first whether fragmentation is in fact a problem which requires regulatory remediation; if so, it asked for comment on six options which could be pursued to address fragmentation. Many of the proposals were specific to the current trading structure in the United States and are of limited application elsewhere. Two of the proposals, however, are worth noting. First was the option of requiring public disclosure of execution quality data. This followed through on the comments made in the Unger Report, and was later reflected in Rules 11Ac1-5 and 11Ac1-6 (discussed in Chapter 5). The second proposal sought to establish a National Linkage System (NLS), which would provide intermarket price/time priority for all displayed interest in a security (the current NMS does not do so).[15] Under the NLS as proposed, all displayed interest would be visible not only to market participants but to the public as well. Trading could be executed automatically (i.e. automatically routed to the market centre with the best price), but the NLS would not itself operate or be regulated as a market.[16] The NLS would, for all intents and purposes, be a Central Limit Order Book (CLOB), administered and operated by a governing board made up of representatives from the public and relevant parts of the securities industry.[17]

The responses to the Concept Release were universally negative towards the NLS. The NYSE rejects the NLS and similar CLOB proposals on the basis that they would actually *increase* fragmentation rather than reduce it, by effectively creating separate markets for retail investors and institutional investors (who tend to trade in blocks, which would be exempt from the NLS).[18] Instead, the NYSE recommended that the best execution policy focused on the obligations of broker-dealers, "insisting that they utilize technology to develop search engines that can route on an order-by-order basis to the best market".[19]

---

[13] *Ibid.*, p. 8.
[14] *Ibid.*, p. 9.
[15] *Ibid.*, p. 20.
[16] *Ibid.*, p. 21.
[17] *Ibid.*
[18] Letter from NYSE to SEC, 31 May 2000, pp. 7–8.
[19] *Ibid.*, p. 8.

These search engines, according to the NYSE, should be constructed so that they are able to consider non-price factors in addition to price when seeking the best market.[20]

Not all respondents to the Concept Release agreed that fragmentation poses a significant problem in the United States. One broker-dealer instead endorsed the idea, largely present in the current structure, of linked markets and best execution responsibilities as the most effective way to address fragmentation.[21] The same sentiment, endorsing linkages amongst markets utilising current technologies, but not a CLOB, was echoed by a number of respondents to the Concept Release. In the end, less intrusive measures were put into effect, and the NLS/CLOB is no longer the subject of serious discussion.

A final point worth mentioning with regard to the US experience in building an integrated market concerns the recent discussion concerning the governance structure of the NMS, particularly with regard to the dissemination of market data. Data dissemination is currently done in accordance with four NMS plans, under which the SROs – the exchanges and the NASD, which operates NASDAQ – act jointly to administer NMS market data. Three of the plans cover equities: one for NYSE-listed shares, one for NASDAQ-traded shares and one for those listed on the AMEX or one of the regional exchanges. The fourth plan governs market data for options. Under these plans, the SROs collect pre- and post-trade market data (quotes, orders and transaction information, for example) and transmit the data to a central processor, who then sends the consolidated information from all the streams to vendors and institutions subscribing to the service.

The plans also govern the prices charged for this market data, the allocation of this revenue to each participating SRO (broadly on a pro rata basis determined by the amount of activity processed through the system), and the governance structure of the plans. The governance structure has been the focus of considerable debate over the past few years, and was one of the major issues considered by the Seligman Committee, established in the summer of 2000 (see also Chapter 5). Two major concerns were raised. First was the concern, expressed primarily by the vendors and institutions who subscribed to the market data, that the contracts and other administrative requirements for participation had become overly burdensome. As the plans had effective monopolies over the market data, subscribers had little power to change these requirements, or for that matter, to negotiate the fees which they were charged. This is not to say that the Operating Committees of these plans were totally unaccountable, though, since the plans and any changes to them are subject to SEC review.

The second concern dealt with the composition and procedures of the governing bodies themselves. These Operating Committees consist of one representative from each of the SROs participating in the plan. Unanimous votes are required for major decisions such as amendments to the operating rules and reductions in fees. Fee increases (or the establishment of new fees), however, only require a two-thirds majority of votes. The requirement for unanimity tends to make the decision-making process unwieldy. Coupled with the exclusive SRO membership of the Committees, the difficulty of subscribers or potential new entrants in influencing the operation of the NMS becomes evident. As the NMS arguably functions as a national utility, these concerns had potentially far-reaching

---

20   *Ibid.*, p. 10.
21   Letter from CIBC to SEC, 26 May 2000, p. 1.

effects for the markets as a whole. The concerns regarding fair access have been addressed by measures such as the provision of Regulation ATS which brings the most active ATSs into the NMS, and by amendments to the NASDAQ plan required by the SEC in connection with its approval of the NASDAQ SuperMontage® system. The competition concerns were addressed by one of the more significant recommendations of the Seligman Committee. In its report, the Committee recommended that the SEC permit competing market data consolidators, eliminating the effective monopoly of the present system. This recommendation was subject to the resolution of certain technical and economic issues, to be addressed as part of a broader market technology review also recommended by the Committee. In a nutshell, the majority of the Seligman Committee favoured a more competition-based, less regulatory approach to the governance of the NMS.

The Seligman Committee's remit was not limited to governance issues, but dealt broadly with issues of market structure and information in general. It is worth noting that the Committee expressly recognised the interconnection between structure and order execution. The report also confirmed the importance of price transparency and consolidated markets as core elements of the securities market in the United States, and of the price display rule mandating the centralisation of market information.

The US experience in constructing an integrated market is instructive on several levels. First, it confirms the importance of transparency and order interaction in achieving market integration. Secondly, it identifies certain infrastructure elements as fundamental to this transparency and interaction, namely, consolidation of pre-trade price and size information, consolidation of post-trade transaction data, and a method by which to route orders for execution on other markets. The US experience has demonstrated that questions of administration and governance are important but can be addressed, even if the passage of time has shown that the particular structures put in place twenty years ago may require revision or wholesale reform.

Caution should be taken of course in transferring the lessons from the United States to other markets, since there are important differences in the regulatory and market environment. Amongst the most important, pointed out also in Chapter 5, is the presence in the United States of a single legislative and regulatory authority to co-ordinate and if necessary mandate actions, which has been a key factor in the successful integration of the US marketplace. But most importantly, the US experience has shown that market integration can be achieved.

This role of regulation bears further mention. The history of the NMS has shown not only the importance of regulation in bringing about cross-market initiatives, but also the methods by which it does so. Initially, the role of the SEC was to facilitate and to co-ordinate. By 1978, the essential elements of the infrastructure, such as the CQS, were in place.[22] But by 1980, it became apparent that more was needed. The market data was being provided, but the markets were not indicating in a clear manner where the best price actually resided (e.g. with a competitor market). As a result, the SEC saw the need to move to a more prescriptive approach, enacting the Display Rule and other measures *mandating* that all vendors and broker-dealers display the NBBO for each security.[23] This demonstrates

---

[22]   Nazareth, in minutes of 10 October 2000 meeting of Advisory Committee on Market Information.
[23]   *Ibid.* See Rule 11Ac1-2, effective April 1980.

the range of approaches available to a regulator (from least to more prescriptive) as well as the necessity in some cases of issuing rules to overcome market inefficiencies and require market participants to take actions which theory would imply they would do of their own accord.

11.3 Pan-European markets

The creation of the European Union and its predecessors provided the original vision for an integrated capital market of a size and sophistication to rival that of the United States. Yet nearly fifty years later, little real progress has been made, particularly in integrating the market for equities. Still, the logic behind a Pan-European market has spawned a number of attempts to build such a market, meeting with varying levels of success.

Unlike the US experience, there has been no real effort by regulatory authorities to impose or co-ordinate the creation of an integrated market. Through the 1990s and into the first decade of the twenty-first century, the main efforts have been by markets seeking to incorporate Pan-European trading into their business plans.

A few Pan-European initiatives are worth a brief discussion. Two of these, EASDAQ and Jiway, tried and failed to build a market almost entirely on the basis of cross-border trading. EASDAQ was founded in the mid-1990s with the ambition of becoming the market of choice for small European growth companies seeking to make their initial public offering – an approach modelled on that of NASDAQ. This effort was undermined by the subsequent appearance of nationally focused growth markets such as the Deutsche Börse's Neuer Markt and the Paris Bourse's Nouveau Marché. Even when EASDAQ attempted to switch emphasis by focusing on cross-market trading in shares already listed on other exchanges (including those traded on NASDAQ), it was unable to attract sufficient liquidity to remain viable. In 2001, EASDAQ found itself in dire financial straits and accepted a takeover by NASDAQ, which then struggled to keep the market viable in its new incarnation as NASDAQ Europe. In the end, NASDAQ Europe ceased operations in 2003.

Jiway was established in 2000 by the OM Group, the parent company of the Stockholm Exchange, and Morgan Stanley Dean Witter. It did not seek to become a market for primary listings, but rather focused on providing technology which would allow price improvement over the displayed prices on the dominant exchanges. In spite of its backing by one of the major investment banks, though, and in spite of technology which was generally acknowledged as state of the art, few orders came to Jiway even when it could provide the best price. Like EASDAQ, Jiway soon fell into financial difficulties and announced in October 2002 that it would cease operations effective from January 2003.

The experience of these two failed markets illustrates the dilemma faced by those trying to create a viable Pan-European market: markets need liquidity in the form of order flow in order to survive, yet few wish to send their orders to a market with little existing liquidity. Even with the backing of major investment houses, both EASDAQ and Jiway fell victim to this chicken-and-egg dilemma. Without any regulation requiring orders to be sent to the best market, liquidity tends to remain in the dominant market in apparent defiance of the laws of economics.

A third market, virt-x, went into operation in 2002 as a joint venture between the SWX Swiss Exchange and Tradepoint, a UK exchange. Tradepoint had been established in the mid-1990s as the first market to compete with the LSE for order flow in LSE-listed securities. In 2000, Tradepoint expanded its business to all blue-chip shares across Europe, though it met the same difficulties that Jiway faced in attracting liquidity. The creation of virt-x with the Swiss exchange provided a stable source of business, however, because the Swiss agreed that trading in the shares of Swiss blue chips would cease in Zurich, making virt-x effectively the home market for these shares.

By ensuring a steady flow of business in the Swiss blue chips, virt-x provided itself with financial breathing space while attempting to overcome the chicken-and-egg inertia which had been fatal to Jiway and EASDAQ. It also increased membership and connectivity, since firms wishing to deal in Swiss blue chips would need to do so through virt-x; it was hoped that dealing in non-Swiss shares would be only a small step further for the traders. As was the case with the other markets, liquidity often remains with the dominant markets even when a better price is posted on virt-x, but its revenues from the Swiss business have enabled virt-x to remain in competition for longer than either Jiway or EASDAQ.

Two other initiatives – Norex and Euronext – have taken a completely different approach. Both have attempted to consolidate existing markets into a larger market with common rules and technology. Norex, established in the late 1990s, includes the Stockholm, Copenhagen, Iceland and Oslo exchanges. Euronext was originally established as a combination of the Paris, Amsterdam and Brussels exchanges, with each of the three taking one sector of trading (blue chips in Paris, derivatives in Amsterdam and small-cap stocks in Brussels). The advantage of this "consolidation" approach is that it overcomes the liquidity problem encountered by other initiatives. There is no need to try to divert liquidity from dominant markets, since the dominant markets remain in place and simply link with each other via a common trading system (though it may take some time before actual cross-border activity amongst the participating exchanges reaches the same level as domestic trading). The limitation of this approach is that its scope is confined to the participating countries. It is extremely unlikely that any single initiative would ultimately include *all* European markets, and so these initiatives are unlikely to become true Pan-European markets.

Each of these two market-driven approaches, then, has inherent limitations which have hindered their success in integrating the European marketplace. True Pan-European markets have difficulty in overcoming the tendency of liquidity to remain with the dominant market, while efforts to consolidate the dominant markets have little or no effect outside the participating exchanges. Given the limited success of market-driven initiatives, a regulatory effort along the lines of the NMS would seem appropriate. Such an effort has been slow to gather momentum, though the European Commission has from the late 1990s renewed efforts to enable an integrated market through a series of some forty-two regulatory measures to be enacted by 2005. This Financial Services Action Plan (FSAP), however useful in removing major obstacles to cross-border capital flows, falls short of creating a European Market System. Though some progress has been made by the market in creating pre-trade quotation montages, the other elements necessary for a market system remain to be assembled. Moreover, the rules needed to ensure the use of the network (Display and Quote rules and price-based best execution, for example) are not amongst the tasks on the FSAP checklist.

Conclusion

The United States and Europe have come by different routes to the structures present in their markets today. Few would dispute that the US markets have achieved a far higher degree of integration, though serious challenges remain. The progress made in the United States reflects a number of factors, such as the presence of a single authority which can co-ordinate and if necessary mandate the creation and use of systems, as well as the presence of integrated clearing and settlement operations. Though the US solutions are now nearly thirty years old, they may nonetheless remain valid in many respects for the present challenges faced elsewhere – old solutions for new problems.

Though many would justifiably advise caution in applying the approach of one market to another, certain lessons can be drawn from the United States and Europe which have general if not universal application. These include:

- Transparency and order interaction are key elements for the integration of markets.

- Certain infrastructure elements are necessary, whatever the market, to facilitate market integration. These include a pre-trade price montage which enables competing orders from all participating markets to be seen, a consolidated tape to validate these prices by showing the actual transactions done on all participating markets, and a means of enabling orders to be routed to the best market. The latter need not take the form of a specific system such as the ITS, though, since modern technology has provided alternatives such as the technologies discussed in Chapter 7.

- The creation of infrastructure alone is not enough. As the United States saw in the late 1970s (and Europe is seeing now) liquidity sometimes defies the laws of economics and fails to move to its most efficient use. Rules are required to overcome these market failures and ensure that the market system overcomes the inertia to create true cross-market trading.

Chapter 7 established that certain systems are necessary for the working of an effective cross-market best execution system. It is no accident that the infrastructure necessary for an integrated market is essentially the same. The two concepts – best execution and market integration – are so closely intertwined that neither can be done effectively without the other. Best execution requires prices in competing markets to be visible, comparable and accessible. Market integration requires effective, enforceable best execution in order to overcome the immobility of liquidity and ensure that orders do in fact flow to the best market.

12 Making Integration Work: *The European Case*

The last four chapters have pointed out some of the issues involved in market integration, and some of the solutions and difficulties encountered in attempting to implement integration strategies. The aim of this chapter is to apply these lessons in a contemporary real-world setting, the goal of integrating European markets. Since the first tentative steps towards European Union were taken nearly fifty years ago, the integration of the markets has been an implied or explicit priority for policy makers, legislators and market participants alike. These efforts have largely proceeded in fits and starts, but have taken on renewed vigour in the last few years.[1]

As measured as progress has been, it must be said that no attempt to integrate national markets has ever been taken on this scale before. The lessons we learn from European integration may prove valuable when, at some point in the future, efforts are begun to integrate markets on a global scale. For this reason, European integration makes a worthy case study for those outside Europe as well as those within.

There are several excellent works detailing the legislative measures which have been taken in Europe over the years, and others which examine in close detail the policy-making process in the European Union. This chapter will not attempt to duplicate their efforts. Rather, it will seek to consider European market integration in the light of the discussion presented in the preceding chapters.

12.1 Treaty of Rome

The original driving force for consolidated markets lies in the foundation of what is now the European Union. The Treaty of Rome,[2] which established the European Economic Community in 1957, enshrined four freedoms as necessary elements of a unified Europe – freedom of movement of goods, services, persons and capital. From the beginning, then, those with the vision of uniting Europe recognised the importance of capital mobility, and that financial integration was as fundamental as political, economic and social integration.

The Treaty of Rome optimistically called for a twelve-year transitional period to make these freedoms a reality, and though the goal of free movement of capital was eventually

---

[1] This discussion will focus specifically on the actions of the European Union. While it is true that the European Union is not synonymous with "Europe", its efforts encompass those of most major European markets (when the nations of the closely linked European Economic Area are included). The major exception is Switzerland, but since its blue chip securities are principally traded on the UK-regulated virt-x exchange, Switzerland is effectively within the EU's sphere of influence at least with respect to major equities.

[2] Treaty Establishing the European Economic Community, which was signed in Rome on 25 March 1957 and took effect on 1 January 1958.

enacted as a matter of EC Law in 1988,[3] capital still does not move freely across borders. It cannot do so until capital markets are integrated – when orders to purchase and sell securities are able to move as freely across national borders as they do within them.

There are many reasons why the free movement of capital has taken so long to achieve. It must be said, though, that the goal has not suffered so much from neglect as from frustration. A number of measures have been undertaken, particularly from the 1990s on, to remove obstacles to cross-border movements of capital. The focus of this chapter is why the efforts thus far have failed to achieve the goal set so many decades ago, to provide a prognosis for current efforts, and to assess what measures are necessary to make market integration work in the European setting.

Amongst the reasons for the failure to achieve a single capital market, three stand out – the process of negotiation and compromise in drafting regulatory instruments, the difficulty in amending existing instruments and the number of instruments necessary to cover the entire range of issues presented in achieving integration.

A financial market is not in reality a single structure, but rather a series of interlocking but independent structures, regulations and practices. In addition to a general ISD, separate Directives have been issued (or at least drafted) in areas such as listing prospectuses, market abuse, clearing and settlement, takeovers and insolvency. Each of these Directives is the product of years of negotiation amongst Member States, amongst the various institutions of the European Union and amongst the market participants. Many initiatives have been held hostage to unrelated political issues – the Directive concerning company takeovers, for example, was held up for more than twelve years partly because of a disagreement between Spain and the United Kingdom over which country would exercise sovereign jurisdiction on the matter in Gibraltar.

The negotiations themselves occur amongst competing interests at several levels – states seeking to protect their national industries or operating from different basic assumptions; market users with a different view of regulation than market operators; and market users seeking advantage over other market users perhaps with different business models. As a result, the various institutions of the European Union (the Commission and the Parliament, for example) negotiate based on positions which themselves have been influenced by the lobbying efforts of competing interests. Under such circumstances, the best that can be hoped for is often a Directive which displeases everyone equally. In some cases, large gaps appear in Directives reflecting the failure to reach a consensus amongst competing parties and especially amongst competing Member States. In other cases, a Directive may contain rules which are confusing or appear to contradict one another. For example, Article 15 of the 1993 ISD provides for securities markets to be able to establish themselves in other Member States, but the following paragraph provides the right for Member States to prohibit the establishment of these markets in their states.

The process of drafting, negotiating and enacting European Union legislation is itself a tortuous one, prone to result in numerous compromises, gaps and contradictions in the legislation. Figure 12.1 is the European Union's own rather simplified illustration of the co-decision process, through which most financial services regulation has been established.

This is not to say that the consultation and negotiation process is inherently bad, but it is this process which often leads to the types of compromises and gaps which limit the effectiveness of

---

[3]   Council Directive 88/361 ([1988] OJ L178/5), adopted in 1988 and taking effect from mid-1990.

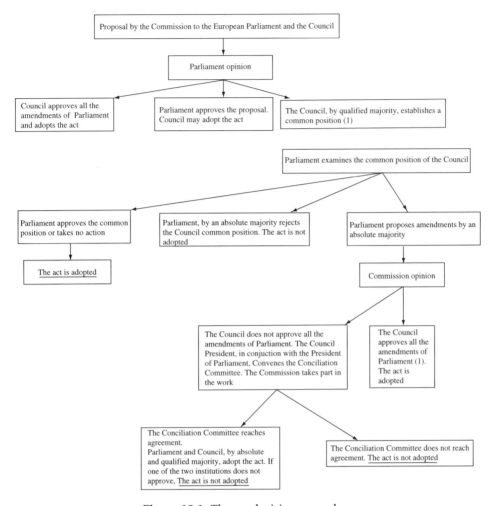

Figure 12.1: The co-decision procedure.
Source: European Communities, www.europa.eu.int.

the instruments intended to bring about integration. Until recently, this has been compounded by the unwieldy process required to update an EU Directive once it has finally been passed and implemented. Typically, Directives can only be changed by superseding them with new Directives – that is, existing Directives could not readily be amended to reflect changes in market structure or technologies. The prospect of enacting a superseding Directive was indeed daunting, as it involved the same process of negotiation and compromise involved in formulating the original instrument. An important (but as yet largely unproven) reform to this proposal came with the final report of the Lamfalussy Committee, which recommended that legislation be founded on framework concepts, with subordinate implementing measures which would fill in the necessary details. Importantly, these implementing measures could be amended as appropriate, without requiring an entirely new framework Directive. The effectiveness of the Lamfalussy procedures is difficult to assess since no Directives promulgated under them has gone through the entire process of consultation, drafting, negotiating, implementation and subsequent amendment. Still, they do hold out the prospect of a regime more responsive to market change, even if they do little to address the problems which might limit the effectiveness of the regulatory instruments in the first place.

The third difficulty – the range of instruments necessary to achieve integration – has manifested itself in the rather piecemeal approach heretofore taken in the European Union to the problem. In 1999, though, the European Commission proposed to address this problem with the publication of an FSAP. Partly in response to the introduction of the Euro across most of Europe, the FSAP provided a road map, or at least a checklist, of instruments deemed necessary to remove the obstacles to the freedom of movement of capital in the European Union. The FSAP also serves as a timetable, and an ambitious one at that, calling for the enactment of some forty-two separate regulatory instruments by 2005 (and for securities markets, by 2003). The complexity and breadth of the FSAP is demonstrated by the number and range of instruments proposed (ranging from revision of the ISD to tax harmonisation and insolvency directives). It is also demonstrated by the degree to which major provisions of the Action Plan were not implemented within their initial target time frame. The effectiveness of the FSAP will be considered later in this chapter.

12.2 Constructing a market system

Towards what object should the regulatory process in the European Union, then, be aimed? Throughout the preceding chapters, the point has been made that certain elements are fundamental conditions for the integration of markets. This is no less the case for European integration than for any other setting.

12.2.1 *Consolidated price montage*

The first and most fundamental element of an integrated market is a place where orders can be brought together to interact. This need not mean a single, monopolistic Pan-European exchange; in fact, such a development would be highly unlikely if only on competition grounds. Instead, it is more appropriate for competing markets to be linked so that their quotes and orders can interact with one another. A consolidated quote montage along the lines of the CQS in the United States is necessary in order to provide the requisite pre-trade, cross-border interaction of borders.

The necessity of this mechanism is best illustrated by observing the consequences of its absence. If a security is traded simultaneously in two, three or fifteen isolated markets, orders for that security will tend to remain in two, three or fifteen separate (national) trading pools. In the absence of linkages bringing these pools together, the security will suffer from the effects of liquidity fragmentation described in Chapter 8, a situation antithetical to the integration of markets. To achieve market integration, orders from across the markets must interact; this interaction requires a common venue for the display and execution of these orders.

If the need for this order interaction mechanism is accepted, certain implementation issues remain and should receive the focus of the regulatory authorities. The first is whether the market will provide a solution of its own accord, obviating the need for regulatory intervention. Vendors have begun efforts in this direction, and the progress of these systems may be judged by regulators to allow for a market-driven solution.

The second, more difficult question concerns participation in and access to the montage. Clearly, the montage should include all regulated exchanges in the European Union. In today's market environment, as we have seen, there are other venues in which orders are executed. Should the montage be open to Alternative Trading Systems? Should ATSs be required to participate? Should internalising firms be required to show orders to the consolidated price montage before executing them in-house? What are the competition issues raised by excluding them – or by including them without regulatory obligations equivalent to exchanges? These issues have indeed been the subject of considerable discussion within the European Union already. The final answer to these questions will depend on the resolution of related issues such as the proper definition and regulation of ATSs.

12.2.2 *Consolidated tape*

A post-trade counterpart to the consolidated price montage is also necessary. While pre-trade information provides essential data as to the level of interest at various prices, a consolidated tape displaying executions on all participating markets shows the prices at which the buy and sell interests meet to create an actual transaction. A consolidated tape validates the pre-trade price montage information.

Some have argued that post-trade information is actually more valuable than pre-trade transparency, since it shows the prices at which people are actually willing to deal. Moreover, they argue, pre-trade transparency can be harmful to those seeking to buy or sell large volumes of a security without suffering the adverse effects of signalling their interest to the market. Certainly it is appropriate to allow for special handling of large orders (as well as delayed reporting of large executions), and this is the norm in many markets already. But it is fallacious to assert that post-trade transparency is sufficient without detailed pre-trade transparency. First, post-trade transparency is inherently dated information, even if only by a few seconds. It shows the price and size at which people *were* willing to deal, whereas pre-trade information shows the prices and volumes at which they *are* willing to deal. Secondly, a consolidated tape itself does not permit the interaction of orders, since it does not indicate where the best open (unexecuted) orders are. While pre-trade information provides both transparency and interaction, post-trade information only provides transparency. In the end, it is necessary to have sufficient levels of both, and it is therefore necessary to have both a consolidated European price montage and a consolidated European tape.

12.2.3 *Order routing*

Transparency is one thing, then, and interaction is something else. While it is necessary to see all orders and trades, true integration only occurs when traders can actually route the orders to the various venues for execution. In the United States, a dedicated ITS was created for this purpose. With network and routing technologies such as those described in Chapter 7, this may no longer be necessary. Constructing a dedicated execution system is only one way to transform visibility to order interaction. The use of existing technologies to provide virtual linkages not only accomplishes this goal, but it does so in a more flexible and adaptable manner.

12.3 Overcoming inertia – best execution as a necessary element of market integration

Once the three basic infrastructure elements are in place, one would think that it would only be necessary to sit back and watch the market integrate itself as the invisible hand moves orders across borders. Experience provides a less optimistic prognosis. There is a fourth obstacle which, if unaddressed, can easily frustrate market integration even if all the infrastructure is set in place. This obstacle should not even exist, according to theory. This is the immobility of liquidity examined in previous pages – a kind of capital inertia which keeps liquidity confined to the domestic markets.

The ECB, reporting on its survey on euro-area equity markets, noted that liquidity is "sticky", tending to remain on the market of first listing for a security.[4] This failure of liquidity (orders) to move to the best price when that price is on another market represents a significant breakdown in the market mechanism. It deprives the investor of the best price, and it impedes order interaction, to the detriment of the price formation process. The findings of the ECB report support two major conclusions of this book. First, market liquidity does not inherently move to its most efficient use, contrary to theory. This represents the type of market inefficiency for which regulatory redress is justified, even necessary. Secondly, the ECB report highlights the fact that technology, in the form of "smart agents" (algorithms), can be used to access the best price on whichever market is appropriate.

As was described in Chapter 8, a survey of industry leaders found several possible explanations for the immobility of liquidity, many of which pointed to potential conflicts of interest within the executing firm.[5] Given their potential effect on fair and efficient trading, these conflicts could be as inimical to the free interaction of market forces as was the pressure placed on stock analysts to provide favourable opinions in order to garner more investment banking business for their firm.

Whether or not one agrees with the reasons for the stickiness of liquidity, there is little dispute over the fact that orders frequently fail to execute across markets when they could do so at a superior price. Leaving it to the "invisible hand" does not work. This brings us to the question of what should be done to ensure that order flows do in fact move freely to the best price.

It is this question which brings us back to the notion of best execution. If the problem is that orders do not move across markets to find the best price, it is logical that a cross-market best execution policy would help to correct this market inefficiency and enable the market linkages to work as theory would indicate. In other words, we come by a different route to the same conclusion reached in the first part of this book – the need for a cross-market best execution policy.

Best execution, then, is not only a fundamental investor protection rule, it is also a necessary element for market integration. Viewed from either perspective, it is necessary that the policy includes a visible cross-market standard in order to make the policy viable.[6]

---

[4]   ECB, p. 39.

[5]   "European Financial Markets 2001: Revolution or Evolution?", Charteris Plc, 2001.

[6]   While the investor protection perspective implies that the policy should be more loosely applied for institutional trading than for retail, a retail-focused policy will, nonetheless, make necessary the removal of conflicts of interest and disallow the inertia which keeps liquidity in general stuck within dominant national markets.

These, then, are the minimum necessary requirements for the integration of the European markets – a consolidated price montage, a consolidated tape, order routing technology and a cross-market standard for best execution. This leads to the question of whether and how the regulatory process in the European Union has facilitated their implementation.

While the regulatory initiatives comprising the FSAP are necessary to remove many obstacles to market integration, there is little specific effort in the Plan to create the necessary infrastructure elements. Of course, the market has made considerable progress in developing elements of the technology without regulatory mandate. Consolidated quote montages are currently available from data vendors, at least in nascent form. Consolidated tapes logically may follow. Order routing (and net-price calculation) technology is available, although it has not yet been taken off the shelf and integrated into the market. Still, it is one thing to have the technologies available, and something altogether different to exploit them to form a workable, integrated market system. There remains an appropriate co-ordinating regulatory role through which a market-led solution may be sped and made more efficient.

Of greater concern is the development of best execution policy within the European Union. In the absence of a clear requirement to route orders to the market representing the best net price, at least for retail orders, it is likely that liquidity will continue to defy the laws of economics and remain stuck, and fragmented, within the dominant national market for each security. Whether caused by inertia, conflicts of interest, both, or neither, the failure to address this problem would significantly retard the development of integration infrastructure since there would be little evidence of its usefulness. Why construct an elaborate system if no one is seen to use it? Even once the infrastructure is in place, the absence of a regulatory remedy to the immobility of liquidity would represent a potentially fatal barrier to the integration of the European market.

Come 2005, the result may well be that the FSAP has been implemented, in that all of the boxes have been ticked, yet the markets have not been integrated. Market integration, after all, is not measured by the absence of obstacles, but by the actual movement of capital – orders and transactions – across national borders with the same ease with which they move domestically. Market liberalisation (capital is free to flow across borders) must not be confused with market integration (capital does flow across borders). If the FSAP merely liberalises the market we would then face the prospect of a second FSAP to integrate the market by addressing the market inefficiencies discussed in this chapter.

12.4 Is a "super-regulator" necessary?

One of the perennial questions in Europe is whether it is desirable or feasible to create a single European securities regulator, usually conceived of as similar to the United States Securities and Exchange Commission. To date, the answer has largely been "no", at least for the time being. Professor Karel Lannoo, in his detailed study of the question,[7] finds that a single European regulator is not only unnecessary, but would likely be ineffective in

---

[7] Lannoo, Karel. "Does Europe Need an SEC? Securities Market Regulation in the EU", European Capital Markets Institute, November 1999.

attempting to regulate the various European markets with their differing structures and traditions. The Lamfalussy Committee generally agreed with this conclusion, calling instead for greater co-ordination amongst national regulators.[8] In its conclusion, however, it recognised that the question should be revisited after the implementation of the FSAP to determine whether such a Pan-European authority is in fact necessary.[9]

Certainly a quasi-SEC would be difficult to enact at the present time given the patchwork of legal traditions, regulatory frameworks and operating practices amongst the Member States of the European Union. It will become no easier with the expansion of the European Union to include formerly communist states. The prognosis might be quite different, though, if one envisions instead a more limited Pan-European authority. It is not necessary to assume that any proposed regulator would have the full range of powers and responsibilities possessed by national regulatory authorities such as the SEC. A Pan-European securities regulator need not be a "Euro-SEC".

We have seen that regulation plays an important role in promoting the creation of an integrated securities market. The same is true of the operation of a market once it has been created. Put simply, someone has to administer and operate the infrastructure, review its effectiveness and mandate modernisation as necessary. This body must be neutral, standing above the commercial and national interests of the participants. The consortium approach used by the NMS in the United States, embodying the single-consolidator approach, is open to criticism on several grounds. It is open to the charge that it serves the interests of the more powerful markets and firms, and lacks sufficient transparency and accountability in its actions, pricing decisions and other areas. It would also be, by its nature, a closed environment constituting a barrier to entry for potential new markets.

Alternatively, a Pan-European regulatory body with powers limited to the operation and administration of the infrastructure could be established. Answerable to the institutions of the European Union, it could be held more directly accountable for its actions. Of course, in the present environment in the European Union, the commercial competition of an industrial consortium could well be replaced by an equally corrosive national competition amongst members of the regulatory body. In this sense, though, it would reflect a weakness inherent in the EU institutions themselves, rather than representing a step towards "regulatory capture" by the industry. Political interference might be avoided devolving regulatory powers from the EU institutions to an independent self-regulatory body (as opposed to a consortium of commercial enterprises) – closer to a "Euro-NASD" than a "Euro-SEC".

Whatever the strengths and weaknesses of each approach, the fact remains that an over-arching authority of some kind will be necessary to ensure the successful creation and operation of the technical infrastructure. More discussion is necessary to determine the precise nature of the authority, but a commitment to achieving this aim is fundamental to the successful implementation of the integrated market. This is true now; it will be doubly so with the expansion of the European Union into central and eastern Europe over the coming years.

What, then, should be the remit of this organisation – and what should it not be? The answers to these questions are best left open to consultation between the Commission, in

---

[8]   Final Report of the Committee of Wise Men on the Regulation of European Securities Markets
      (February 2001), available at http://europa.eu.int/comm/internal_market.
[9]   *Ibid.*

whom the authority resides, and market participants and technology firms, in whom the expertise largely resides. Still, certain roles can be envisioned which would be appropriate. In the first stage, the organisation should be responsible for overseeing the implementation of the intermarket infrastructure. This would initially involve general instructions as to how the infrastructure should be constructed, the performance parameters and other necessary guidance.

The detailed proposals should be left to those in the industry with intimate knowledge of current market practice and technology. Their input could come either in the form of a public consultation process or, more likely, via a standing committee with representatives of the appropriate sectors, which would be established to support the work of the regulatory organisation (in this respect, similar to the organisation of the Securities Committee and CESR in the Lamfalussy process). The composition of the body would likely consist of industry trade organisations rather than specific firms, in order to avoid the perception that a participating firm benefits from exerting its influence over the proposals. For example, organisations such as FESE and APCIMS-EASD would represent the interests of their sectors, rather than one or two "privileged" firms having a seat in the advisory committee.

Once the industry, under the guidance of the implementing organisation, has provided a workable plan, the role of the organisation would likely be one of co-ordination and continued consultation. For instance, once the advisory committee has recommended various standards and protocols, the implementing organisation could make their use mandatory, overcoming the "critical mass" hurdle which often defeats the implementation of new standards and technologies.

Once the infrastructure is in place, the organisation would play the important role of administering it on an ongoing basis. This role would include administration and financing (and determination of fees) and an ongoing assessment of the state of technology to determine from time to time whether and how the infrastructure should be updated.

It would be a step too far at this point to speculate in further detail on the specific structure and duties of the regulatory organisation. The point remains, however, that there is a strong case to be made for a European regulatory authority tasked with facilitating and administering the construction of the technical infrastructure necessary for true integration of the European securities markets. In the absence of such an agency, efforts to establish the necessary integration infrastructure, with its component technologies and standards, would be threatened by the piecemeal fashion in which they could be expected to proceed. A high-level co-ordinating and standard-setting body is therefore necessary in order to take the existing technologies off the shelf and make real the development of an integrated market. An agency of this nature is an altogether different animal from the Euro-SEC which has been discussed and rejected in the financial community. Its powers would be limited to those necessary for the implementation of the necessary market infrastructure; broader enforcement and supervision matters would remain in their present bodies. The debate should therefore shift from "do we need a Euro-SEC" to "do we need a limited authority to co-ordinate and set standards"?

The establishment of a limited Pan-European authority is not so much a step onto the slippery slope that leads to overregulation and state control of the markets. Rather, it is recognition of the fact that some degree of regulation is necessary at that level in order to allow the market to overcome its own inherent inefficiencies and to perform as an unimpeded market should. The traditional argument against state regulation holds that it is to be avoided because it impedes the free operation of the market. This may be generally true, but outside the textbooks markets have their own manifest impediments, and regulation may be necessary to overcome these obstacles. In so doing, the visible hand of regulation accomplishes the very goal that classic *laissez-faire* market liberals seek: the free functioning of market forces.

Conclusion

The integration of securities markets is an enormously complex undertaking. In the European case, it is made even more complex by the fact that the markets to be integrated reside in different nations with different legal structures, business cultures and financial structures. Yet we can see past this complexity if we break the problem down into the minimum fundamental components necessary for an integrated market, in which orders and transactions flow without hindrance across these national borders.

Drawing from the lessons and conclusions of the previous chapters, it is inevitable to conclude that elements of integration infrastructure – consolidated price montage, tape and order routing mechanism – require further development and exploitation. This infrastructure will likely remain an empty road without a cross-market best execution policy which addresses the tendency of liquidity to remain on the dominant market. Even if this policy only applies directly to retail trading, it will help to build up the necessary critical mass to make the integrated market system viable, as well as highlighting any residual conflicts of interest which militate against cross-border executions.

At the same time, the FSAP should remain on course in order to address those more visible obstacles to integration. Rationalisation of clearing and settlement, tax harmonisation and other structural reforms should remain high on the European Commission's list of priorities. The critical point is that the FSAP reforms represent a necessary, but not sufficient, condition for European market integration.

Lastly, a Pan-European regulatory authority with limited powers would be able to provide the necessary co-ordination and standard-setting tasks needed to make the market system a reality. Such an authority should only have those powers required to co-ordinate, and if necessary to direct, action across the markets which are necessary to achieve the goal of market integration. Appropriate tasks for such a regulator would be the establishment of technological, data and other standards and the co-ordinated study of issues central to market integration. These include questions of governance and finance, best practice and technology. An important question for this body would be that of whether conflicts of interest do in fact impede the movement of liquidity away from the dominant markets, and if so how these conflicts can best be mitigated. A second key role for this authority would be the regular review of technology and market structure necessary to keep regulation apace with the progress of the markets.

Market Integration: Conclusions

The integration of securities markets has been the focus of much of the regulatory debate over the last several years. Few question the importance of the goal, since integration feeds the efficiency of the markets, and because capital cannot move freely as long as the capital markets themselves work in isolation from one another. More at issue are the methods by which markets can be integrated in a way which does not unduly limit competition or risk investor protection.

Much of the discussion has centred on the idea of reducing market fragmentation, seeing the simultaneous trading of securities in separate venues as the antithesis of integration. This is true as far as it goes, but it has led us down the wrong path in certain respects. It fails to distinguish between *separate* markets and *isolated* markets. The difference between the two is order interaction – markets may be separate from one another, but if their orders and transactions are able to interact they are not isolated. The focus for market integration then should not be to prevent market fragmentation (separate markets), but instead to prevent liquidity fragmentation (isolated markets) in which orders cannot interact.

When orders are able to interact freely, it should make little difference whether they are located in one market or ten. Indeed, competition is enhanced by the elimination of the natural monopoly presented by a single market dominating trading in a security. In reality, though, there are obstacles to the free interaction of orders across markets. Many of these are legal and regulatory in nature, especially when the markets to be integrated reside in different countries (as in Europe). It is the remediation of these obstacles that has occupied most of the time of policy makers concerned with market integration. This is time and effort well spent. Yet the actual integration of markets – orders across borders – requires more.

It requires an infrastructure consisting of, at a minimum, mechanisms to perform three processes. First amongst these is the actual consolidation of pre-trade information (e.g. quotes and orders) into a single montage where prices can be viewed and compared (ideally net of costs). To this must be added a means by which these prices can be validated – a consolidated tape showing executed transactions on all relevant markets. The third element is a mechanism by which orders can actually be routed across markets to execute against each other, and current technology and networking capabilities may mean that a formal trading system is not necessary to accomplish this task.

Yet infrastructure alone is not sufficient. If these elements are in place, market integration has been facilitated but it has not necessarily been activated; the market has achieved transparency but not necessarily interaction; the market is liberalised but not necessarily integrated. Market laws tell us that capital naturally flows to its most efficient use, and therefore orders will naturally flow to the market where they can receive their best execution. Yet experience and observation show this is not the case. Even once the legal and regulatory differences have been neutralised, liquidity still tends to stay with the dominant market – to the evident detriment of investors and the markets alike. Regulation is then appropriate to overcome this market failure and to ensure that the markets achieve the efficiency they should.

In other words, actual achievement of market integration requires a regulatory mandate that overcomes inertia and ensures that orders flow across markets, interact and execute at the best price. This has brought us back to the idea of a best execution policy, though its necessity has been arrived at by an entirely different logical route than the investor protection route taken in the first part of this book.

The creation of the infrastructure and accompanying regulation requires a high degree of co-ordination and the setting of standards, even if most of the work is accomplished through market solutions. Especially in environments where there is no single regulator (i.e. in multinational environments), a regulatory authority is likely to be necessary to perform this role. This does not imply that it would be necessary to establish a super-regulator with all the powers and responsibilities of a national regulator. The powers of this regulatory authority should be sufficient, but limited in scope to its goal of achieving market integration.

In conclusion, the major lessons drawn from these chapters on market integration are:

- The integration of markets is necessary for the optimal efficiency of the markets and to assist in broader economic integration by allowing capital to move more freely across borders. The key to this integration is the cross-market interaction of orders.

- True fragmentation occurs when markets are isolated from one another, preventing order interaction. Measures opposing the existence of separate pools of liquidity serve not to encourage integration, but only to discourage competition. Efforts should be aimed instead at the development of market linkages which will facilitate the interaction of orders across markets.

- These linkages should consist, at a minimum, of a consolidated price montage, a consolidated tape and a mechanism for the routing of orders across markets.

- To achieve integration, rather than just facilitate it, regulation is necessary to overcome market inefficiencies such as the immobility of liquidity. This is accomplished by the same best execution policy which is necessary for investor protection.

- In the case of Europe, a limited Pan-European market authority is likely to be necessary to perform the co-ordination and direction functions of a single regulator.

Part III
Making Market Integration Work

The following section will seek to take a broader, strategic view of achieving market integration, drawing on the lessons from the previous sections on best execution and market structure. Two themes in particular will be examined – the roles of the state and the market in bringing the necessary policies and processes to fruition, and the centrality of order interaction.

13 State vs Market – Who Regulates the Integrated Market?

In Chapter 2, the grounds on which regulation may be justified were explored in some detail. What can we now say about the role of regulation in the markets, and more specifically about the role of government regulation vs pure self-regulation by the market?

Even those who take a purist, "invisible hand" approach to markets generally agree that there is an inevitable role for state regulation, even if this role is restricted to the absolute minimum of involvement. The question then becomes not whether there should be state regulation of markets, but rather in what areas and in what form this regulation should be established.

There are three primary areas in which state regulation can actually facilitate, rather than hinder, cross-market activity. The first arises from the fact that markets are not "perfect" in either the economic or the broader sense. Economic models of markets are just that-models which are simplified and stripped of imperfections in order to demonstrate fundamental principles. In practice, of course, imperfections exist, and one role of regulation is to address these imperfections. Many of these imperfections arise from the workings of a competitive marketplace itself, and therefore are better addressed by an entity such as the state which is "neutral" in the competitive battle. An example of such an imperfection is the incentive of traders to send orders to the market on which their market-share, and therefore their compensation, is based. More mundane imperfections such as the commercial inertia which drives firms and individuals to business on their own domestic market, rather than on a foreign market, must also be addressed. The list of market imperfections which are appropriate for regulation is extensive, and the logic behind regulation as a remedy to market imperfections is generally (though not universally) accepted.

The second area in which state, rather than market, regulation may be appropriate is in the setting of standards and the mandated use of these standards. We have seen that a lack of standardisation poses a real obstacle to market integration in several contexts. From a technical point of view, standardisation is necessary in such areas as pre- and post-trade data flows to permit consolidation and dissemination to the marketplace. Similarly, standardisation is a key element to the harmonisation and interoperability of clearing and settlement systems. From a regulatory point of view, changes in permitted business practices may need to be mandated across the industry at more or less the same time, since the first mover in such a reform may disadvantage himself with respect to his competitors. This requirement is perhaps an unspoken basis for much of securities regulation, when one considers recent regulation in the United States and the European Union. Actions such as those mandated by the Order Handling Rules would not likely have been generated by firms themselves were it not for a regulatory requirement forcing all firms to do so at the same time, so that none was disadvantaged with respect to the others.

Related to this idea of standardisation and co-ordination is the creation of a common infrastructure to be used by all. In the sense that the infrastructure is used by all or most of the market, and new joiners benefit from the infrastructure at no additional cost, common market infrastructure is a "public good". Construction of consolidated montages and tapes, and of cross-market clearing and settlement systems, benefits the entire market in this way and the burden of their construction and maintenance should not be borne by a few market participants. Conversely, their control and pricing should not be left in the hands of a few (as with the Operating Committees of the NMS).

Of course, some could point to the construction of the NMS and object that it was constructed by the industry, not the national regulatory authority. While this is true, it is also true that the market players only constructed the System when the SEC required them to do so, and even that occurred only after legislative action by Congress. Whether the market would have constructed linkages amongst exchanges if left to its own devices is an open question.

These two areas – market imperfections and standardisation/co-ordination – are necessary in order to facilitate market integration. The third area in which state regulation is appropriate is that of investor protection. The protection of investors, particularly individual retail investors, is a necessary imperative in its own right. Yet as we have seen in the preceding chapters, investor protection in the form of cross-market best execution is also a necessary ingredient in the integration of markets (in this sense, it also serves the function of addressing market imperfections by overcoming interfering factors to drive orders to the market of best execution).

In these three areas, then, regulation by the state is necessary to the proper functioning of the market. It is important to consider, however, what exactly we mean by "state regulation".

The most important element of state regulation is that it brings with it the *authority* to require an action to be taken. That is, state regulation carries with it a level of authority which resides above that of the various participants to whom the regulation applies.[1] This is most easily seen with respect to the legislation of the European Union, where Directives are superior to the national regulations of the Member States and therefore reach across boundaries to apply to all participants. This authority is, at least in principal, free of the competitive considerations which could be seen to taint market self-regulation.[2] What distinguishes whether state regulation is appropriate? The answer lies in whether this level of overarching authority is necessary.

While authority is the strength of state regulation, detailed knowledge often is not. Experienced though individual staff members may be, regulators in general do not have the day-to-day, up-to-date familiarity with the markets that market participants do. Consultations are a useful tool in transferring some of this knowledge, but it should be acknowledged that consultations are also a means of competitive lobbying by the participants. Once the focus moves to the level of detailed regulation, it is likely more effective that market participants construct the regulations. In some instances this may be done through SROs,

---

[1] "State" regulation need not be performed directly by the state, since the powers and authority of the state can be devolved to a subordinate, non-state institution. For brevity's sake, though, "state" regulation is used here to denote both direct and devolved regulation from the state.

[2] States themselves are often perceived to be tainted by their concerns to promote or protect the interests of those market participants established in their jurisdictions. The extent to which this is true, or to which it is a factor, is appropriately covered in other research.

while in other cases through advisory bodies proposing standards to the state statutory regulatory body.

State regulation has also been accused of being too unwieldy for an industry as dynamic as securities markets. This criticism is largely justified if the regulatory process is cumbersome. The broad and powerful authority that is the strength of state regulation requires that new regulations, or amendments to existing ones, not be done lightly. The process of doing so is therefore deliberate, often to the point of being unwieldy. The European Union recognised this to be the case, particularly in the light of the first ISD. The Directive was negotiated through the early 1990s and came into force in May 1993, with the requirement that Member States enact enabling legislation by July 1995. By the time the Directive reached full effect, then, nearly half a decade had transpired since the original negotiations. By the end of the decade, it was clear that changes were required to the Directive, both to address its inherent shortcomings and to bring it up to date with market developments. As we have seen previously, this was not possible with the legislative structure as it stood at the time, as the only way to modify such a Directive was to negotiate, draft and implement an entirely new Directive. The Lamfalussy process was meant to address this legislative bottleneck, and constituted a recognition of the danger posed by the "regulatory lag" manifest in the state regulatory process.

Put simply, the strength of state regulation is its overarching authority and the strength of market self-regulation is its detailed knowledge of the market. Ideally, it can be supposed that the best approach would combine the authority of the one with the expertise of the other. When viewed in this light – of the strengths and weaknesses of state and market regulation – one answer appears to be a regulatory division of labour.

Envisioning such a division of labour is not a theoretical exercise, since it has been put into practice already, on both sides of the Atlantic. The creation of the NMS involved the state (via Congress and the SEC) mandating the achievement of identified goals, while the construction of the infrastructure was left to the markets. In Europe, the Lamfalussy process seeks a rather modified form of this division of labour. The promulgation of general goals and principles is the domain of the European Union (via the Directives agreed by the Commission, the Parliament and the Council) whilst detailed implementing measures are left for the national authorities sitting in the form of the Securities Committee and its supporting CESR. While these are both committees of *state* regulators, they are specifically charged with seeking input from market participants through formal consultations.[3] The Lamfalussy process is still in its infancy, and it remains to be seen whether this modified division of labour will be effective.

If it is true that there is a valid role for state regulation, we might well ask how it is best applied, and the previous chapter addressed this question in the context of European regulation. Though the final report of the Lamfalussy Committee held out the possibility of a Pan-European regulator should the Lamfalussy process be seen to fail in its goals, the idea of a "Euro-SEC" has met considerable opposition. The desirability of a multinational regulator depends in part on how the organisation is conceptualised. As much as the idea of a Pan-European regulator has been debated, the quality of the debate has been limited by

---

[3]   Article 5, European Commission Decision Establishing the Committee of European Securities Regulators, available at http://europa.eu.int/comm/internal_market/en/finances/mobil/com1501en.pdf.

the presumption that this regulator would possess all the powers and responsibilities of a national regulator – a Euro-SEC.

It is true that differences in legal frameworks, local market practice and other factors would make it well-nigh impossible for a unified regulator to function effectively in the European Union of today. However, a Pan-European organisation with a more limited area of competence is not only possible, it is necessary. A Pan-European authority with narrowly targeted responsibilities could effectively perform those functions for which it is necessary without treading in broader areas for which it is not appropriate.

In the end, it is clear that state regulation is critical to the achievement of market integration, even if its role is limited. A Pan-European authority is appropriate and necessary for overseeing the establishment of a truly integrated European market. Its responsibilities would be targeted to those areas in which its authority is necessary, such as overcoming market imperfections and co-ordinating the establishment of the technical infrastructure necessary to facilitate the free flow of capital across borders. It should not be assumed that this authority need be created from a blank sheet of paper. Rather, it may be appropriate to expand the responsibilities (and resources) of CESR to fulfil this role. Expanding the role of CESR may also be more politically acceptable than the creation of a new bureaucracy within the already byzantine EU structure. The principal question would be whether CESR, which is after all composed of representatives from the various Member States, could rise above national competitive considerations to fill this role fairly and effectively. In this regard it should be noted that remarkably little criticism has been levelled at CESR (or its predecessor, FESCO) along these lines. Alternatively, state powers could be devolved to an independent self-regulatory body, free of national political interference as well as commercial bias. Ultimately, the important point is that the creation of a limited Pan-European authority is necessary, and the question of whether it is to be an expanded CESR or a new organisation is subsidiary to this point.

Conclusion

This book has addressed why capital does not flow as freely across borders as would be expected in a perfect market. In addressing this question from a number of angles and in conjunction with several related issues, it has identified certain actions which are required to overcome the inherent obstacles to cross-border order interaction. These include a cross-market best execution policy, technical standardisation and infrastructure development, and interoperability of back office operations across borders. Each of these requires to some extent the overarching authority of a state regulator; in the European context, a limited Pan-European authority. The achievement of true market integration should be a matter for the markets, with co-operation, authority and direction of appropriate state regulation.

14 Conclusions

This book has examined two issues which on their surface are separate – one a matter of investor protection, the other a matter of market inefficiency. It has been shown, however, that they are closely intertwined both in their action and in their solution. Integration is a tool for investor protection, and investor protection a tool for market integration. More specifically, best execution cannot be effective unless the markets are integrated, and market integration requires a cross-market best execution policy. Following two different paths of logic – the need for an effective best execution policy and the need to integrate markets – these chapters have arrived at the same fundamental conclusions. These include the fundamental necessity of cross-market order interaction and the need for an execution policy which sets a clear enforceable standard for the routing of orders to the market on which best execution resides.

An underlying theme of this book has been the appropriate role of regulation in this process. Perfect markets work perfectly; all others require some degree of regulation. While it is axiomatic that markets should be as free as possible, it is not always clear from what they should be free. In the minds of many, they should be free from the interference of regulation, hence the momentum behind "deregulation" in all of its forms. Observation and experience show us, though, that markets must also be free from the inefficiencies inherent in their real-world operation which hinder (or preclude altogether) the operation of beneficial market forces. In the end, totally free markets are a thing more wished for than actually experienced, and regulation is generally accepted as a necessary evil for the operation of markets. The question is what role regulation should play, and how it should do so.

The necessity of certain regulatory roles speaks for itself. Amongst these are the protection of investors (who are inherently disadvantaged), the promotion of competition and removal of factors which limit the efficient operation of the markets. These responsibilities are manifestly in the interest of the markets, and thereby the economies and societies in which they operate. The integration of markets is an unequivocal imperative of those seeking to ensure that financial markets fulfil their critical role in the economy and society. The importance of the subject speaks for itself, and the legislative and regulatory record on both sides of the Atlantic demonstrates the gravity with which policy makers view this responsibility.

This premise lies as the foundation of the discussions in this book. Whether protecting investors through best execution or promoting an integrated market of competing but linked markets, regulatory policy plays a critical role in the marketplace. It must be done right. Yet the issues are individually complex and collectively entangled. The best way to approach this Gordian knot is to boil the issues down to their fundamentals, and to deal with them together rather than separately.

We have also seen that regulatory policies must be set in the context of current, and anticipated, technology and market structure. Moreover, the regulatory processes them-selves must also be responsive to change. This requires two elements – a regulatory process which is open to amendment and interpretation (as the Lamfalussy process demonstrates), and regular comprehensive review by the regulatory authorities to assess developments in technology and market structure. The aim of these reviews should not only be to identify and anticipate problems, but to seek ways in which things can be done more efficiently.

The notion of a core standard approach to regulation was also developed, primarily with regard to best execution. Those who repeatedly decry "one-size-fits-all" policies often are really just seeking a larger size – that is, the application of loose, non-prescriptive standards appropriate to institutions but providing no real enforceable protection to retail investors. The core standard approach focuses on those who most need protection, and provides various means of exempting those to whom retail regulation does not fit.

A closely related principle is that of regulatory clarity. The establishment of clear standards is in the best interests of all. Retail investors benefit from more certain enforceability of the standards. Firms benefit by the avoidance of disputes and litigation, and because their internal controls can be more efficiently based upon the relevant standards. Markets benefit from increased confidence. And in the case of best execution, a clear benchmark results in the reduction of the immobility of capital, thus enhancing order interaction and the efficiency of the markets.

Though fragmentation is indeed the antithesis of integration, the concept is commonly misunderstood. "Fragmentation" of the marketplace into separate, simultaneously operating markets is not inherently contrary to market integration. It is the isolation of markets from each other – the lack of interaction – which defeats integration. It is the fragmentation of liquidity, not of the market, which is inimical to integration. To oppose separate markets simply because they are separate is not only based on a fallacious assumption of isolation, but it is anticompetitive in that it promotes the monopoly position of dominant markets.

The fundamental principle in market integration, underlying all others, is order interaction. All other factors are relevant only to the extent that they contribute to the interaction of orders across markets. Measures which promote transparency, for instance, but fall short of order interaction also fall short of integrating the market.

Also fundamental to the integration of markets is the distinction between liberalisation and integration. Liberalisation is accomplished through the establishment of the necessary structure (pre-trade and post-trade consolidation, order interaction technology) and the removal of legal, tax or other regulatory barriers. It merely creates an environment in which capital is free to flow across markets. Actual market integration will not occur until the inherent inefficiencies of the market are overcome so that capital actually moves to its most efficient use. An effective best execution policy, following the principles enumerated in these pages, would likely accomplish this.

Focusing on the integration of Europe, we have seen the need for legislation to mandate and facilitate the consolidated market infrastructure, accompanied by the requisite policies (i.e. best execution). Whether through market initiatives or regulatory fiat, this will be a complex task. A complex task, to be sure, but no more so than adopting and converting to the Euro, or the establishment of the NMS in the United States. It is in large measure a matter of political will and market consensus. For this reason, a concise plan for the implementation of these measures should be issued, accompanied by a clear statement of their necessity. In other words, a second FSAP is likely to be necessary to make integration a reality. It is also likely that a Pan-European regulatory authority, with powers limited to those appropriate for the task, will need to be established to provide the necessary functions associated with co-ordinating efforts to build the structure necessary for an integrated market.

The integration of markets is about more than the theoretical efficiency of an abstract price formation process. It is about removing barriers and allowing economies to benefit from each other, to lift the artificial constraints which have left markets and economies unnecessarily isolated from one another. If one believes in the concept of free markets and free trade, it is difficult to argue against the goal of financial market integration. Much, therefore, depends on the success of policy makers in devising ways in which to ensure that market integration is not only facilitated, but it is *achieved*.

This success will depend amongst other things on boiling the complex notion of market integration down to its essential components or principles. The principles can and should serve as the starting point for concrete proposals for action. They should be as basic and objective as possible. Any undertaking as far-reaching as market reform will necessarily affect the interests of a number of competing parties. For any measure proposed, some will benefit and some will lose. Moreover, honest and intelligent people will differ fundamentally on the approaches to take, though their shared interest in the overall good of the market is unquestioned. A discussion centred on simple and objective principles would help to keep the debate focused on the ultimate goal of market integration.

In that vein, this book has sought to address complex issues by reducing them to these fundamental principles. At the same time, it has endeavoured to construct both a practical and a theoretical perspective to the issues involved. It has endeavoured to construct a coherent approach to achieving market integration, in the hope that it can at least serve as a basis for consideration and debate. It does not answer all questions, nor could it; rather, it seeks to highlight the principles and provide a new perspective from which to view long-standing problems.

Appendix A

Selected Best Execution Terminology

Austria	"...at best price on the relevant market within a reasonable period of time..."
Belgium	"Orders must be executed as rapidly as possible and at the best conditions."
Denmark	"...a securities dealer must always have a universal obligation to ensure the customer the best possible price"
Finland	"...shall execute...in the customer's best interest without undue delay."
France	"ensure that its orders are executed in the best manner possible."
Germany	"...to obtain the best price on the relevant market..."
Greece	"...within reasonable time period...firms will seek the best price available..."
Ireland	"...deal to the best advantage..."
Italy	"...best possible conditions considering price paid, received and other costs..."
Netherlands	"...as fast as possible in the best possible manner..."
Norway	"...the client shall be given the best price that the firm considers..."
Portugal	"perform the transactions in the best conditions of market feasibility."
Spain	"in the best terms..."
United Kingdom	"price which is the best available for the customer order in the relevant market at the time for transactions of the kind and size concerned"
United States	"...a member shall use reasonable due diligence to ascertain the best inter-dealer market for a security and buy or sell in such market so that the resultant price to the customer is as favourable as possible under the prevailing market conditions."

Source: Best Execution, FSA Discussion Paper, April 2001; FSA Handbook of Rules and Guidance: Conduct of Business, Section 7.5; NASD Rule 2320.

Appendix B

Proposed Best Execution Policy

There should be a clearly identifiable standard – the best price.

A benchmark is necessary to provide a standard against which execution can be judged. It is necessary both to provide guidance to the trader and to make the policy enforceable. For this reason, the proposed best execution policy should have a clear benchmark, the best price.

The best price should be the best net price, including all identifiable costs to the investor.

Proceeding from the best displayed price, other quantifiable factors should be considered in determining best execution. These are those costs which:

- affect the final price paid or received by the investor (*not* the intermediaries)
- are knowable before the execution of the trade
- are readily quantifiable.

The best price should not be limited to the "home market" for the security – it should be the best *intermarket* net price.

Clearly, in today's environment, more than one venue should be checked. Data vendors are already consolidating price information from multiple venues, and these consolidated displays are available on some of the most widely accessed systems.

Best execution protection should focus on the needs of the retail investor.

The assumption should be made that, in the absence of any indication to the contrary from the investor, the intermarket price standard should be the "default" criterion for best execution. For the retail investor, the bottom line – quite literally – will be the price received when selling the security less than the price paid when buying it. All other factors are relevant only to the extent that they contribute to this equation.

While institutions are themselves intermediaries for individual customers, these customers are best protected by ensuring that the fund managers responsible for their investments do not operate under incentives such as soft commissions which present a conflict of interest in the execution of trades.

Investors to whom best execution is owed should be able to affirmatively waive best execution.

Nonetheless, there are occasions in which one or more of the non-price factors will be of greater priority for the retail investor than price. Flexibility and customer choice must be built into the policy to account for these situations. The way to address this, however, is not to dilute the policy to the point that it no longer provides an adequate standard for the rest of the investors. Rather, the policy should allow for investors to affirmatively waive the best execution requirement. This can either be done on a one-off basis, or as a standing order. It should be done prior to the trade, and should be documented in a manner which will facilitate monitoring during on-site inspections.

Further Reading

There are many excellent books and articles on market integration, order execution and related subjects. Those interested in exploring these areas further may wish to read the works listed below. Several of these books (and their authors) have been particularly influential in helping to shape the discussion on these issues.

Alcock, Alistair. *The Financial Services and Markets Act 2000: A Guide to the New Law* (Bristol: Jordan Publishing Ltd). The most comprehensive and comprehensible summary of securities regulation in the UK, which also includes a succinct analysis of the European Union framework and its implementation via national legislation.

Ferran, Eilís and Charles A.E. Goodhart, (eds). *Regulating Financial Services and Markets in the 21st Century* (Oxford: Hart Publishing) 2001. A forward-looking collection of papers from some of the most senior policy makers in financial regulation. Includes chapters on regulatory reform, international regulation and the challenges to regulation posed by technology.

Goodhart, Charles, Philip Hartmann, David Llewellyn and Liliana Rojas-Suarez. *Financial Regulation: Why, How and Where Now?* (London: Routledge) 1999. An important analysis of the nature and goals of financial regulatory policy.

Hallam, Nicholas and Nick, Idelson. *Breaking the Barriers: A Technological Study of the Obstacles to Pan-European Best Execution in Equities*, TraderServe Limited, March 2003. The only report to date which thoroughly analyses the role of technology in facilitating best execution.

Lee, Ruben. *What is an Exchange? The Automation, Management and Regulation of Financial Markets* (Oxford: Oxford University Press) 1998. Addresses one of the most fundamental questions in the regulation of markets, drawing on elements from economic theory, law and practical analysis.

Lofchie, Steven. *A Guide to Broker Dealer Regulation* (Fairfield, NJ: Compliance International, Inc.) 2000. A comprehensive summary of US securities regulation, with excellent analyses of ATS regulation and order handling rules in particular.

Moloney, Niamh. *EC Securities Regulation* (Oxford: Oxford University Press) 2002. An equally comprehensive summary of current regulation in the European Union. An invaluable reference, particularly with respect to the ISD and protective regulation of retail customers.

Schwartz, Robert A. (ed.) *Regulation of US Equity Markets* (Boston: Kluwer Academic Publishing) 2001. Provides views on current regulatory issues in the US by, among others, senior policy makers with the NYSE, AMEX, NASDAQ and the SEC.

Steil, Benn *et al. The European Equity Markets: The State of the Union and an Agenda for the Millennium* (London: European Capital Markets Institute) 1996 (Distributed by the Brookings Institute). An in-depth, comprehensive analysis of obstacles to equity market integration. Of particular value is the chapter on integration, fragmentation and the quality of markets.

Selected Bibliography

Autoriteit Financiële Markten. *Position Paper: In-House Matching* (2002).

Bacidore, Jeffrey, Katherine Ross and George Sofiano. "Quantifying Best Execution at the New York Stock Exchange: Market Orders". NYSE Working Paper 99-05, December, 1999.

Bentson, George J. *Regulating Financial Markets: A Critique and Some Proposals – Hobart Paper 135* (London: Institute for Economic Affairs) 1998.

Blundell, John and Colin Robinson. *Regulation Without the State – Occasional Paper 109* (London: Institute for Economic Affairs) 1999.

Board, John, Charles Sutcliffe and Stephen Wells. *Market Regulation in a Dynamic Environment*, London School of Economics, September 2002.

Bresiger, Gregory. "Regulator Looks Again at Best Execution: Buysiders Grapple with a Difficult Standard", in *Traders Magazine*, June 2002.

Charteris Plc. *European Financial Markets 2001: Revolution or Evolution?*, 2001.

Committee of European Securities Regulators (CESR). *A European Regime of Investor Protection – The Harmonisation of Conduct of Business Rules*, CESR/01-014d (2001).

——*Standards for Alternative Trading Systems* ("CESR ATS Standards"), CESR/02-086b.

Davies, Howard. "Why Regulate", speech to City University Business School, 4 November 1998.

Davydoff, Didier, Carole, Gresse and Laurent, Grillet-Aubert. *Internalisation of the Order Flow* (2002).

Euronext Amsterdam. *Internalisation* (2002).

European Central Bank (ECB). *The Euro Equity Markets*, August 2001.

European Commission. *Proposal for a Directive of the European Parliament and of the Council on Investment Services and Regulated Markets*, COM (2002) 625(01) (2002).

——Final Report of the Committee of Wise Men on the Regulation of European Securities Markets (2001).

Federation of European Securities Commissions (FESCO), *Standards and Rules for Harmonising Core Conduct of Business Rules for Investor Protection*, Consultation Paper (2001).

Financial Services Authority (FSA). *Best Execution*, Consultation Paper 154 (2002).

——*Best Execution*, Discussion Paper ("FSA Discussion Paper") (2001).

——*Best Execution*, Issues Paper ("FSA Issues Paper") (2000).

——"FSA Chairman Calls For Broader Debate on New Market Structures", Press Release FSA/PN/046/2000, 4 April 2000.

Foley and Lardner. LLC analysis of Newton *vs* Merrill Lynch http://www.foleylardner.com/brokerdealer/139838.html.

Goodhart, Charles, Philip Hartmann, David Llewellyn and Liliana Rojas-Suarez. *Financial Regulation: Why, How and Where Now?* (London: Routledge) 1999.

Hallam, Nicholas and Nick, Idelson *Breaking the Barriers: A Technological Study of the Obstacles to Pan-European Best Execution in Equities*, TraderServe Limited, March 2003.

Keenan, Denis and Sarah Riches. *Business Law*, Fifth Edition (Harlow, Essex: Pearson Education Limited) 1998.

Lannoo, Karel. "Does Europe Need an SEC? Securities Market Regulation in the EU", European Capital Markets Institute (1999).

Lee, Ruben. *What is an Exchange?* (Oxford: Oxford University Press) 1998.

Levitt, Arthur. "Best Execution, Price Transparency and Linkages: Protecting the Investor Interest", in *Washington University Law Quarterly*, Vol. 78, pp. 514–515.

——"The National Market System: A Vision That Endures", speech at Stanford University, 8 January 2001.

Lofchie, Steven. *A Guide to Broker-Dealer Regulation* (Fairfield, NJ: Compliance International Inc.) 2000.

London Stock Exchange. "Price Improvement and Best Execution", in *Stock Exchange Quarterly with Quality of Markets Review*, Spring 1992.

Moloney, Niamh. *EC Securities Regulation* (Oxford: Oxford University Press) 2002.

National Association of Securities Dealers, Inc. (NASD). 1999 Annual Report.

——Notice to Members ("NTM") 01-22.

——NTM 02-40.

—— NTM 97-57.

——SuperMontage® Release 1.0 Functional Description.

New York Stock Exchange, 2000 Annual Report.

Patel, Simit. *Direct Access Execution: ECN's, SOES and Other Methods of Trading* (New York: McGraw-Hill) 2001.

Schwartz, Robert A. and Steil Benn. "Controlling Institutional Trading Costs: We Have Met the Enemy, and It is Us", in *The Journal Portfolio Management*, Spring 2002.

Securities and Exchange Commission (SEC). *Inspection Report on the Soft Dollar Practices of Broker-Dealers, Investment Advisors and Mutual Funds*, 22 September 1998.

——*Institutional Investor Study Report to Congress* (1971).

——*Minutes of 10 October 2000 meeting of Advisory Committee on Market Information.*

——*Minutes of 12 April 2001 meeting of SEC Advisory Committee on Market Information.*

——*Minutes of 16 April 2001 meeting of SEC Advisory Committee on Market Information (Subcommittee on Alternative Models).*

——*No-Action Letters to Instinet*, 8 September 1986 and 6 December 1991.

——*On Line Brokerage: Keeping Apace of Cyberspace*, Special Study, November 1999.

——*Order Execution Obligations*, 62 SEC Docket at 2242-43.

——*Policy Statement on the Structure of a Central Market System* (1973).

——*Report of the Advisory Committee on Market Information* (the "Seligman Report") (2001).

——*Report to the Congress: The Impact of Recent Technological Advances on the Securities Markets* (1997).

——Securities Exchange Act Release No. 33-27611.

——Securities Exchange Act Release No. 34-42212.

——Securities Exchange Act Release 34-42450.

——Securities Exchange Act Release No. 34-43590.

——Securities Exchange Act Release No. 34-43863.

——Securities Exchange Act Release 34-43963.

——Securities Exchange Act Release No. 37619A.

Securities and Exchange Commission (SEC). *Statement on the Future Structure of the Securities Markets* (1972).

Securities and Futures Authority (SFA). Board Notice 280.

SFA Board Notice 437.

SFA Board Notice 488A.

SFA Board Notice 542.

SFA Board Notice 600.

Securities Industry Association. "Achieving Cross-Border Trade Processing Goals" Research Reports, Vol. 2, Nos. 3 and 4 (2001).

Securities and Investments Board (SIB). "Regulation of the United Kingdom Equity Markets" (1995).

SIB. Report of the Review of Best Execution (1995).

Schwartz, Robert A., Robert A. Wood, and Deniz Ozenbas. "Volatility in U.S. and European Equity Markets: An Assessment of Market Quality" in *International Finance*, Vol. 5, No. 3, pp. 437–461.

Underhill, Geoffrey (ed.) *The New World Order in International Finance* (New York: St Martin's Press) 1997.

United Nations Conference on Trade and Development (UNCTAD). *Trade and Development Report 2001.*

US Senate Banking Committee. Subcommittee on Securities, Hearing on the Changing Face of Capital Markets and the Impact of ECNs, Testimony of Arthur Levitt, 27 October 1999.

US Senate Banking Committee. Hearing on The Financial Marketplace of the Future, Testimony of Charles W. Schwab, 29 February 2000.

Wallman, Steven M.H. "Information Technology & the Securities Market: The Challenge for Regulators", in *Brookings Review*, Winter 1998, Vol. 16, No. 1, pp. 26–29.

Laws, regulations and cases

European Union

Treaty Establishing the European Economic Community, 1957.

Council of the European Union, Council Directive 93/22/EEC (Investment Services Directive).

Council of the European Union, Council Directive 88/361 ([1988] OJ L178/5).

United Kingdom

Financial Services and Markets Act 2000.

Securities and Futures Authority (SFA) Rule 5-39.

Securities and Investments Board (SIB), Core Conduct of Business Rule 22.

United States

Securities and Exchange Act of 1934.

Securities Acts Amendments of 1975, HR Rep. 94-229 (1975).

Public Law 94-29, 89 Stat. 97 (1975).

SEC Rule 11Ac1-1.

SEC Rule 11Ac1-2.

SEC Rule 11Ac1-4.

SEC Rule 17a-23.

National Association of Securities Dealers, Inc. (NASD) Rule 2320.

Charles Hughes and Co. vs SEC, 139 F.2d 434(2d Circuit 1943), cert. denied, 321 US 786 (1944).

In the Matter of Duker vs Duker, 6 SEC 386 (1939).

Newton vs Merrill Lynch, 135 F.3d at 271 n.3.

Index